I0585649

TERRITORIALIZING THE CHINESE NATION-STATE

This book is the first annotated translation of the travelogues of Huang Maocai. A trained Chinese cartographer in the service of the imperial Qing state, he was officially deputed to ascertain the Tibet–India land route and the geopolitical status of British India in the nineteenth century. His travelogues are the first authoritative modern Chinese texts exploring the physical and ideological connections between China and India. Unpublished for a long time, and so far, unavailable in an English translation, these texts provide meaning to many key issues that enshroud the concepts of civilization and nation.

An important contribution to the study of Sino–Indian interactions, it demonstrates Huang Maocai's keen observation of the geopolitics of the region. His vivid descriptions of Kolkata and nearby regions enlighten the Chinese perception of colonial India. This book will be an indispensable resource for students and researchers of nation, nationalism, civilization, empire, frontiers and borders, modern history, translation studies, Chinese studies, and Asian studies.

Kamal Sheel is Professor (Retd.) of Chinese at Banaras Hindu University, Varanasi, India.

Ranjana Sheel is Professor of History at Banaras Hindu University, Varanasi, India.

TERRITORIALIZING THE CHINESE NATION-STATE

Cartography, Geopolitics, and Huang Maocai's Mission to India (1878–1880)

Edited and translated by
Kamal Sheel and Ranjana Sheel

Routledge
Taylor & Francis Group

LONDON AND NEW YORK

Designed cover image: Engraving by Louis Delaporte (1842-1925). The image was sourced from the Alamy Inc.

First published 2025
by Routledge
4 Park Square, Milton Park, Abingdon, Oxon OX14 4RN

and by Routledge
605 Third Avenue, New York, NY 10158

Routledge is an imprint of the Taylor & Francis Group, an informa business

© 2025 selection, translation and editorial matter, Kamal Sheel and Ranjana Sheel; individual chapters, the contributors

The right of Kamal Sheel and Ranjana Sheel to be identified as the authors of the selection, translation and editorial matter has been asserted in accordance with sections 77 and 78 of the Copyright, Designs and Patents Act 1988.

All rights reserved. No part of this book may be reprinted or reproduced or utilised in any form or by any electronic, mechanical, or other means, now known or hereafter invented, including photocopying and recording, or in any information storage or retrieval system, without permission in writing from the publishers.

Trademark notice: Product or corporate names may be trademarks or registered trademarks, and are used only for identification and explanation without intent to infringe.

British Library Cataloguing-in-Publication Data
A catalogue record for this book is available from the British Library

ISBN: 978-1-032-82625-7 (hbk)
ISBN: 978-1-032-82618-9 (pbk)
ISBN: 978-1-003-50539-6 (ebk)

DOI: 10.4324/9781003505396

Typeset in Sabon
by Deanta Global Publishing Services, Chennai, India

CONTENTS

PREFACE

This book focuses on Huang Maocai's [1843–1890] travelogue on the mapping of the Southern Silk Route. This is the second book of our translation series on Chinese travelogues on modern India, and it follows the earlier work published with the title *Kang Youwei Engages India: His Travel Narratives (1901–1902) and Predicaments of Civilisation and Nation.*

Huang Maocai is credited with writing the first Chinese travelogue on modern India. He was a Qing cartographer and official who led in 1878 a delegation to India at the behest of the Imperial Court during the reign of Emperor Guangxu [1875–1908]. He traveled overland from Chengdu [Sichuan, China] to Kolkata [Bengal, India] through the Southern Silk Route via Yunnan and Myanmar. He was assigned the task of updating and drawing boundaries of China's southwest frontiers, employing modern cartographic tools, collecting geographical and ethnographic information on the region, and rectifying old placenames and other signifiers in Chinese maps with new currently used ones. This was to be done for the better management of China's southwest frontiers. The urgency was then due to the whole area becoming vulnerable to the western trader-imperialists' growing interests in the region to search for a profitable overland route for trade.

The age-old reputation of the Southern Silk Route as a carrier of flourishing trade of horse and tea, silver and cowrie, and ideas and culture to vast regions between China, Southeast Asia, and India galvanized traders as much as explorers and seekers of various hues and color. The route was difficult and arduous but shorter and faster than the Central Asian routes. As such, it offered promises of further expansion of trade and control of market, and potentials for laying a railway line and developing river routes were explored. During his two years [1878–1880] sojourn in the region, Huang made extensive notes and maps which were submitted to the Imperial Court after his return. Huang also studied in detail rivers and waterways along the Southern Silk Route. His travel records were published in 1886 in two volumes. One was entitled *Xi you ri-ji [Records of Travel to the Western Region]* and the other was known as *Yin-du za-ji [Reading Notes on India]*. This book presents an annotated translation of the two volumes with an editorial introduction.

Huang's narratives initially became a significant source of information for India in China. Kang Youwei specifically refers to reading those in preparation for his journey to India. Yet, Huang's books also provoked the ire of Qing conservationists who disapproved of his admiration of the British colonial state in India and support for the idea of a nonhierarchical world order in the management of international relations. While China was moving from an empire to a nation-state, conservationists were still beholden to the conduct of foreign relationships characterized by a hierarchical tributary system with China at the top. It is therefore not surprising that Huang's book after its first run almost disappeared, and its maps became extinct. It was only later that local bureaucrat admirers from his homeland in Jiangxi retrieved dilapidated woodblocks and scrolls to restore and publish a fresh edition of his works. More recently on the occasion of his 100th birth anniversary he was treated as a 'youth hero'.

Apart from introducing Huang's 'modernist' ideas, perceptions, and descriptions of regions he visited from China to India, these books provide some observations on the early Chinese attempt to territorialize the frontier region for the upcoming Chinese nation-state. As frontiers and empires began to fade away with the onset of a new world order, exercises to demarcate boundaries of the empire employing modern cartographic tools became crucial to legitimize the reach of the state. Vast tracts of semiautonomous frontier regions with varying degrees of simultaneous control of local tribes and states over land and trade thus became the subject of contention and rivalry of competing states. Huang Maocai's information gathered from frontiers, once listed, and categorized, became part of the fresh mapmaking process of the nation-state. In addition, Huang's books also reflect upon early Chinese nationalist intellectuals' discursive responses to the West.

Huang's works have received inadequate attention from scholars and much information about him is missing. He has not found a place in writings on modern India and China discourses during the late nineteenth and early twentieth century. We are indebted to the two professors of Peking University, Ji Xianlin and Lin Chengjie, for introducing these texts several years ago. In fact, Professor Lin's remarkable book on the history of cultural relationship between India and China in modern times with an excellent introduction to Huang has enthused us to take up this work along with our earlier translation of Kang Youwei's travelogue.

In doing this translation, our effort has been to present the work in an easily readable format. Annotations are added to explain events, place names, and other not much known details for readers unfamiliar with Chinese or Indian history and culture. Further, at places, we found Huang's transliteration of Indian names in Chinese problematic and far off from the original phonetic rendition making it difficult to locate actual local names. We have kept those names as rendered in Chinese phonetics.

This work has been made possible due to the generous help and support of many friends and institutions. We cherish our interactions with Prasenjit Duara, Sugata Bose, Anand Yang, Tansen Sen, Brian Tsui, Zhang Ke, B.R. Deepak, Sabaree Mitra, Madhavi Thampi, Dhrub Kumar Singh, Sarfaraz Alam, and our students who read the present manuscript in part or in full and made useful comments and suggestions from time to time. Professor Xue Keqiao (Peking University) and Professor Chu Hongyuan (Academia Sinica, Taipei) helped us locate useful materials and provided valuable inputs to comprehend complex passages in the texts. Huang Weimin and Huang Zongyang have been of immense help since the beginning of the translation project. We are grateful to them. Dr. Satya Prakash, a young and dynamic geographer and cartographer at Banaras Hindu University, prepared the two maps of the route followed by Huang Maocai. Alamy Images permitted us to use an 1868 engraving of the Southern Silk Route by Louis Delaporte. Fellowships to work at the China Central Library and the Academia Sinica and a translation project by the Indian Council of Historical Research facilitated our work. Dr. Shashank Shekhar Sinha, the Publication Director of Routledge India, readily offered to take up its publication. Anvitaa Bajaj, Antara Ray Chaudhury and Sanjeevi Nagarajan provided all the necessary help and support. We are thankful to them. We are also grateful to the anonymous reviewer for useful suggestions and corrections in the text.

Our grandchildren, Jayan and Anika, as ever delightfully kept pushing us to complete the work and enjoy their antics. Our families gave us their full support. We dedicate this work to our teachers, both in India and abroad, and to our parents. Finally, we take full responsibility for all the errors in facts, interpretations, and translation and seek readers' indulgence.

Kamal Sheel and Ranjana Sheel

MAPS OF HUANG MAOCAI'S TRAVEL ROUTES FROM CHINA TO INDIA AND BACK

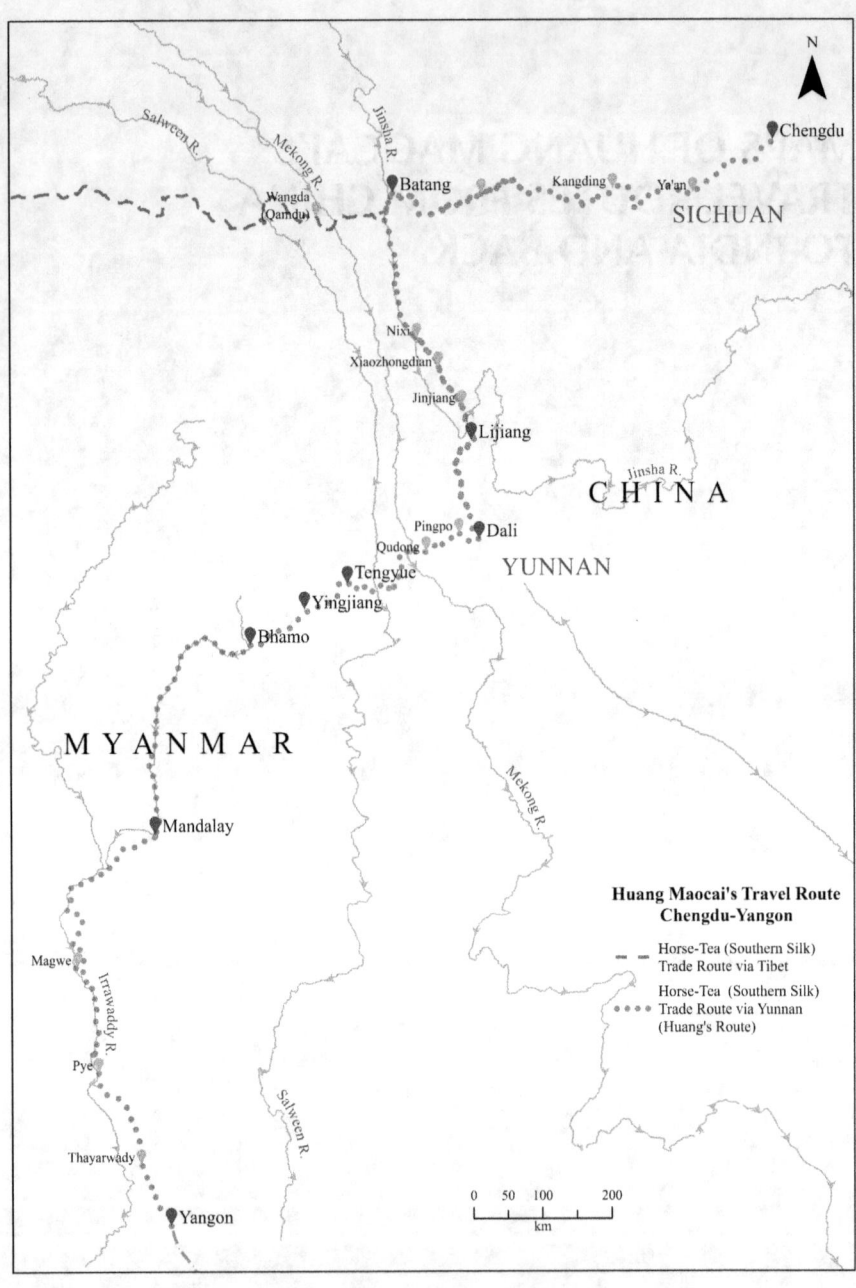

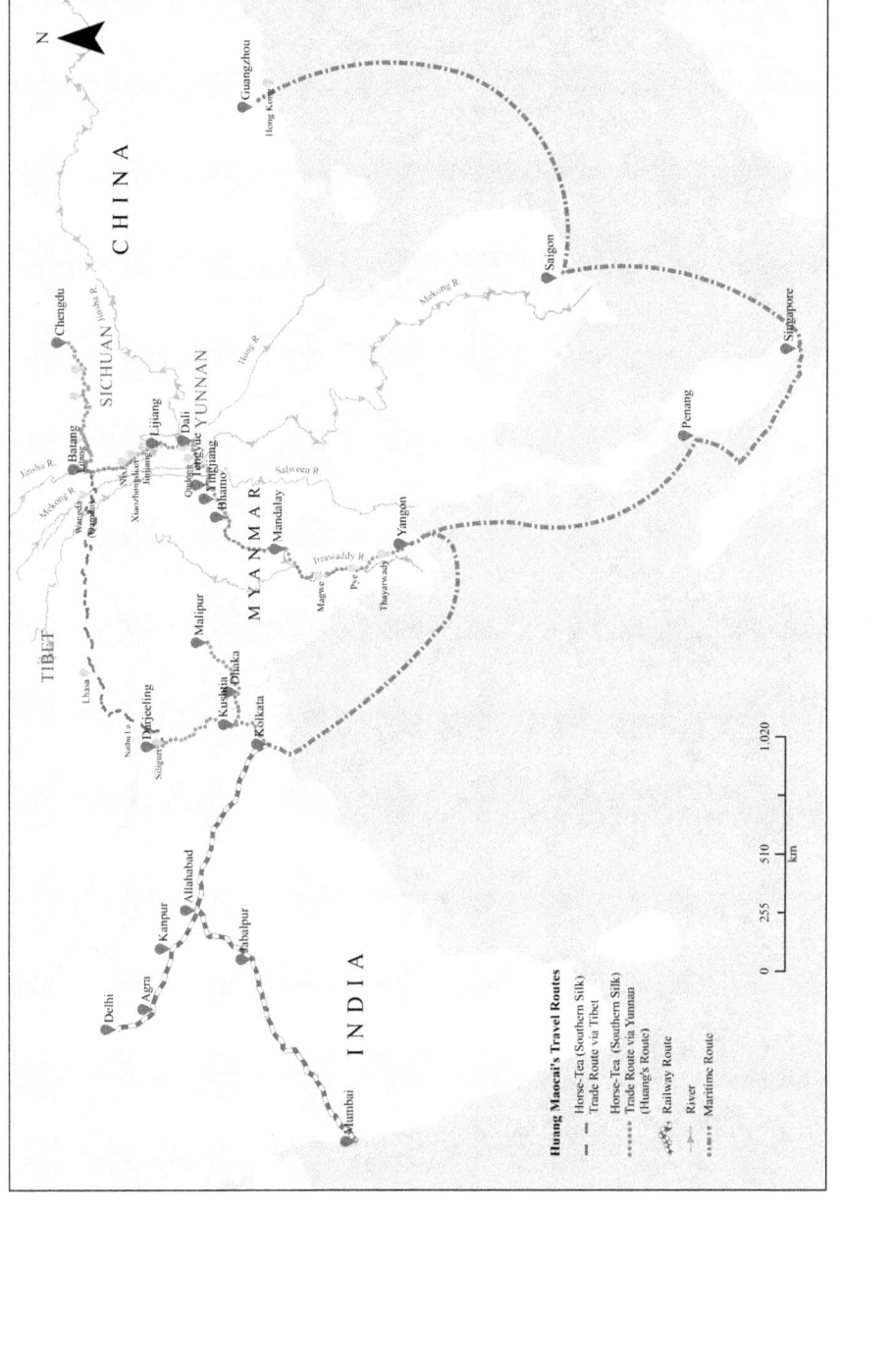

Huang Maocai's Travel Routes

- – – Horse-Tea (Southern Silk) Trade Route via Tibet
- ● ● ● ● ● Horse-Tea (Southern Silk) Trade Route via Yunnan (Huang's Route)
- ⋆⋆⋆ Railway Route
- River
- ◆◆◆◆◆ Maritime Route

0   255   510   1,020
km

CHINA

TIBET

SICHUAN

YUNNAN

MYANMAR

INDIA

N

Chengdu

Batang

Lijiang

Dali

Tengyue

Longling

Bhamo

Mandalay

Yangon

Pyay

Thayarwady

Magwe

Irrawaddy R.

Salween R.

Huang R.

Mekong R.

Jinsha R.

Jinsha R.

Mekong R.

Wangda

Lhasa

Nathu La

Siliguri

Darjeeling

Malipur

Kushna

Dhaka

Kolkata

Jabalpur

Allahabad

Kanpur

Agra

Delhi

Mumbai

Penang

Singapore

Saigon

Guangzhou

Hong Kong

1

INTRODUCTION

Huang Maocai, Cartography, Geopolitics, and the Travel Narratives

A trained Chinese cartographer and maverick intellectual-official, Huang Maocai (1843–1890),[1] visited Tibet and India during 1878–1880. His description of travel routes and sociocultural and politico-economic observations of the 'western region' provide the first Chinese glimpse of modern India. His travel narratives, published in 1886 in two short volumes with the titles *Xi-you ri-ji* [*Records of Travel to the Western Region*] and *Yin-du za-ji* [*Reading Notes on India*], are the first travelogues on India in modern China. Besides these, he also wrote *Xi-jiao shui-dao* [*Waterways in Western Borderland*] and *You-li chu-yuan* [*My Humble Opinion on Travels*]. All four volumes were compiled in *De-yi-zhai za-zhao si-zhong* [*A Collection of Varieties of Sundry Records*]. Huang's writings were in line with long narratives produced by earlier illustrious monk-travelers such as Faxian, Xuanzang, and Yijing who traveled to India in their quest for exploration of Buddhist scriptures and provided useful geographical and political information of the region travelled in the age of empires. In fact, so accurate were their observations that later archaeologists and historians used them to find significant Buddhist sites and construct history. Huang's narratives were, however, written with modern cartographic observations, and motivated by geopolitical ideas for strengthening and protection of the Chinese nation-state.

Huang Maocai was born in the 23rd year of the Qing Emperor Daoguang [1843] in Tianxin village, Shanggao county, Jiangxi province. He was a native of Dou-men house. His other names were Hao Bo and Bai Ting. His family was poor but he was diligent and excelled in studies. He received public funding to study at the Yuzhang Academy[2] in Nanchang. At the age of 16, he completed 'xiu-cai'[3] [the middle-level civil service] examination. The

DOI: 10.4324/9781003505396-1

mid-nineteenth century in China was the period when Western education and especially science and mathematics became part of the modernization movement for the dynastic 'self-strengthening'. This received further impetus with Protestant missionaries' deeper inroads in China. They broke the monopoly of the Jesuit-controlled forays in science-education and emerged as a better rival in introducing a whole range of western scientific subjects. Popular science books in translation became easily available in treaty ports and metropolitan cities.

This naturally, increasingly attracted some of the bright Chinese young students to abandon old Confucian civil-service-oriented education for a more patriotic and exciting science-based education.[4] Huang was no exception. He discarded the idea of preparation for the coveted preferred path for the higher civil service position and decided to study science in order to serve the country. He read widely. In addition to studying the classics and history, he was especially devoted to 'the study of the world' that included mathematics and astronomy. Biographies and descriptions of 'barbarians' and their land in the books of past dynasties interested him. He was proud of China's thousands of years old ancient civilization. Increasing foreigners' encroachment and the declining strength of China since the Opium War disturbed him.

At that time, Shanghai was a prosperous metropolitan city with many international business concerns in the foreign concession areas. Huang Maocai felt that he should first go there to learn and understand the method and style of foreigners' operation. On March 21, 1866 [i.e., the fifth year of Tongzhi], he arrived in Shanghai. After being recommended by others, he worked in the Education Bureau founded by the Yulian Village Society. He gained training in translation in Shanghai and interned at the Tianjin Machine Manufacturing Company. Since then, he devoted his main energy to studying the society there and paid attention to current affairs. Moving frequently to lanes and bye-lanes of the city in search of the detailed life and activities of foreigners, he visited theaters and brothel houses; witnessed signs of rampant social abuses; and encountered crowded translation houses, foreign companies, and churches. In more than a year there, he learned in detail the politics, economy, military, and culture of the then globally active countries such as Britain, France, Germany, Russia, Japan, Italy, Austria, the Netherlands, and Portugal. He wrote about what he saw and heard in a two-volume book entitled *Hu-you-sheng-ji* [*Record of Successful Wandering in Shanghai*]. This attracted the attention of the literati and officials and turned him into a public figure.

In the first year of Emperor Guangxu [1875], Huang encountered the chief provincial education officer, Li Wentian, who examined him in Ruizhou, Jiangxi for eligibility for official training. Highly impressed by his 'good character and fine scholarship', Li recommended Huang to his successor,

Xu Gengshen, to put up his case for an official position at the Imperial Court. Xu too was happy with Huang's excellent contribution in the provincial affairs as well as his high academic performance, especially in mathematics and sciences. He promoted him and presented a memorial to the [Guangxu] Emperor to send him to the Tong-wen-guan [Foreign Language and Translation Academy][5] in Beijing or to the Confucian Wu-jing [Five Classics] Academy [Han-lin Academy] for advanced training for the highest degree of the civil service examination. Huang chose to join the Tong-wen-guan after passing the examination. He studied diligently and meticulously. Along with learning English, French, German, Russian, Japanese, and other foreign languages, he actively enriched himself in western scientific knowledge. He especially focused on cartography and improved his surveying and drawing skills, turning into an accomplished cartographer.

This was the time when imperialist powers were exploring various routes to enter China to expand their trade and commerce as well as political hegemony employing various pretexts. Incidents like the killing of a British missionary-diplomat-explorer Augustus Margery provided such a pretext. On February 21, 1875, Margery while traveling through the ancient Southern Silk Route to China through India–Myanmar, Tibet, and Yunnan was killed by the locals in the Yunnan–Myanmar area. This traditional trade route to China was lucrative but physically not very safe for traders and travelers not moving with large contingents or caravans. It passed across a large semi-independent frontier area that was full of steep mountains and gushing rivers, and was inhabited and ruled by various tribes who frequently defied and rebelled against Han hegemony and sought to control the route through protection fees or other benefits. Margery was probably on a secret mission to explore the feasibility of opening channels of communication, probably a viable railroad connection, between India and China over the traditional Yunnan–Burma–India route. His deeper encroachment in China through this route led to apprehensions regarding the British opening up a southern land route to China. These trepidations were much more immediate and serious among the local people, traditionally inhabiting and controlling the volatile frontier region or borderlands, who possibly attacked and killed Margery and his assistants in their area.

Enraged by the Margery incident of 1875, the British used it as a pretext to draw more concessions from China. They negotiated the Sino-British Treaty of Yantai in 1876[6] which guaranteed the British right to travel to Tibet and China from the southern land route from India. This led to various concerns. Chinese feared for the security of their territory as the British and other foreigners both independently and officially began to encroach on Tibet through various routes in the entire long frontier by the third and fourth year of Guangxu (1877 and 1878).[7] Some traveled through the southern route to the middle of Sichuan, privileging the provisions of the Yantai

Agreement[8] exploring trade and communication routes through Tibet and Yunnan. The frequency of such explorations further increased after the British occupation of Darjeeling in north India. Governor of Sichuan, Ding Baochen, dreaded the impact of opening a route from Darjeeling to Tibet for foreign trade on the security of his state. Further, as China began to be surrounded by foreign imperialist forces, its status as an empire-state began to be increasingly threatened. This necessitated the opening up of a special office, the Zongli Yamen, in 1861 to deal with foreign affairs as a nation-state with a recognized and accepted national boundary. Consequently, the territorialization of the mostly customary frontier area became imperative. Thus began the exercise to draw fresh or updated maps using modern cartographical methods. Ding Baochen memorialized the Guangxu Emperor to send a qualified imperial official to explore and map the borders for strategic purposes. The Emperor approved the dispatch of a Chinese official delegation under the leadership of Huang Maocai to survey and map the southern land route from Chengdu, Sichuan, to Tibet and 'Five India-s'. He bestowed upon Huang, a fourth-ranked official, full power and authority of a second-ranked officer of the Qing bureaucracy. This was the first official mission from China to India in modern times. Huang was then 35 years old.

Huang Maocai and his entourage of six persons consisting of subordinates, servants, and cooks set off from Sichuan on the seventh day of the seventh lunar month in 1878. He took the overland route from Chengdu–Tibet–Xi [Sikh-land/Punjab]–India, which was shorter. Traveling on a rugged arduous mountain route, he reached Ba-tang.[9] The hostility of the local Tibetan groups, who were highly suspicious of his motives to travel to India, however, forced him to take the alternative but longer Yunnan–Myanmar–India route. Turning to the south, he journeyed on this no less perilous but relatively safer route for 211 days from Zhong-dian,[10] and passed Li-jiang, Da-li, and Yong-chang prefectures to arrive at Teng-yue [Momein],[11] the famous custom town in Baoshan city located on the China and Myanmar border on the eighth day of the second month of the following year [1879]. From there, he reached Xin-jie and boarded a steamer and plied on the majestic Irrawaddy River to the port city of Yang-guang [Yangon/Rangoon] via the capital city of Myanmar, Awa. In the course of his travel, he noted the location of each place that he visited in modern geographic coordinates of latitude and longitude and provided their significant physical and ethnological descriptions in brief. He stayed in Myanmar for close to a month and detailed his observations of the area and its history, culture, and present status under the British occupation in his diary. On the 27th day of the 3rd month of 1879, he left by ship for Kolkata, India. He spent more than six months in India, staying a good amount of time in Kolkata, the ultimate colonial city at the time. From there, he also made a trip to Darjeeling ostensibly to meet the higher colonial officials in the summer capital and areas under the British occupation in the northeast. Later, he embarked on a journey to India's hinterland covering Allahabad, Agra, Delhi, Mumbai, and other places. He was thus able to get more than a bird's overview of India and conveyed his impressions in his writings. He, however, clarified that he would not list all which were already listed in earlier works on India in China but focus on the contemporary situation.

Huang set off on his return journey from Kolkata by the maritime route on the first day of the tenth month in 1879. His delegation crossed the Bay of Bengal, passed through Penang, and had stopovers in Singapore and Saigon for more than half a month each. On the second day of the eleventh month of 1879, when he and his entourage took the ship out of Saigon to cross the seven seas, they suddenly encountered an unprecedentedly strong hurricane. The turbulent ocean with massive waves kept the ship dangerously dangling and passengers on tenterhooks for five days and nights without adequate ration and cooking materials. They managed to survive and finally in the first month of the sixth year of Guangxu [1880] arrived in Guangzhou. The whole trip lasted for two years, completed a journey of 50,000 *li*, and left footprints over a large area of south and southeast Asian terrain. The trip was most remarkable and successful. Huang himself avers that such a survey of the frontier region with unimagined hardships was most rare in China. It was indeed a brave feat that facilitated achieving goals of diplomatic and strategic pursuits.

Huang meticulously noted the contemporary physical, socio-political, and economic situation in Tibet, Yunnan, Myanmar, and India and drew fresh maps using contemporary place names. These were published in several short and separate notes, essays, and volumes. It may however be noted that as travelers' tales they were written keeping in mind their particular audience in China, and were influenced by the contemporary Chinese ideological and cultural fervors. They gathered selective information and presented a report that resonated with the requirement of their home settings. Hence they were inherently biased. Yet, in so far as they contributed to historical information on interactions and connectedness they enrich our knowledge and comprehension of both source and target countries to develop a 'connected or integrative' history. Huang admitted at the very beginning of his Opening Remarks for travel narratives that he recorded what he saw and experienced, and ignored such details which were generally in the public domain. His reports were published as separate volumes in his *Collected Works*.[12] The first volume was entitled *Xi-you ri-ji [Records of Travel to the Western Region]* and consisted of four short chapters. This recorded the existing situation of travel from Sichuan to India through the mountains, rivers, and roads and also described culture, customs, and ethnological information that Huang gathered on his way. The second volume, entitled *Yin-du zha-ji [Reading Notes on India]* provided in two short chapters, namely, 'Yin-du zha-ji' [Reading Notes on India], Part I and Part II, various snippets from India along with significant features of physical and political geographies of the five regions of India, known in Chinese records as 'Wu Yin-du' [Five India-s]. The last chapter contained short poems that he composed reflecting on his trip. It was entitled 'Yin-du za-xing' [My Humble Opinion on Travels]. The third volume, *Xi-you shui-dao [Records of Travel to the Western Region]*, was a detailed description of rivers flowing in the western frontier area, namely, Jin-sha, Ya, Yue, Lan-ying, Lu-jiang, Long-chuan, Bing-lang, Yu-long-hei-shui, A-lu-da si-shui, Da-he, and others. He corrected the wrong description of the water flow and river basin of the Indus existing in the earlier Chinese records, and also provided suggestions for harnessing these and other waterways for various purposes. The next volume, You-li chu-yan [My Humble Opinion on Travels], contained eight short essays or summaries which included You-li yin-du shi-mo [The Story of Travel to India], Wu Yin-du xing-shi [A Panoramic View of Five Indias], Teng-yue bian-jiao [Frontier Region of Teng Yue], Xi-you xing-sheng [Favorable Geographical Spots of the Western Region], Nan-yang xing-shi [Situation of the South Sea], E-guo tu-shu [Illustrated Russia], He-lin kao [Examining He Lin], and Xi-you tu-shuo [Illustrated Western Region]. The fifth volume, *Hu-you sheng-ji*[13] *[Victorious Records of Shanghai]*, and the sixth and seventh volumes, respectively concerned his random thoughts on various diverse subjects in *Ping-zheng-lu [Notings for Fair and Peaceful Politics]* and *De-yi zhai-wai-ji [Collection of Knowledge Gained from the Outside]*. The latter was painstakingly reconstructed after the original was lost or suppressed.[14]

In the present work, in view of our focus on the connectedness of India and China, we have limited our translation to two of Huang Maocai's most referred India-specific volumes and chapters, namely, *Xi-you ri-ji [Records of Travel to the Western Region]* and *Yin-du zha-ji [Reading Notes on India]*, and an India specific chapter of the volume entitled *You-li chu-yan [My Humble Opinions]*.

The Qing court ordered on November 1, 1880 to keep in the court Huang's two books of maps and illustrations on India. In the process, maps attached as annexures with the volumes became unavailable as they were either transferred to the executive branch or to collections in the First Archives in the Beijing Palace Museum or the relocated National Museum and Archives in Taipei, Taiwan.[15] Presently, it is difficult to ascertain the whereabouts of the maps attached to the original edition.

The first edition of Huang's works was published as *De-yi-zhai-za zhu si-zhong*《得一斋杂著四种》and was then never seen.[16] In 1886, it was compiled and republished by Jiang Biaozi from the Hanlin Academy. It was then appraised to be 'accurate in description', 'supported by rich verified textual research', and 'an indispensable book for those who talk about border or

frontier affairs'. The demand for this book far surpassed the number of copies produced. In 1896, the 22nd year of Guangxu, another issue was brought
out by the efforts of Jiang Shaotang who during his tenure as the County
Magistrate at the Shanggao District of Jiangxi personally visited Huang
Maocai's house to solicit his papers for research. He found that most of
the original copies were badly termite-infested and almost totally decayed.
It was painstakingly restored and published as a supplement together with
his volume entitled *Hu-you qi-ji [Humble Records of Travel to Shanghai]*.
These volumes were included in the impressive and influential late Qing
encyclopedic work on world geography by Wang Xiqi, ed., *Xiao-fang hu-
zhai yu-di cong-chao [Collected Works on Geography from the Studio of
the Small Square Jug]* series, Vol X, and published in Shanghai between
Qing Guangxu 17 [1891] to 23 year [1897], and republished in several edi-
tions later. Some of Huang's provisionally preserved illustrated writings
could be traced here. It was estimated that besides partially restored *De-yi
zhai-wai-ji [Collection of Knowledge Gained from the Outside]*, his more
than 20 works were lost. These include *Xiang-shu-xin-li* 象數新理 *[New
Principles for Calculation of Stars and Constellations]*, *Ji-qi-lue-shi* 機器
略釋 *[A Brief Explanation of Machines]*, *Hai-guo-jian- wen-lu* 海國見聞
錄 *[Records of Knowledge from the Overseas]*, *Hu-you-yin-cao* 滬遊吟
草 *[Wild Chantings on Travels in Shanghai]*, *Jiang-chen-yin-cao*江城吟草
[Wild Chantings on Jiangcheng (Yunnan)], *Zhi-yan*卮言 *[Wine-talks/Tid-
bits]*, *Jiang-xi gui-du-biao* 江西晷度表 *[Sun-dial Meter of Jiangxi]*, and 丙
寅至壬申年日記 *[Annual Diary from Bingyin (1866) to Renshen (1881)]*.
An attempt was made to compile and print all his rescued and available
writings under the title *Huang Mao-cai wen-ji [Collected Works of Huang
Maocai]* as his 100th Death Anniversary Volume by a group of editors at his
home county Shanggao in Jiangxi.[17] Editors of this volume proclaimed that
although Huang Maocai was an intellectual of the feudal era, his meticulous
academic spirit, ardent patriotism, and strong belief in honest and just government could still be worthwhile to introduce for the sake of posterity and
high moral integrity. The present translation of Huang's writings on India is
based on the originals from this volume.

We may add that the *Collected Works of Huang Maocai* were full of novel
ideas based on intensive thoughtful study of the contemporary domestic and
international situations and his extensive travel experiences in hitherto rarely
touched China's southwest region and Southeast Asia. His observations and
nationalistic or 'reformist' views and pleas for a just and honest style of government were influenced by the currents of West-inspired nationalism and
modernity. In the contemporary scenario of the Qing nation-making efforts
they appear as appropriate alternative views. The state however apprehended
their impact on raising people's participation in politics at home and in exac-
erbating further encroachment of foreign forces from the outside. Though

praised for presenting authentic surveys and maps, Huang's ideas did not receive much attention and his presentation of new 'nationalist' ideas failed to awaken the Qing state dominated by the ideals of State Confucianism. He was kept at a distance and posted in Yunnan – more than a thousand *li* away from the capital city of Beijing. He successively served for four years in Ping-yi[18] county and Mi-le[19] county as the county magistrate and earned a name for his careful management of the area and honest and uncorrupted administration. Because of his academic foundation in science and economics, and frustrated by the routine civil administrative work, he later sought a transfer to the capital city. Finally, he was posted at the Hui-dian-guan[20] [Office for the Compilation of Statues/Maps] for rectifying and reforming the survey work and illustrating maps with the additional charge of inspecting defects in Tong-wen-wu. Unfortunately, Huang did not live long to leave his mark in his new position. In the 16th year of Guangxu (1890), he died at the young age of 47 after a brief illness in Shanghai.

Huang's nationalist and modernist streaks cannot be better comprehended unless we disaggregate three broad areas or themes of his travel writings and examine them separately. The first relates to the Sichuan–India or the Southwest Silk Route. The second concerns frontier region, cartography, and demarcation and territorialization of the Chinese nation-state. And, the third is about India and its configuration as the colonial state under the British rule.

Sichuan–India or the Southwest Silk Route (SSR)

Published in 1886, Huang's travel narratives presented the first direct official report on India in China. They corrected many of the fallacies in the existing Chinese records on the Five India-s and updated descriptions of various places and traditional names on the Southwest Silk Route from Sichuan, China to India via Tibet, Yunnan, and Myanmar. As such, they became the must-read materials for any Chinese traveling to India in the late nineteenth and early twentieth century and contributed to the formation of Chinese views on India. For example, Huang's book was one of the first books which Kang Youwei read before he embarked on his famous tour to India in 1901.[21] This facilitated comprehension of borderland policies and contemporary debates and dilemmas over the issues of civilization, nation-state, and modernity. Huang's descriptions raised various issues starting from India's civilizational legacy and enslavement by the British to skillful modern management under colonial administration conveying exemplary lessons for China. His works have, however, remained untranslated and thus hardly find any reference in the context of the history of modern interaction between India and China. Also, in studies of Silk Roads, Huang's survey and maps of the traditional Southwest Silk Route (SSR) connecting China,

Tibet, Myanmar, and India have somehow remained ignored despite the fact that since the mid-nineteenth century European powers had begun to explore this traditional route in their quest to monopolize and manage it for the cross-regional trade.

To understand the context and urgency that persuaded the Qing state to depute Huang Maocai for the comprehensive survey and mapping of the Southwest Silk Route (SSR) from China we need to slightly digress to throw some light on the historical significance of this route. The name, the Southwest Silk Route, owed its origin to Han General Zhang Qian's famous official exploration of China's western region, mentioned in Sima Qian's *Record of History*, which alluded to another Silk Route that connected Southwest China with India and brought Sichuan cloth (*Shu-bu*) and bamboo cane (*qiong-zhu*) to Da-xia (Bactria). Some, as Bin Yang notes, also used names like *Xi'nan si-chou zhi-lu* (Southwest Silk Road) or *Nan-fang si-chou zhi-lu* (South Silk Road), while others preferred the more descriptive *Nan-fang Lu-shang zhi-lu* (Southern Overland Route) or *Dian-mian-yin gu-dao* [The Ancient Road Connecting Yunnan, Burma, and India]. This was also more specifically referred to by its traditional name, *Shu-yin-du dao* [Sichuan–India Road] or *Chuan-Dian-Mian-Yin* [Sichuan–Yunnan–Burma–India] road which was the area that it covered. Its other branches connected Yunnan via Sichuan to Tibet and India; and with Laos, Thailand, and Cambodia; and also with Vietnam. Because of the movement of tea, horses and cloth it was also called Tea and Horse Road or Sichuan Cloth Road.[22]

One of the important links to the SSR was Yunnan. Bin Yang's study[23] demonstrates Yunnan's crucial role in long-distance cross-regional trade and its Eurasian interaction from several centuries before the Christian era to modern times. This contributed to its rise as a non-Han multiethnic state with special characteristics and historically integrated with China or the China sphere and prevented it from following the path of other neighboring Southeast Asian regions that became independent countries such as Burma, Thailand, Laos, and Vietnam.[24]

Yang refers to various material and documentary evidence of historically continuing and flourishing trade between Sichuan, Yunnan, Tibet,Burma, and India through the Shu-Yan-du [Sichuan–India] Route in Tang and post-Tang periods. Xuanzang and Yijing both mentioned this route in their respective works. Yijing also indicated its many Buddhist connections. The existence of a large monastery there alluded to frequent peaceful movement of both Chinese and Indian monks of Theravada/Hinayana, Mahayana, and Vajrayana sects through this passage that painted this and the area beyond it with various Buddhist colors.[25] D. P. Singhal[26] in his *India and World Civilization*, for instance, mentioned both overland routes through Nepal and Tibet to China, and through Assam and Upper Burma to Yunnan.

Economic and commercial importance of this route has been described by scholars of numismatic studies such as John Deyell and Nisar Ahmed who narrate in detail the movement of silver, gold, cowries, tea, cotton, salt, and horses on this route between China and India.[27] Despite the abundance of Chinese sources identifying the movement of a variety of trading goods through its various branches, accurate information on the trade volume and the orbit of its arteries, especially in the frontier region bordering Burma and Assam, only scantily existed.

By the mid-nineteenth century, the political and commercial expansion of European power in Southeast Asia, and the discovery of this overland trade route avoiding a long and arduous sea voyage by the straits and Indian archipelago presented a better prospect of expanding and profiting through the trade via western China. Media reports and tales of adventurous treks fired popular imagination of rich returns. In his travelogue pertaining to this region, an early explorer John Anderson thus wrote: 'A direct interchange of our manufactures for the products of the rich provinces of Yunnan and Sz-chuen [Sichuan], might well seem to be advantages which would richly repay almost any effort to accomplish this purpose'[28]. While fluctuating volume of the trade, the complex and difficult terrain of the area, the Indian Mutiny, the shifting focus to the Middle-East and Africa, the Panthay [Moslem] Rebellion in Yunnan between 1856 and 1873, and the difficulty in negotiating inter-regional trade permission with the Burmese kingdom initially inhibited both the Indian and British governments to commit any major investment for this road. However, by 1860, the global situation began to change and the race for the global routes and markets began. The Manchester Chamber of Commerce started pressurizing the British government to open the Southwest China route for the export of its machine-made cotton textiles and woolens. The completion of the American transcontinental railroad in 1869, the opening of the Suez Canal, the French plan to connect Saigon with Dali in Yunnan through a railroad, and the beginning of the restoration of the Qing control over Yunnan required a speedy response to emerging emergencies to deal with global and local currents.

Along the road, the construction of a railroad between India and China via Burma also picked up demand. Captain Richard S. M. Spyre of the British Army was in fact the first to raise such a demand in 1833.[29] This demand kept popping up at short intervals from many quarters because of often hyped up and reflected popular fantasies over the integration of the global market and creation of a market hub in the region.[30] In the heyday of global imperialist expansion and market integration, there was a strong feeling that the link route via Burma 'between the 250,000,000 inhabitants of India and the 300,000,000 inhabitants of China should be opened up to trade'. Davies (1909:10 ff.), the leader of the first completed British official exploratory mission during 1894–1900, poignantly remarked,

[I]n an age when railways are penetrating to the most out-of-the-way places in the earth, it is impossible to suppose that India and China – the two most populous countries in the world – will be content to remain side by side without being connected by railway. I think I am quite safe in asserting that any such railway must pass through Yunnan.[31]

The vague geographical details of the local and regional topography, however, required massive surveying and cartographic exercises before taking up the mammoth task of creating communication channels. Before 1867, it was known that a regular traffic existed between Mandalay and China, especially in the supply of cotton to the interior, which was reserved as a royal monopoly, and the steamers and numerous flotilla plied on the Irrawaddy supporting caravans traversing the overland route via Yangon to Yunnan; yet no cartographic details were available. Major explorations of this route began with the British and French pioneers attempting to officially or privately track the route. The French were the first to move from Saigon to Yunnan and carried out a major expedition in 1866–1868 under Ernest Doudant de Lagree, Francis Garnier, and Louis de Carne.[32] The first British expedition set off in 1868 under the leadership of Colonel Edward B. Sladden. It, however, could not proceed beyond the city of Momien [Tengyue][33] – the first town on the Chinese side of the Burma–China border. Wooed by both the Panthay Governor [*woon*] of Momien and the rival Chinese and Panthay bandits or rebels, and also harassed by them because of their mutual jealousy and mutual competition and opposition, Sladden found it safer to return. After the failure of Sladden's mission to make any headway, another official expedition with Colonel Horace Browne was organized in 1875. To assist him on the trip, a young official from the British consular office in Shanghai with excellent proficiency in the Chinese language and considerable knowledge of Chinese culture and customs, Augustus Raymond Margary[34] was attached to the mission. He had earlier worked in the consular office at Taiwan, Peking, and Chefoo. He was to reach Bhamo at the Burma—Yunnan frontier from Shanghai by the overland route and await there to join Colonel Browne's mission coming from the British Burma. He moved immediately with the concurrence of the Chinese government and an imperial Chinese passport, and safely traversed the overland route and joined Browne's mission much in time, which started early in February 1875. However, as this large mission entered the first frontier town Seray near the first major frontier city Mawyun [Tengyue] in China from the valley of Nampoung in Burma, they were, as mentioned earlier, attacked by the local stakeholders of the route and Margary was killed on February 21, 1875. Subsequent to the Margary incident and in the face of growing local opposition, the mission abandoned the exploration journey and returned. It was finally a mission led by a British Army officer, Henry Rodolph Davies in 1894–1900, which succeeded in completing the survey of the region's geography, society, diverse indigenous cultures, economy, and politics. His comprehensive work earned him the Royal Geographic Society's Murchison Award [instituted in 1882 in honor of the Scottish geologist Sir Roderick Murchison (1792-1871) for contribution to geographical science] for being the first published authentic report on the region.

To be sure, the long continuity of this trade route, connecting rich Chinese border provinces to the outside world and opening alternative entry points to the internal China market, made it sufficiently lucrative for all the stakeholders despite its geographical location in a perilous highland region and its administrative control by relatively autonomous local forces in the large southwest frontier region. Its emergence on the scanner of global trade threatened the historically developed customary trade system and the power and authority of both the local forces and the Central State. Efforts by the outsiders to survey the region and the trade route alarmed the Qing state and necessitated the urgency to territorialize it in maps for the Chinese nation.

Frontier Region, Cartography, and Demarcation and Territorialization of the Chinese Nation-State

This historical highland frontier region typically characterized spatial peculiarities of what Scott calls Zomia[35] a 'contested borderland' with minimal reach of successive states developing and pursuing their own more or less autonomous lifestyles and connections to manage power and authority on both sides of the frontier. The single distinguishing trait of Zomia, Scott writes is that it is relatively stateless and ungoverned or self-governed. Chinese, Burmese, Panthay, Kakhyens, Shan, and other indigene local elites, merchants, and inhabitants thrived on taxes, levies, and various fees collected from the caravans passing through the route. For all of them, the overwhelmingly floating and prevalent ideas of the European encroachment of their area for the construction of the railroad raised various serious apprehensions – both true and imagined, for the loss of their customary freedom, power, and control.

The nineteenth century, as C. A. Bayly[36] and others demonstrate, was the period of the:

[T]erritorialization of the globe in large part through the slow process of surveying land and water, conceiving of nature as sets of systematized objects, mapping the result of that process, and using that information, in turn to redefine the degree to which the state 'saw' the space it attempted to control.

Further, in the era of empires disintegrating into nation-states and the gradual shift from universality to particularity of the political order, as Kyle Gardener[37] writes, 'geography not only transformed into science, but also became a political science' in defining and designating states through such technologies of new forms of knowledge as cartographic mapping and surveying. Maps became a signifier of permanent territory of the nation-state that were often invoked in the political discourse of nationalism. Mapping provided a territorial imaginary of the nation that was to be defended and preserved.

In the late nineteenth century, Chinese attempt to define/ demarcate its borders with the British, European and other colonizing or emerging states was part of a rapid and aggressive global shift from the civilizational-state to the nation-state. Among the contemporary Chinese intellectuals, Xue Fucheng, a diplomat in London in the 1890s, realized and affirmed the significance of maps in negotiation with foreign powers. He advocated a shift in the way the Qing dealt with the West in China. Xue writes, as quoted by Bussche, 'All countries in the world are interconnected. We must follow West's examples in forging alliances rather than acting unilaterally and in isolation. We may not be able to force foreigners to comply with Chinese law but we can use Western law to govern Westerners'. Accordingly, his strategy envisaged expansion through the military incorporation of tributary states, encouraging emigration, and protecting Chinese commercial interests in Southeast Asia. As Vanden Bussche notes, Xue 'was aware that the map was the medium through which the Europeans constructed and negotiated space', and 'he had to use a map rather than written sources to advance Chinese territorial claims'.[38] In the case of Burma, its practice could be seen in the policy of border dispute as the first step towards wresting Burma away from the British and transforming this tributary state into a colony. Mapping the territory thus became a fundamental part of the discourse on nation, nationalism, and modernity to stand in line with the overwhelming European world order, and follow the art and science of the emerging era of geopolitics. No wonder in solving border issues Chinese often presented the 'Burmese model' of border negotiation and resolution as 'ideal'.

To digress a little, it may be noted that the major issue in mapping sovereign national territory was in defining and demarcating frontiers which by its very nature historically often remained 'ambiguous', 'malleable', or 'overlapping'. Frontier or borderland, as Thongchai Winichakul conceptualizes, are pre-national state spaces encompassing a 'sovereign zone' (where state exercised full power), an 'inner frontier zone' (where state power was intermittently projected), and an 'outer frontier zone' (where there was a vacuum of authority with no definite claims of contingent states). In such a space, the extent of state power was not determined by a boundary line, but by a dynamic overlapping boundary that was continuously reconfigured by a fluid web of power relations at the local level.

Further, in the area of cartography in China, there has been an alternative disposition to also produce, what has generally been called, the 'Humiliation Maps'. They are part of efforts to superimpose 'real' or 'perceived' territories of the civilisational-state to the nation-state, where both the late imperialist Chinese concept of 'unbounded domain (jiangyu)' and the 'modern understanding of bounded sovereign territory (chuquan lingtu)' fuse together 'often in a creative tension' – to draw the PRC's twenty-first century geo-body taking into account the Chinese imagination. These Chinese maps of humiliation, as William A. Callahan[39] aptly demonstrates, are the product of 'creation of imaginative and aspirational maps, inscribing territories that are not under state control - but could and should be part of China's sovereign territory.'

Thus, growing external focus on China's southwest region and the traditional SSR required a strengthened internal vigilance and a robust enterprise of territorialization of the Chinese nation-state through modern cartographic principles and tools. This became urgent and necessary due to increasing footsteps of the foreigners in the region and their frequent surveying expeditions. After all, maps turned indispensable as China began to shift from the empire to the nation-state and consequently from the frontier to the foreign policy. The greater reach of imperialist countries over the multiple frontiers across China rendered a coordinated frontier policy ineffective.

The earlier Kangxi Survey map of Qing did not place much weight on the maps as evidence regarding territory beyond Qing's control. The geography of foreign lands remained imprecise until the early nineteenth century. Huang Maocai in *Yu-li-chu-yan* [My Humble Opinions] mentioned that a variety of Chinese names were used for India.[40] It included names like Tian-zhu, Shen-du, Yin-du, Fo-guo, Wu Yin-du [Five India-s], Xin-du, Xin-du-si-tang, [Hindustan], etc. Words like Wu Yin-du [Five India-s], for example, evolved from ancient Chinese texts by combining two separate words and were not at all in common use; Enetkek [United Province/India] originated from the Mongolian/Manchurian language texts, and several others like Hen-du-si-tan or Wen-du-sit-an came from the Muslim region. Even Yindu [India] and Hindustan were considered two separate entities. The map of non-imperial territory, as Matthew Mosca points out, 'was enmeshed in the matrix of corroboration ... and formed by weaving together strands from various sources, (including European maps widely regarded as dubious) without first hand evidence from a trusted observer in the Qing elite' [Mosca: 125]. The Qianlong Emperor's ambivalence toward European geography is amply demonstrated in the use of the Buddhist place names like *Jambudvipa* in his writings.[41] But, as Mosca writes, 'never, as far as I can determine, did he refer to 'Asia'.' Further, 'the survey map's utility in regard to foreign territory was also limited by its regional origin on a single frontier'. In areas like Xinjiang, which were charted in great detail, preferred use of local lexicon of

Inner and Central Asian informants for geographic nomenclature, rendered maps operationally inadequate. [Mosca: 123ff].

> It was of no use for warfare or diplomacy along other parts of the frontier with India, such as the Eastern Himalayas. Bengal was left almost entirely blank, its river systems grossly distorted to fit the needs of reconciling the Kangxi ssurvey of western Tibet with European maps. Calcutta was excluded, as were most other major European ports trading to China.
>
> *[Mosca: 126]*

The lack of a universal name for India in various Chinese maps limited their influence in the management of the frontier. By the 1840s, as Mosca [305] writes, 'developments in geographic and geostrategic thought allowed a foreign policy to emerge as an alternative to the previously dominant frontier policy'. This witnessed the rise of new institutions like Zongli Yamen [Office for the General Management of Affairs Concerning the Various Countries] in 1861, and schools/arsenals for training in western languages and sciences that included cartography and the undertaking of large projects for map-making. By 1886, a specialized and independent 'Office for the Compilation of the Statues/Maps' [Hui-dian-guan] took over the task of the production of official maps.

As mentioned earlier, Huang Maocai was a part of the movement for new [Western] learning and the emergent West-inspired nationalism. As an official cartographer and leader of the Qing state-commissioned official expedition, he was to undertake a full survey of the southwest region and the SSR, remove existing lacunae in the traditional Chinese atlas, and draw fresh maps using modern cartographic principles and tools for the protection of Chinese territoriality. His task was not only to situate places along the SSR according to modern cartographic practice based on a geographic coordinate system that measured in degrees of latitude and longitude, but to also update old and unrecognized place-names by their current appellations. It was thus to nationalize the unidentified, un-demarcated, and relatively ungoverned territories of its southwest frontiers to counter contemporary British and French expeditions to open Southwest China for the commercial and national interest of their countries. It was driven by geopolitical concerns of the Chinese nation-state and the anxiety to consequently frame a coordinated foreign policy.

These map-making activities at the frontiers while strengthening territorial claims of the nation-state, 'impacted central control over the empire's borderlands and it can be hypothesized that a diminished sensitivity to local perspectives in pursuit of a foreign policy designed to counter Western imperialism played some part in the upheavals within the Qing realm in its last decades'.[Mosca: 310] Scholars have contested its impact on the state. Yet, its Janus-faced nature cannot be discounted. For some, such fresh mapmaking efforts in the wake of foreign threats facilitated a more homogeneous centralized administrative structure laying the foundation of a modern nation-state. Any inaction in this matter would imply weakening control of the state. However, for those still skeptical of the impact of shifting global geopolitics, such a fundamental reconfiguration of Beijing's assertion of greater control over the periphery led to a breach of precedent, undermining the dynasty's right to rule.

India and its Configuration as the Colonial State under the British Imperialist Rule

Not unlike other modern Chinese travelers to India, Huang lamented the disappearance of Buddhism in India. The wisdom and precepts of Buddhism that illuminated India and China for thousands of years and that intelligently and compassionately guided people and society in both the countries were not visible in the country of its origin. In one of his poems on India, he writes that earlier Chinese travelers crossed thousands of hurdles to visit Sravasti and other holy Buddhist places and searched for true knowledge in *Tripitaka*. All these places exist even now. 'The Ganges with its many tributaries flowed towards the East and received many foreign heretics from regions of the West and the Lu-ye garden [The Deer Park] and the Ling Vulture Mountain [the Holy Vulture Peak] have all endured many changes'.[42] Yet, now there was no Ananda, the famous senior disciple of Buddha, to present Buddhist discourses and talk about past events. He at the same time admitted that the motive of his journey was not to collect relics of Buddhism but to draw maps of this vast country. His narratives, therefore, skipped general knowledge of India in texts available in China.[43] Huang's study of India, as Idier (2020) notes, 'was progressivist-oriented and not so negative' and recommended 'looking carefully at the modernization processes that he witnessed in India'.[44]

British India greatly intrigued Huang. He was fascinated by the colonial state's use of modern methods to administer the vast territory under its rule. Various new technical devices, products of western scientific discoveries, and various modern systems of communication like telegraph and telephone that provided swift and efficient communication from the top to the bottom chain of administration were impressive. He liked the power of steam engines and railways that facilitated the fast movement of people and materials over long distances. Kolkata's clean and wide roads and streets with gas lamps appeared very convenient. The supply and control of water everywhere in the city through chains of water pipes and water taps were a novelty. The dissemination of modern knowledge through the museum, the zoo, and the botanical garden appealed to him. Rigorous trainings and discipline at the modern schools especially the Western art school where, unlike the Chinese style of painting, the emphasis was laid on drawing mirror-like representation of the object captivated him. He noticed the efficient police administration and the 'humane' and transparent judicial system. Taxes were heavy. But the state expenditure of these funds for public conveniences kept people happy and quiet. Huang felt that the local Indians perceived the British rule as a welcome change in comparison with the cruel and lawless administration of the earlier native rulers. On the whole, Huang found the colonial local administration less corrupt, more efficient, and equitable.

The colonial flavor in Huang's writing, Zhang Ke [45] aptly writes, was most notably because of his failure 'to distinguish between Britain and India, often confusing the political structures of Britain with India to compare them with China', and his selective portrayal of India 'as a country dependent on the British and a model representative of British governance in Asia'. His writings therefore featured very few views of Indians themselves and projected interpretations that were conveyed by the colonial state. Huang's criticism of the British upper class in India as people 'pursuing pleasure without any restriction' was not a critique of colonialism, but merely a curiosity about the lifestyle of the people he seemed to admire and convey to his Chinese readers. Yet, on the flip side, Huang also negatively reacted to the state's maximum possible extortion from the ordinary masses and the extravagant lifestyle of the British officials. Huang's commitment to the West-inspired nationalism imbued with the spirit or ethics of capitalism in the Weberian sense is fully evident when he makes a distinction between China and the West. Highlighting such strains in Huang's ideology, Zhang Ke notes that this appeared because of his belief that 'China's political structure benefits the poor first, while the Western government supports the rich. Perhaps in the Western tradition being poor is shameful, and so Western people are all working hard to get rich'.[46]

While Huang did not detail customs and practices of native Indians in his narratives, he noticed the beginning of westernization among the higher echelon of the local people due to British influence. They were the ones who practiced the western ethics to get rich. There was however not much change in the practices of the common people from what was described earlier in Wei Yuan's *Hai-guo tu-zhi* [Illustrated Records of Maritime Countries] or Xu Jiyu's *Ying-huan zhi-lue* [A Short Account of the Maritime Sphere] written in the 1840s, which included descriptions like Indians wearing a white cloth to cover the lower portion of the body, winding it over to cover the upper front, and then using the remaining portion to cover the head; or they wore turbans of either white or red cloth, daubed their forehead and/ or spot between the eyes with ornamental or sectarian marks, and maintained the caste system, etc.[47] Huang realized that the slow pace of social transformation in India originated from the lesser intervention of the British in the characteristic Indian social system after the Great Rebellion of 1857. This event ended the rule of the East India Company and brought in direct control of the British crown, which pursued the policy of supporting the feudal setup and minimal interference in religious customs and beliefs on the one hand, and the opening up of the economic domain on the other hand. This is evident, for example, in the British segregation of the British Indian Army based on religion and castes to maintain their control and other such administrative acts. Their motives remained focused on turning India into an 'ideal' colonial capitalist market.[48]

It is true, as Zhang Ke notes,

> Huang's perceptions of British India were driven by his curiosity about the new things he was seeing in a foreign land. Moreover, what he reported in his travelogue was highly selective and intended to serve a particular purpose. His eagerness to imitate Westerners, his preference for Westernization and his exaggerated descriptions of the exotic were quite usual among late Qing Chinese travellers in foreign lands. Similar accounts and descriptions can be found, for example, in the works of Guo Songtao and Wang Tao both of whom visited European countries.[49]

One may see similar fascination for these colonial establishments and objects also in Kang Youwei's travelogues.[50] Colonial wonders indeed generated admiration in the eyes of those who either believed in the west-inspired nationalism and modernity or sought 'hybrid' modernization and reform to rejuvenate China. Huang's travelogue, Zhang Ke (2021) concludes, failed to generate much direct impact on his contemporaries and represented an idealized view, not altogether rare among Qing officials, of British rule in India. Not surprisingly, Huang's unabashed admiration for the British Indian state appeared uncharitable to the Confucian state and might have placed hurdles in his rise to higher active positions of administration during the Qing.

Yet, Huang was not oblivious to the encroachment and movement of the western imperialist forces and its consequences on the rise of China as a strong nation-state. He noted disastrous consequences of the Assam tea production in the British-controlled tea gardens on the traditional Sichuan–Tibet–Yunnan tea trade through the Southwest Silk Route. The British had planted a large number of tea bushes in Assam with the help of Fujian and Zhejiang tea planters. They imitated the production of tea from Sichuan and Yunnan which was exported to nearby Tibet. Ding Baozhen, Governor of Sichuan, was worried that the development of Assam by the British would cause it to send troops from the local area to encroach on Tibet in case of any obstacle to this trade. Huang's visit to Darjeeling, Assam, and nearby tea-producing regions in northeast India confirmed the wide-expanding tea production there. He was in fact the first whistleblower regarding the possibility of Chinese dominance in the world tea trade getting overturned. In fact, by the beginning of the twentieth century, India's tea exports surpassed China and became number one in the world. This revelation was shocking for the members of the Imperial Court in the late Qing. So much so that in 1905, Zhou Fu, the Governor of Liang Jiang, sent an overseas tea industry delegation to India and Sri Lanka to investigate local tea production and trade there.[51] However, Huang's solution to the problem was different. When somebody raised the issue of closing the SSR trade route to defend the country from the possible foreign invasion, he responded that 'I don't know if the circulation of commercial goods is enough to enrich the country and protect the border. How could its closure be prudent for the defense of borders?' Using the same reasoning, he becomes the first Chinese to support the construction of railway to connect Yunnan with Southeast Asia. In his travel narrative, he proposed that if a railway was built from Burma and extended to Yunnan, 'the distance by land and water would not exceed ten days, and it would be only one-third of the distance from Nanyang to eastern Guangdong'. Therefore, 'this road is not only for the benefit of the British, but also for the benefit of the Chinese'. For him, the capitalist free market and free trade were not bad if they were managed well by the state.[52]

Huang's strong patriotic enthusiasm and knowledge of contemporary geopolitics were apparent in his description of the historical evolution of the long frontier in the western part of China and neighboring countries. He informed that any possibility of a threat of British invasion of China through Tibet and the Southwest frontier region lurked primarily from a narrow pass in the Himalayan region of Darjeeling and Sikkim located between Bhutan and Nepal. Having acquired the Hill tract from Sikkim and established a Darjeeling district, the British finally annexed Sikkim and made it their protected state. Huang noted the construction of military blockhouses and stationing of foreign troops as well as the laying of a direct rail track there from the plains thus being done with a long-term plan. He observed that the unrestrained heavy investment in railways, the settlement of Fukienese and Cantonese people, and the covetous eyes on the Tibetan territory and the trade route were ominous signs for China. The British colonizers would seize any opportunity that promised financial benefits. They first craftily extended their power with commercial dominance, then infiltrated and interfered in local politics, and finally forced all to follow them. Their present stance indicated forming a bond with Bhutan through the offer of heavy financial aid on the one hand, and dismembering Sikkim gradually on the other hand. The possibility of their indulgence in a clash on the frontier should, therefore, not be taken lightly. In order to save China, he advised Sichuan Governor Ding Baozhen to protect Jiangze [Gyangze/Rgyal rtse], Ding-ri [Dingri zd zong], and Bhutan, and develop a good friendly relationship with Nepal by supporting its rise as a solid buffer state.[53]

Conclusion

Huang's writings covered a vast canvas in his geopolitical observation of regions surrounding China. While returning to China through the maritime route, he passed through Rangoon, Penang, Singapore, and Saigon and made brief stop-overs there. That helped him comprehend the actual situation in the Nanyang region. He analyzed the expansion of Western imperialist forces and the contemporary strategic importance of the Southeast Asian countries. He drew the attention of the Imperial Qing Court to current developments in the Nanyang region and emphasized the need to play an active role there. Unlike in the past, the Nanyang region must now be adequately taken care of. There were more than a million Chinese staying in these foreign lands for an extended period of time. These overseas Chinese were often 'bullied by natives or abused by foreign states'. They must be provided proper consular protection as Chinese citizens as practiced by the other modern nation-states for their nationals. His strong pleas to the Qing court to establish more and more consulates of the Chinese nation also indirectly signaled an end to the fast-eroding system of 'hierarchical' tributary relationship in favor of emerging 'non-hierarchical' equality-based global reality.

Huang noted that after the end of the ban on the overseas-travel, diplomatic communications, and trade activities between China and other countries expanded. Developments of maritime routes and plying of safer and faster steamships reduced the time and distance of travel. Distant countries interacted much more frequently with China for various purposes; yet, there was no corresponding vigorous effort in China to study Western sciences and new knowledge. He emphasized to the Court to urgently expand specific programs to train and scout 'talents' in foreign languages and studies. He also prioritized a program for strengthening of maritime defense through the wide exploration of the sea and the detection and use of new sea lanes to raise commercial and political power. His views echoed contemporary views of strategists like Alfred Thayer Mahan and others on the significance of building naval power and supremacy.

Another area that drew Huang's attention was the concept of buffer states in foreign policy. The eighteenth century Western theory of the balance of power along with the concept of the buffer state as part of the strategy and diplomacy in foreign policy received his appreciation and approval. He realized problems in maintaining the traditional Chinese worldview and its application through tributary relationships. In his narratives, he recommended connecting with Nepal and developing it as a strong buffer state between British India and China. Observing the growing importance of the Southeast Asian countries, he favored their treatment as equal partners in the world of nation-states. Adopting a foreign policy based on 'contacting and connecting with countries to strengthen barriers', he believed, would protect and strengthen China's status in Southeast Asia. Huang's narratives and other available essays put him among those contemporary 'modernist' intellectuals who looked ahead of time and sought an alternative discourse for China's predicaments.

To be sure, the context, time, method, and narratives of Huang's cartographic mission from China to India evince the complexity of the Southwest Silk Route and the borderland. Most of all, it manifests the Qing state's active effort to territorialize the imprecise/ 'malleable'/ 'nebulous'/ 'overlapping' frontier region in view of many contesting claims from both inside and outside. In China, the mapping of place, space, and territory of the empire constituted one of the most significant part of making and preserving the modern nation-state and the projection of an ideology of nationalism. Duara perceptively tells that the novelty of the modern state and its ideology of nationalism lies not in political self-consciousness but in the recognition of a world system of nation-states as the only legitimate form of polity.

> It is a political form with distinct territorial boundaries within which the sovereign state, 'representing' the nation-people, has steadily expanded its role and power. The ideology of the nation-state system has sanctioned the penetration of state power into areas that were once dominated by the local authority structure.[54]

In the face of various outside and inside threats, territorialization intricately linked the construction of the nation-state with nationalism, modernity, and imperialism, prioritizing and overwhelming other signifiers of China's legacies. In this context, the mission of Huang Maocai was crucial.

Yet, the problem arose as the rules of cartography differed. Unlike the Western cartography's emphasis on putting down the location on the map showing longitude and latitude, 'Chinese mapmaking practices', Bussche informs, 'did not emphasize mathematical projections. For the Chinese, a map was a broad illustration of a region based on written sources. For instance, 19th-century Chinese maps depicted landmarks and trade routes, but didn't feature distance measurements'. Huang's narratives did put measurements employing geographical coordinates through the calculation of longitude and latitude. However, the maps which he subsequently produced and presented to the Imperial Court are not in circulation. A definite observation on the true content and character of his maps thus could not be made.

Finally we could say that Huang completed the state-assigned project as a true nationalist and modernist. Nowhere in his writing one finds recourse to the universality of the 'boundless' Tianxia world order and the Confucian political order. His commitments to the particularity of the nation – defined by boundaries and as a part of the world system of nation-states, and a compatible reform in the political system – along the lines of the administrative structure of the British India remained profound. These might not be so compatible with the contemporary worldview and the dominant political structure of the Qing state. This is evident in the limited circulation of his maps and the post-expedition postings in the borderlands. Yet, his works and commitments make him an important foot soldier moving a step ahead of his more illustrious predecessors Wei Yuan and Xu Jiyu in the presentation of a geopolitical scenario, and in paving a space for later eminent reformers like Kang Youwei who juggled with a hybrid form of nationalism that attempted to fuse civilizational sensitivities with 'perceived' modern nationalist essentialities. His efforts at territorializing the nation thus opened up one more window to facilitate and strengthen the process of construction of the modern state in China even at the cost of emulating the Western path. Many of the leftover and unresolved tensions emanating from the process of movement from empire to nation, contestation between the frontier and the border, the tributary relations and foreign policy, local ethnic identity and national identity, and traditional and other signifiers of the nation however still haunt contemporary China.

A young admirer of Huang Maocai, in an essay commemorating 140 years of the latter's overland mission, poignantly sums up that Huang was a scholar:

> who had dreamt of studying to become an excellent official, and who had studied sages hard under the cold window. Encountering great changes unseen in a thousand years, he resolutely went to Shanghai to study in a new school [for western learning], and obeyed Ding Baozhen's assignment to lead a small team [for the expedition to southwest China from Sichuan to India]. Only when we travel the long way to the west will we find that the great changes of the times have also brought more choices in life. And Huang Maocai's choice just responded to the most unforgettable theme of that era: 'Mountains and rivers fall into a dream [Our beautiful land is turning illusive], save the nation and ensure its preservation'.[55]

Notes

1 The middle character of Huang Maocai's [黄楙材] 'mao [楙]' is also sometimes written as 'mao [茂]'. Not much biographical details on Huang Maocai are available. Most of the information here has been culled from Preface of the book by Zhengxie shang-gao-xian wen-shi zi-liao wei-yuan-hui, eds. 1989. *Huang Maocai wen-ji [Collected Works of Huang Maocai]*. Shanggao, Jiangxi: Jiang-xi di-zhi ce-hui yin-shua-chang; and from materials in Lin Cheng-jie. 1993. *Zhong-yin ren-min you-hao guan-xi shi: 1851–1949 [A History of Sino-Indian Friendly Relations: 1851–1949]*; Zhang Ke. 2021. 'Through the "Indian Lens": Observations and Self-Reflections in Late Qing Chinese Travel Writings

on India', in Tansen Sen and Brian Tsui, eds. 2021. *Beyond Pan-Asianism: Connecting China and India 1840s–1960s*. Oxford: Oxford University Press.

2 It was one of the famous ancient private learning academies established during the Song Dynasty to provide Confucian teaching. It was taken over by the state during the Ming period and turned into a semi-government school. (See Sarah Scheneewind. 2006. *Community Schools and the State during the Ming China*. Stanford: Stanford University.)

3 Bright students [sheng-yuan] with high academic potential were known as Xiucai [distinguished talent] and were granted state subsidies to complete education for the civil service examination.

4 See for an enlightening and detailed description, Banjamin A. Elman. 2006. *A Cultural History of Modern Science in China*. Cambridge, MA: Harvard University Press.

5 Tong-wen-guan was the first official foreign language school established following the opening of Zongli Yamen [Office of the Foreign Affairs] in 1861 to teach western languages and prepare native interpreters to communicate with foreign powers. In 1866, the study of astronomy and mathematics was included in its curriculum. By 1870, it conducted a comprehensive eight-year teaching program that started with the study of three years of a foreign language and five years of western science and knowledge. Its branches were later expanded to Shanghai and Guangdong. In 1902, this school was merged with the Imperial University.

6 In English, it was also known as the Chefoo Convention. It was a treaty between Qing China and Great Britain, signed by Sir Thomas Wade and Li Hongzhang in Zhifu (a district of Yantai) on August 21, 1876.

7 Lin (1993: 17) notes that in 1877 two foreigners Jiweili [William John Gill] and Beidelu [Father Blettery] sought permission to go to India from Sichuan via Yunnan and Tibet to explore trade and inter-regional trade. For Gill's account of his expedition from Chengdu, China through Sichuan, along the eastern edge of Tibet via Litang, to Bhamo in Burma, a region little explored by westerners before him. See Capt. William John Gill. 1880. *The River of Golden Sand: Being the Narrative of a Journey through China and Eastern Tibet to Burmah,* in two volumes. London: John Murray.

8 Besides agreeing to the indemnity payment to Raymond Margery's relatives, the Agreement provided more extraterritorial rights to the British citizens as well as approval for the opening of new trade ports.

9 Located in the Garze Tibetan Autonomous Prefecture in the Sichuan Province of China, Batang town was an important stopover point on the Sichuan–Tibet–India route. As tea and horses were carried for trade through this road, it was also known as the Tea Horse Road.

10 This refers to Tibetan Gyeltang town. It was in Diqing Tibetan Autonomous Prefecture in northwest Yunnan. Its former name was Xiang-ge-li-la Xian [Shangri-La county].

11 It was the famous custom point at the junction of China–Myanmar border on the old trade route from Bhamo to Yunnan. Its Burmese name was Momein [also written as Momien]. Under Momein was the frontier town of Manwyne, where Margary was assassinated in January 1875.

12 Zhengxie shang-gao-xian wen-shi zi-liao wei-yuan-hui, ed. 1989. *Huang Maocai Wenji [Collected Works of Huang Maocai]*. Jiangxi: Jiang-xi di-zhi ce-hui yin-shua-chang; hereafter referred to as Huang Maocai Wen-ji.

13 Elsewhere entitled Hu-you qiang or kong-ji.

14 See Chinese Editor's preface in *Huang Maocai Wen-ji*

15 See notes 37 and 38 later in this chapter. Bussche's (2014) states about the availability of declassified original Chinese maps but also the British maps of the

Southwest China and Myanmar of the late Qing period with detailed notes in Chinese, added by the Qing negotiators and surveyors.

16 See Preface in *Huang Maocai wen-ji*.

17 See Huang Maocai Wen-ji.

18 This is the present Xinping Yi and Dai Autonomous counties located in the central part of Yunnan.

19 This is named after the Maitreya Buddha and is a county in China with a Buddhist name and a Maitreya temple. It is located in Honghe [Red River] Hani [tribe] and Yi [tribe] Autonomous Prefectures/counties bordering with Vietnam.

20 On Huidianguan and other developments in the history of cartography in China, see Iwo Amelung. 2007. 'New Maps for the Modernizing State: Western Geographic Knowledge and its Application in the 19th and 20th Century', in Francesca Bray, Vera Dorofeeva-Lichtmann, and Georges Métailié, eds., *Graphics and Text in the Production of Technical Knowledge in China*, The Warp and the Weft: 79 (Sinica Leidensia, Vol. 79). Leiden: Brill, 685–726.

21 Kang Youwei, however, found Huang Maocai's travel narratives not very useful and even refused to enlist Huang's work in line with the works of illustrious ancient monk-travelers like Faxian, Xuanzang, and Yijing. Instead, he proclaimed himself to be the fourth eminent Chinese traveler to India.

22 See Bin Yang (2008): 284–293. These names, as Yang (292) cautioned, must be seen from a temporal perspective as they 'emerged in different times, they functioned variously, and their sub-branches changed course through history'. In the period of World War II, it became also strategically important and became known as Ambassador/Royal Road, Burma Road, The Hump, Ledo Road, and Stilwell [after allied general Joseph Stilwell] Road.

23 See for a detailed history and description of the circulatory cross-regional trade on the Southwest Silk Road SSR, Bin Yang. 2008. *Between Winds and Clouds: The Making of Yunnan – Second Century BCE to Twentieth Century CE*. New York: Columbia University Press; and Bin Yang. 2004. 'Horses, Silver, and Cowries: Yunnan in Global Perspective', *Journal of World History*, Vol. 15, No. 3.

24 Examining Yunnan from a global perspective as well as in the context of Turner's 'frontier thesis', 'Sinocentrism', western imperialism, Yang (2008) argues that 'a national approach to a frontier area such as Yunnan is too simplified. In most cases, if not all, the simplification aims to build a national legend. Likewise, it is similarly dangerous to categorize Yunnan as part of East Asia or Southeast Asia. After all, history was born much earlier than nations'.

25 See Tansen Sen. 2003. *Buddhism, Diplomacy, and Trade: The Realignment of Sino-Indian Relations*. Honolulu: University of Hawaii Press; and Tansen Sen. 2018. *India, China and the World: A Connected History*. Delhi: Oxford University Press. Another good account is available in Har Prasad Ray. 1993. *Trade and Diplomacy in India-China Relations: A Study of Bengal during the Fifteenth Century*. Delhi: Radiant Publishers.

26 D. P. Singhal. 1972. *India and World Civilization*. London: Sidgwick and Jackson.

27 See John Deyell. 1994. 'The China Connection: Problems of Silver Supply in Medieval Bengal' in Sanjay Subhramanyam, ed., *Money and the Market in India, 1100–1700*. Delhi: Oxford University Press; Nisar Ahmed, 1990. 'Assam Bengal Trade in the Medieval Period: A Numismatic Perspective' *Journal of the Economic and Social History of the Orient* Vol. 33(Jan. 1990: 169–198); also quoted in Bin Yang. 2008. *Between Winds and Clouds: The Making of Yunnan – Second Century BCE to Twentieth Century CE*. New York: Columbia University Press. Also see James Z. Lee. 2000. *A Frontier Political Economy:*

Southwest China, 1250–1850 (Vol. 190 of Harvard East Asian monographs). Cambridge: Harvard University Press.

28 See John Anderson. 1876. *Mandalay to Momien: A Narrative of the Two Expeditions to Western China of 1868 and 1875 under Colonel Edward B. Sladden and Colonel Horace Brown.* London: MacMillan and Co., p. 2, and also Chapter I: 2–37 for the background to the expedition on the SSR route from British Burma.

29 For details of various proposals for the railroad construction, see H. R. Davies. 1909. *Yunnan: The Link between India and the Yangzi.* Cambridge: Cambridge University Press; Ralph C. Croizier. 1962. 'Antecedents of Burma Road', *Journal of Southeast Asian History*, Vol. 3, No. 2; also see 'Mr. Holt Hallett on Burmah and the Shan States', *The Manchester Guardian*, 20th January, 1886; Holt S. Hallett. 1892. 'The Remedy for Lancashire: A Burma-China Railway,' *Blackwood's Edinburgh Magazine*, September 1892, quoted in Frances O'morchoe. 2020. 'Tracing the More Than Century-Old Dream of Building a Myanmar-China Railway', *The Irrawaddy*, 17 March 2020. In fact, amateur private enthusiasts like Archibald Ross Colquhoun along with Holt S. Hallett made a survey of the area on their own in the race to beat the French in the construction of the rail route. Colquhoun presented their travel record in an 1883 book *Across Chryse: Being the Narrative of a Journey of Exploration Through the South China Borderlands From Canton to Mandalay,* 2 Volumes. Whitefish, Montana: Kessinger Legacy Reprints, rpt. 2010.

30 Frontier towns of Bhamo and Dali were imagined as future global entrepots like Shanghai, Calcutta, and Saigon in French writings. These were touted as the 'Louisiana of the East'.

31 H. R. Davies. 1909. *Yunnan – The Link between Indian and the Yangzi.* Cambridge: Cambridge University Press.

32 The report of the French expedition appeared in a volume by Francis Garnier. 1873. *Voyage d'exploration en Indo-Chine, 1866–68.* Translated with an introduction by E. J. Walter, 1996–2001. *Tips as The Mekong Exploration Committee Report, 1866–1868.* Bangkok: White Lotus Press. This is a most valuable record of the political and economic situation of the region.

33 Momien in Chinese was known as Teng-yue, which is now renamed as Tengcheng.

34 See for details, Augustus Raymond Margary and Rutherford Alcock. 1876. *The Journey of Augustus Raymond Margary from Shanghae to Bhamo and Back to Manwyne: From His Journals and Letters with a Brief Biographical Preface.* London: MacMillan and Co.; For a description of both the expeditions see also the report of another explorer and a naturalist, John Anderson (1876), who was part of both the expeditions. (John Anderson. 1876. *Mandalay to Momien: A Narrative of the Two Expeditions to Western China of 1868 and 1875 under Colonel Edward B. Sladden and Colonel Horace Brown.* London: MacMillan and Co.)

35 See James C. Scott. 2009. *The Art of Not Being Governed: An Anarchist History of Upland Southeast Asia.* New Haven: Yale University Press. See also, Kyle Gardner, 2021. *The Frontier Complex. Geopolitics and the Making of India–China Border, 1846–1962.* Cambridge: Cambridge University Press; Jagjeet Lally. 2021. 'Salt, Smuggling, and Sovereignty: The Burma-China Borderland, c. 1880-1935', *The Journal of Imperial and Commonwealth History*, Vol. 49, No. 6, 1047–1081) who have demonstrated the state's response to Zomia by tacit understanding of its spatial peculiarities and devising and deploying newer tools of geography like cartography and maps to assert their control and authority. Also some scholars have emphatically argued that unlike Frederick Turner's frontiers, frontiers existing at the edges of the two empires or larger dominant

civilizational area are relatively autonomous territories that contest and resist appropriation through deft sociocultural and political negotiations and interactions. In this sense, James C. Scott's 'zomia' or Owen Lattimore's 'dynamic frontier zones' present an apt characterization of China's Southwest border region. See Owen Lattimore. 1940. *Inner Asian Frontiers of China*. New York: American Geographical Society; and Peter Perdue. 2005. *China Marches West*. Cambridge, MA: Harvard University Press. The state in China identified and created these zones way back during Han dynasty and since then the frontier defense and management have been an important activity.

36 See C. A. Bayly. 2003. *The Birth of the Modern World, 1780–1914: Global Connections and Comparisons*. London: Wiley-Blackwell.

37 Quoted from Gardner, Kylie (2021): 14. Recently, several illuminating studies providing a new framework for the study of frontier, border, and borderlands in connection with cartography, discourse of nationalism, and modernity have been published. One of them is by Bussche, Eric Vanden whose *PhD dissertation* entitled 'Contested Realms: Colonial Rivalry, Border Demarcations, and State Building in Southwest China, 1885–1960', Stanford University 2014, 'draws on recently declassified Chinese maps from the 1880s and 1890s to examine the role of cartographic practices and spatial discourses in defining borders between the Qing and European colonial regimes. To advance their territorial claims, the Qing formulated new spatial discourses of the disputed border regions by employing a vast array of sources that included European maps, Chinese imperial gazetteers, and secondhand geographical knowledge gleaned from border inhabitants. Through the use of such diverse sources, the Qing produced new maps of their borderlands that at first glance resembled the ones of their European counterparts'. These maps should, however, 'not be viewed as an enthusiastic embrace of Western cartographic practices by the Qing officials. Aware that maps were the political medium through which Western powers constructed and negotiated space, the Qing produced their own versions of European maps to convey their concepts of territorial sovereignty to their counterparts and aggressively legitimize their border claims'. Bussche's work advances hypotheses raised in Iwo Amelung. 2007. 'New Maps for the Modernizing State: Western Cartographic knowledge and its Application in the 19th and 20th Century China', in Francesca Bray, et al., *Graphics and Text in the Production of Technical knowledge in China: The Warp and the Weft*. Leiden: Brill, 685–726, and Cordell D. K. Yee. 1994. 'Traditional Chinese Cartography and the Myth of Westernization', in J. B. Harley and David Woodward, eds., *The History of Cartography*, Vol. 2, Book 2, Chapter seven. Chicago: University of Chicago Press. Another interesting work on the connection of Cartography and nationalism is James Leibold. 2021. *Reconfiguring Chinese Nationalism: How the Qing Frontier and its Indigenes became Chinese*. London: Palgrave Macmillan. The Qing dispatch of Huang Maocai's mission could be seen in these perspectives.

38 Quotations from Bussche (2015) have been collected from his e-presentation, 'On China's Map and Boundaries', in *Kamalashow.com* hosted on youtube .com on January 30, 2015 and from Bossche (2014) interaction in *Stanford Report* (May 29, 2014), 'Stanford historian sees new perspectives on Chinese border disputes in declassified Qing dynasty maps'. Also see important works by C. Paterson Giersch. 2006. *Asian Borderlands: The Transformation of Qing China's Yunnan Frontier*. Cambridge, MA: Harvard University Press; Eric Tugliacozzo. 2005. *Secret Trades, Porous Borders: Smuggling and States along a Southeast Asian Frontier, 1865–1915*. New Haven, CT: Yale University Press; Frances O'Morchoe. 2019. 'Mobility, Space and Power in the Making of Burma's Borders, C.1880-1961', *Ph.D. Thesis*, Somerville College, University of Oxford.

39 William A. Callahan. 2020. Sensible Politics, *Visualising International Relations*. London, Oxford University Press.

40 As quoted in Lin Chengjie. 1993. *Zhong-Yin ren-minyou-hao-guan-xi shi 1851–1949 [A History of Friendly Relations between India and China]*. Beijing: Beijing da-xue chu-ban she, 20.

41 For detailed discussions on names of India, see the first two chapters of Matthew W. Mosca. 2013. *From Frontier Policy to Foreign Policy: The Question of India and the Transformation of Geopolitics in Qing China*. Stanford, CA: Stanford University Press; and also P. C. Bagchi. 1948. 'Ancient Chinese Names for India', *Monumenta Serica*, Vol. 13, 366–375.

42 See the authors' translation of the poem in the Chapter III. 3, entitled 'Sundry Thoughts on India', pp. 123–126.

43 See earlier discussion and full reference to Huang's Preface as translated in the next chapter.

44 See para 17 on Huang Maocai in the internet text of Nicolas Idier. 2020. 'Kang Youwei and India: The Indian Travels of a Cosmopolitan Utopian', in Anne Cheng and Sanchit Kumar, eds., *India–China: Intersecting Universalities*. Paris: College de France: Published on Open Edition Books.

45 See Zhang Ke 2021: 136–137.

46 See Zhang Ke 2021: 136–137.

47 See Lin 1993: 7–16 and 28.

48 Lin 1993.

49 See Zhang Ke 2021: 136; also Lin Chengjie 1993: 26.

50 See Kamal Sheel and Ranjana Sheel, 2024. *Kang Youwei Engages India: His Travel Narratives (1901-1902) and Predicaments of Civilization and Nation*. Routledge, New Delhi.

51 See for details, Liu Zhangcai. 2019. 'Jin-dai you-li "yin-du di-yi ren"- Huang Maocai yan-zhong de yin-du cha-ye' [Indian Tea Industry from the Eyes of Huang Maocai- the first person to travel to India]. In Cha bo-la [Extensive Reading on Tea], 2019: 8 (http://www.cnki.com.cn/Article/CJFDTotal-CBLZ201908017 .html); also, Fan Huichuan and Shi Yunli. 2018. *Qing -mo min-chu de jing-wai cha-ye kao-cha ji ji-ying-xiang* [On the Overseas Investigation of Tea Industry and Its Influence in the Late Qing and Early Republic of China Period] in Zhong-guo nong shi [Agricultural History of China] 2018.2. Anhui: Hefei.

52 See Lin 1993: 12; Also see a laudatory account by Nie Zuoping. 2019. 'Shan he ru meng: 140 nian qianqing chao kao-cha dui chuan-yue heng-duan-shan zhi xing" [Mountain and River Fall into Dream: 140 years ago the qing Dynasty expedition traveled through Hengduan Mountain] in *Peng Pai* (the Guangdong Communist Youth League's paper) distributed by Xin-hua mei ri dian xun [Xinhua Daily Electronic dispatch] on Nov 14, 2019. Available on the internet.
This recorded mountains and rivers that Huang crossed in the course of his tortuous journey for spiritual pursuits. The title of the article and its style of writing appears to have borrowed or been influenced by Ge Fei's famous avant-garde novel of the same name that characterized a detached and alienated author's self-doubt on the reality of existence and the placement of memory, history, myth, and reality in an indeterminate space in the writing. Nie thus enlivens the joy and melancholy of Huang's journey.

53 Lin (1993: 27) collates Huang's ideas.

54 See Prasenjit Duara. 2009. *The Global and Regional in China's Nation-Formation*. London: Routledge, 103–104. This is an insightful study providing a comprehensive framework to comprehend the process of state formation in China.

55 Nie Zouping (2019).

Translation

11

HUANG MAOCAI'S INTRODUCTORY REMARKS

Travel to the Western Region and India

Introduction to Records of Travel to the Western Region

The Zongli Yamen's [Foreign Office] notings:

Xu Gengshen, the Chief Justice of the Imperial Qing Court of Judicial Review, while serving as the Head of the Education Office in Jiangxi, noted Huang Maocai's excellent contribution to the provincial affairs, his good character and fine scholarship especially in mathematics and science. He presented a memorial to the [Guangxu] Emperor to recommend Huang to the Translation Academy in Shanghai and Machine Manufacturing Factory in Tianjin for further training and preparation for placement in an important imperial position at the opportune time. On the first day of the 12th month of 1876, the Minister of Military Machinery [Li Hongzhao] received the order of Emperor Guangxu requesting Liu Bingzhang [then Governor of Jiangxi] to immediately send Huang Maocai to Beijing to have an audience with the Zongli Yamen [Foreign Office] in compliance with the order of the Emperor in the matter.

Earlier to that, the Zong-du [Governor-General][1] of Sichuan, Ding Baozhen, had presented a memorial to the Emperor stating that Tibet was very close to India, and the British occupation of Du-ji-lin [Darjeeling], had extended its influences to the 'protected' Wei-jing [Lhasa and high plateau of Tibet] region through some carefully and attentively drawn plans. Ding Baozhen requested for the Emperor's approval to depute Huang Maocai to India to take stock of the ground reality and to draw a map of the mountains and rivers along the way as a reference for formulating a foreign policy with [British] India. The Emperor agreed to Ding Baozhen's request and ordered Huang Maocai to travel to India and survey the region. Huang Maocai departed from Chengdu, Sichuan Province in the seventh month of

DOI: 10.4324/9781003505396-3

1878, and returned in the seventh month of 1880 after completing the mission. The map and travel notes drawn by Huang Maocai were sent to the Department handling confidential military and political affairs. After reading them, the Department acquiesced that Huang's maps and travel narratives presented in detail the Indian landscape with mountains and rivers and also comprehensively reported on the local situation on the route travelled and region visited.

His report included a map of the entire territory of India, another map of 12 divisions and 13 territories of the Western Region, as well as route maps of the itinerary from Sichuan to Tibet and Yunnan to Myanmar. These were placed in volumes entitled *You-li-chu-yan* [*My Humble Opinion on Travels*] and *Xi-jiao-shui-dao* [*Waterways of the Western Frontier*]. They were then reported to the Emperor [Guangxu] for perusal. The Emperor ordered Governor Ding to depute Huang to Beijing for a comprehensive debriefing by the Department handling confidential military and political affairs and making a final report of the situation in accordance with the procedures of the Zongli Yamen.

On the first day of the 11th month of 1880, the Chief Secretary of the Military Intelligence Department, Li Hongzao, complying with the Emperor's orders temporarily stacked these maps and travel narratives in the library of the office of the confidential military and political affairs.

Preface to *You-li-chu-yan [My Humble Opinion on Travels]*: You-li yin-du shi-mo [Story of Travel to India]

Since the abolition of restrictions on maritime trade and travel, China's interior became accessible to the whole world. Foreign countries flocked together there leading to the beginning of a completely new phase. England, after colonizing India, gradually expanded its power and influence to several island countries of the South Pacific and firmly established its hegemony over the seas. India and our Xizang [Tibet] province are closely linked together. According to a legal provision of the Yantai Convention [Chefoo/Zhifu Convention][2] China permitted England to open up a convenient land route to China via Xizang [Tibet]. Following this, the English began to activize the Xizang land route to enter Sichuan. But the local Tibetan people strongly resisted and obstructed their movement. The English did not take this lying down, as they had worked out a long ambitious plan to swallow China. They had an eye over Xizang [Tibet] and on opening Yunnan - Sichuan communication channel for the smooth conduct of their trade through the land route. Taking into account the long-term thoughtful view of the contemporary world situation, the Sichuan Governor, Ding Baozhen, especially appointed me [Huang] to investigate the situation in Tibet and India as a surveyor and cartographer and to draw maps. The appointment was reported to the Court and received imperial approval. The Emperor also specifically ordered the Minister-in-charge of the Zongli Yamen to issue me a passport and seek a visa from the British embassy.

I [Huang] set off from Chengdu on July 7, 1878. Packed lightly, I traveled towards the southwest with six servants. After passing through Qiang-zhou [present Sichuan's Qiong-lai town] and Ya-zhou [present Sichuan's Ya-an town], climbing up to Da-xiang-lin[3] and Fei-yue-feng[4], crossing over the Da-du River, and walking through 12 road stations, our entourage arrived at Da-jian-lu[5]. We then realized that the Tibetan landscape was very different from the interior mainland. Our dynasty's gold and silver currency had no use-value here. Throughout the journey, we used tea leaves or Ha-da [Cowrie – white slugs] for the purchase of usual daily items. Or, encountering a guest or during celebrations, we, like the local people, used a kind of cotton cloth to greet and convey blessings.

Fortunately, Si-ma [Minister of War][6] Bao Zhi-yong has arranged everything for us thoughtfully and satisfactorily. Besides that, he also gifted us good horses for riding. On the eighth day of the eighth month in 1878 [November 5, 1878 in Gregorian calendar] loaded with food and other materials, we left the place. The Tu-si [local headman][7] Jie-ao also supplied us with serf labor. From Zhe-duo mountains we turned west. The mountain landscape was precipitous and the road was hard to travel. Smoke, rain, and noxious air filled the atmosphere making the eye bleak and desolate; except for locally stationed soldiers at the checkpost, nobody could smoke. Everywhere there were steep cliffs and waterfalls which appeared suspended like one half of a strong and robust jade dragon. The snow-capped peaks stood far away like a silver screen, the images of which presented undoubtedly a rare spectacle of beauty and grandeur.

After moving on ten stop-stations road, we reached Li-tang County[8] in Xuan Fu Division[9], and traveled further to another eight stop-stations to arrive at Ba-tang County[10] in Xuan Fu Division. This was the border town between Sichuan and Tibet. There, Peng Shou-bei[11] of the forward Jiangka [river checkpost][12] Camp informed us that the road to Tibet was blocked by Tibetans and we could not proceed further. There was no way but to report the situation to the government. The officials then permitted us to take a diversion route passing through southern Yunnan. The Zhi-fu [prefect][13] there, Zhao Yanwu, was very affectionate and wanted to accompany us further. However, he had to decline as it was heard that a fighting between the Tibetans in the area of Dong-wang [Shangri-la Township in present Yunnan] and Xiang-cheng [today's Xiangcheng county in Ganzi Prefecture, Sichuan] had just erupted. Added to this was the infestation of indigenous savages and bandits in the area. Because of that, two Tu-si [local hereditary headmen] with Han and Tibetan soldiers and their gu-cao (personal guards) accompanied us carrying dry food on their backs in sacks through Liu-yu and

Zou-dui[14] villages. After passing through Liu-yu and Zou-dui, we descended along the Ba-long-da River[15]. The road passed through wild deserted mountains and uninhabited roads. Traveling through deep mountains and dense forests, ghastly trees, perilous cliffs and precipices, heavy snow and hailstorms, crossing skyrocketing rivers and streams in kayaks, and narrow and difficult wooden paved roads, we often had to abandon the sedan chair to ride a horse or get down even from the horse for walking. The cold north wind blew on our faces, and formed ice on our beards. The mountainous landform was as hideous and terrifying as an evil spirit. We often slept in the wild, and both people and horses were exhausted.

After traveling for 18 days, we reached Zhong-dian City[16] and rested there for six days. While Prefect Zhao returned to the north still following the same road, we proceeded south to Li-jiang Fu [a prefecture in Yunnan]. The scenery here was like the inland again, and the weather gradually turned slightly warmer. We arrived at Jian-chuan Fu [a prefecture][17] just in time for the Chinese great lunar year festivities. After passing through the counties of Da-li [Yunnan][18] and Yong-chang [Yunnan][19], we crossed the Lan-cang River, Lu-yin River[20], and Long- chuan River[21] and innumerable iron-chain bridges. Traveling from Zhongdian to Teng-yue[22], we reached the southwest border of China. The area was rich in products and was famous as the land of prosperity in Yunnan Province. In addition, this was connected by road with Meng-yang[22] and Bao-jing[23]. In the past, pearls, jade stones, colorful jadeite seals, amber, emerald, and ivory were all found here. In recent years, because of the more convenient sea routes, more and more business people set off from Guangdong, and cotton was the only bulk product that entered the customs from Myanmar. The custom duty was only two to three percent. On February 16, we set off from Zhou-cheng and passed through Nan-dian, Gan-ya, and Zhan-da[24], the three administrative posts of the Xuanfu chieftain office. All of them were on both sides of the Bin-lang [Penang][25] River and were mostly vast plains with fertile soil. The locals belonged to Bai-yi-zu [Bai and Yi ethnic minorities]. Their folk customs were simple, people were hardworking, and the area was prosperous.

Teng-yue [Deng-chong][26] had jurisdiction over seven chieftains. Its Southern Road was called Long-chuan[27] that included Xuan-fu Tu-si [chieftain] as well as three chieftains[28] of Hu-sa[29], La-sa[30], and Meng-mao.[31] For years this was a part of the tribute-carrying road from Myanmar that originally entered through Hu-ju-guan, passed Meng-mao, and joined the great Southern Road at Long-chuan. In the past ten years, it changed and passed through Xin-jie to join the Northern Road. During the Ming Dynasty, Myanmar frontier residents repeatedly violated our borders, and several chieftains turned arrogant and overbearing, so the 'eight to nine checkposts and strategic passes'[32] were built to manage the boundary. Myanmar was now very poor and weak, and the border checkposts were gradually relaxed and abandoned. However, the world is changing. It is necessary to take preventive measures in advance, restore the border management system as soon as possible, and recruit the local indigenous people. It is hoped that the officials managing the border would pay attention to that.

We passed through four road-stops to reach Man-yun[33], which was the border between China and Myanmar. After crossing that, we entered the territory of the indigenous savages. Without a group of people to accompany us on the journey, I would not at all dare to move there. So we stopped for ten days and recruited 40 musketeers and polemen. There were also more than 500 armed bodyguards straddled on horses with a caravan of about a 1000 camels before we dared to walk out on the embankment along the narrow bamboo pass. Traveling through the Huo-yan Mountain, the road was narrow and dangerous with space for only a horse or a camel to move in a single line. The forest was covered with dense overgrown weeds; wild beasts and monkeys constantly howled; native savages [tribe-men] with unkempt hair and dirty faces were ready to waylay and rob; and every time we passed a mountain village, everyone had to dismount from their horses and walk slowly and cautiously. There were three roads there. The lower one was the riverside road, the middle was the stone-steps road, and the uppermost was the Huo-yan mountain road. The lower road was comparatively convenient and nimble for movement, but the mountain road, laid with more and more wooden logs, was shorter and easier to walk, so merchants and tourists preferred to travel on that road. After walking for four days, we arrived at Man-mu[34] and entered the Myanmar territory. There was a Chinese Street on the main road along the river. About 30 Chinese people lived there. After arriving at this place, the terrain gradually turned flat, and the weather became very hot. The scene was totally different from what we had walked through so far.

The Myanmarese people carved holes in large logs to make small boats. The two small boats were tied together and covered with a straw canopy. The river was wide and shallow, and we sailed about 120 miles by boats to Xin-jie. More than 300 Chinese people lived there, and there was also a Guan-shen [Frontier Pass Protector God] temple. Myanmar had set up a post for Yunji [first-grade official] here, and the British had an office for Yayeban [consular officer]. The great Jinsha-jiang [Jinsha River][35] originated from the Gang-di-se[36] mountain in the A-li [Ngari-s prefecture] region of Tibet. There was also a river called Ya-lu-zang-bu [YarlungTsangpo / Brahmaputra][37] which flowed through the expanse of Tibet and regions of Nu[38], Qiu [Drung or Tulung][39], and Mo-yu[40] ethnic groups [in southern Yunnan][41]. Turning to the south and flowing downwards to Meng-yang was a river which after entering the territory of Myanmar was called the Yi-la-wa-di [Irrawaddy], and which from Meng-gong[42] town flowed windingly northward and rushed through a rocky canyon where no boats could ply.

It passed Xin-jie[43] and became a vast and broad river with a width ranging from a few to more than ten *li* after other rivers like Cha-shan, Ma-li, Pi-nang, and Long-chuan converged with it. On March 18, we took a steamer and traveled further southward for three days. While passing through the capital city of Awa[44], the Myanmarese King sent officials to our boat to welcome us ashore, but we politely declined. More than 3,000 families from Yunnan lived in Awa. Most of them had married local Myanmarese women. We changed here to another ship and traveled south for five days to reach Bie-mou [Bhima/Bhamo?][45] and entered the territory under the jurisdiction of the British. There were no less than 10,000 merchants from Guangdong, while those from Yunnan numbered only about ten or so. In the last years of Daoguang (between 1830s and 1840s), the British and Myanmarese had fought incessantly[46]. The Myanmarese set up wooden fences to defend the capital. Unaccustomed to the environment and climate of the new place, the British army was often defeated and originally planned to retreat. But they were able to finally repulse the Myanmarese and advanced side by side by both land and water routes straight towards the city of Awa. The Myanmarese King was highly ftightened and agreed to cede land for peace. He surrendered without a fight. From then on, the British gradually kept invading and expanding to these most prosperous coastal areas. After the British annexed Myanmar, they went west to Bengal and east to Ma-liu-jia [Melacca]. Their territory stretched to more than 5,000 miles.

The British sent an important high official to escort us. His name/title was Ge-wu-na [Governor/Commander?] and was called Yunji in Myanmarese. We together arrived at Yang-gong [Yangon/Rangoon], where Yunji invited us to his mansion. He was very courteous and thoughtful. We stayed there for 14 days before taking a steamer to the northwest. We sailed for five days and five nights to reach a port at Bengal, East India. The British called it Kolkata [Ka-ni-ge-da]. It is the number one seaport city in the southwest. Fujian [Fukienese] people were first to start some family shops here, but Guangdong people [Cantonese] opened up more than a 1000 shops, most of which were engaged in handicraft businesses. India was a vast area with more than 4,000 miles in length and width. It bordered with Myanmar in the east, Afghanistan and Bi-lu-zhi [Baluchistan] in the west, sea and oceans in the south, Cong-lin [Pamir] mountain ranges in the north, and Ni-po-luo [Nepal] in the northeast. Tribes of Xi-jin [Sikkim] and Bu-lu-ke-ba [Bhutan ?] were vassals of our country [China] and were next in hierarchy to those of the Tibet region, but they were separated in the middle by thousands of snow mountains and difficult and dangerous roads. This was how heaven created natural barriers to separate China from foreign countries. During the Qianlong period [1735–1796],[47] the British invaded and occupied Bengal. Taking advantage of their conquest, they either annexed most of the tribal areas of the north, south, and west to their British territory or reduced them to vassal states with the obligation to pay them tributes every year. The British also built piers and started railway lines and trains in India. The water and land transportation were spread in all the directions. Goods piled up like mountains in various cities. Taxes were heavy. The British turned India into their colony. Its important cities were Man-da-la-sa [Madras], Meng-mai [Mumbai], Ya-jia-la [Agra], and Si-nan [Ceylon/Sri Lanka] island. The British set up officials and stationed heavy troops, all under the jurisdiction of the British Governor-General at Bengal. They especially dispatched their trusted aides as senior officials with full powers to manage important cities. In the summer and autumn seasons, the governor would go to Xin-la [Shimla] to escape the heat, and in the event of encountering certain urgent matters he used the telegraph to send instructions.

We traveled in India for half a year, arriving in the east to Ya-shan or A-sa-mi [Assam] state, going up north to Darjeeling (the entrance point of the passage into Tibet), and then journeyed along the Ganges river to E-na-te [United Province/India?][48], Ya-chia-la [Agra], Meng-mai [Mumbai], and other places. During the travel, we observed mountains, rivers, and landscapes, and explored the society and folk customs. But the language was difficult to understand, and the pronunciation of the hired interpreter–translator was sometimes beyond a point not comprehensible. This was a matter of great regret while traveling. I investigated and discovered that the ancient name of India was Tian-zhu, and it was also called Shen-du or hen-du-si-tan [Hindustan].[49] Since the Han and Tang Dynasties, India and China have been in diplomatic relations. There was also a constant stream of Chinese Buddhist monks going to India in search of Buddhist texts and dhamma. For example, Fa Xian[50] during the Jin Dynasty [266–420 CE], Hui Sheng in the Northern Wei Dynasty[51] [386–534 CE], and Xuanzang[52] at the time of the Tang Dynasty [618–907 CE] came to India and wrote their respective detailed travel narratives of what they saw in India. Between the ancient to the modern period, India was divided and united at different times, many different languages were added and changed in the course of a constant process of translation and interpretation. Consequently, every person spoke differently and presented a rough approximation of the original. India did not have a standard original language for translation.

India also did not have an initial standard pronunciation. After the Yuan Dynasty [Mongol/Mughal] Emperor Sai-ma-han [Shahjehan ?] annexed India, place names were all named in Meng-gu [Mongolian/Persian][53]. In modern times, it changed to English, keeping the pronunciation of place names close to or the same as the original names. A true rendition of the original was obviously impossible. Affairs of the world varied with each passing day. The maps I drew noted all presently used names. Even if they differed from the previous names, people with extensive knowledge would definitely be able to distinguish them. We returned from India to China by sea route and took a steamer which sailed through Nanyang's[54] Bin-lang-yu [Penang], Xin-jia-po [Singapore], and Ma-liu-jia [Melacca], and then passed by Champa [Zhan-cheng], Vietnam [Yue-nan], and other countries. It took a total of 64 days to reach Guangzhou [in China]. All were mentioned in the detailed diary, so I would not say any more here. In this journey of about 50,000 *li*, it is impossible to describe all the condition and customs, such as the severe cold of Tibet, the scorching heat of India, the malarial fever of Lu-jiang [Nu-jiang] River region, food and night at the Savage Mountain, reckless biting of mosquitoes and insects, as well as headaches and earaches at the countryside, custom of carving tattoos, tongue-twisting incomprehensible languages, diet of zan-ba [Tibetan tsampa] barley and cheese, and the inexhaustible range of most special landscape and scenery of the world. I had never experienced all that in my whole life. The most difficult and painful experience was passing through the hurricane of the seven continental seas and oceans, when rows and rows of huge waves battering the sides of the ship like a rock wall tossed it violently. Consewuently we suffered unbearable pain scorching all internal organs. In addition, food in the ship was already all consumed, no coal was left to use, and all the wooden utensils and other materials on the ship were burnt leading to reluctantly utilizing cotton instead of fuelwood to cook for survival. Fortunately, we finally reached the coast safely and it was like rebirth for all of us. Our fellow travelers were Zhang Hongjun from Gao-an [Jiangxi], Nie Zhensheng from Changsha [Hunan], Qiu Zuyin from Cixi [Zhejiang], and two servants.

[This is the author's foreword.]

Notes

1 During Ming and Qing dynasties Zong-du [Governor-General] administered more than one province.
2 The Chefoo Convention, known in Chinese as the Yantai Treaty, was a treaty between Qing China and Great Britain, signed by Sir Thomas Wade and Li Hongzhang in Zhifu (now a district of Yantai) on August 21, 1876.
3 It is in the south of present Sichuan's Ya-an town with an average height of 3000 meters with its highest point reaching to 3552 meters and is the watershed between Da-du River and Qing-yi River.
4 Luding County in Garze or Kandze, Tibetan autonomous prefecture, Sichuan (formerly in Kham province of Tibet).
5 Dardo or Kangding County, which was the political and economic center in present Sichuan's Garze or Kandze, Tibetan autonomous prefecture.
6 During the period of Ming and Qing dynasty, this referred to a civil official position whose functions were the management of salt administration at the prefectural government, the arrest of criminals and robbers, and such administrative matters as coastal defense.
7 Refers to Government-appointed hereditary tribal headman in Yuan, Ming, and Qing dynasties.
8 Li-tang County in present Sichuan's Garze or Kanze Tibetan Autonomous Prefecture.

9 In the Yuan Dynasty, Xuanfu Division was set up in remote minority areas as a local administrative agency. During the Ming and Qing Dynasties, they were all hereditary officials of the chieftain.

10 Ba-tang County in present Sichuan's Ganze or Kanze Tibetan Autonomous Prefecture.

11 These local officials belonged to the fourth and fifth grade positions in hierarchy and were set up in the minority areas in the early Qing Dynasty for guarding military attaches, managing camp affairs, and supporting food and salaries.

12 This is in the eastern part of the Tibet Autonomous Region. Originally set up by the local government of Tibet, it is an important military area in Tibet, and a pot road that passes through the Southern Silk Road or the ancient Tea-Horse Road.

13 The Zhi-fu [prefect] was the fourth grade official and the chief executive of the state government at the prefectural level

14 This refers to two villages of Xiang-cheng County of Ganzi Tibetan Autonomous Prefecture.

15 This is the present Ba-qu River in Ganzi Prefecture.

16 It is the capital of Diqing Tibetan Autonomous Prefecture in Yunnan Province.

17 It is today's Heqing Autonomous Prefecture in Yunnan Province and has jurisdiction over counties of He-qing, Lan-ping, Jian-chan, Bi-jiang, and Fu-gong.

18 Presently, it is the capital of Dali Bai Autonomous Prefecture in Yunnan.

19 It is Bao-shan city of Yunnan.

20 Lu-jiang River is today known as Nu-jiang River, which is one of the bigger rivers in southwest China. The upper reaches of the river are called Na-qu River in Tibetan and originate from the southern foot of Tang-gu-la Mountains on the Qinghai-Tibet Plateau. After entering Yunnan province, it flows southward into Myanmar and is renamed as the Salween River, and finally flows into the Andaman Sea [Bay of Bengal].

21 The Long-chuan River is a first-class tributary merging on the south bank of the Jin-sha River.

22 Today's Kachin state in northern Myanmar.

23 Presently it is Myanmar's Meng-gong (also known as Mogok).

24 Three of the five Xuanfu Division (Nan-dian, Gan-ya, Zhan-da, Long-chuan, and Zhe-fang) were under the jurisdiction of Yong-chang House in the Qing Dynasty.

25 Known also as Hai-ba River in ancient times and located in Ying-jiang County of Yunnan, the Bing-liang River is a right tributary of the Da-ying River that merges into the Irrawaddy in Myanmar.

26 Teng-yue is presently known as Deng-chong and has also been earlier called Teng-Chung, Ting-yueh, Teng Yueh, Momein, and Momien. British missionary Margary was murdered here on February 21, 1875 and this led to the Chefoo Convention.

27 Long-chuan called 'Mengwan' in Dai language, means the place where sun shines. Today it belongs to De-hong prefecture, Yunnan province.

28 It was the name of the local authority. The Yuan Dynasty had set up a 'Barbarian/Tribal Chief Commanding Officer'.

29 Hu-sa A-chang Township is located in the northwest of Long-chuan County, bordering Ying-jiang County to the north and Myanmar to the west.

30 It now belongs to Qian-liu-yi township in Lancang Lahu Autonomous County, Pu'er city, Yunnan Province.

31 The Nan-wan River Delta area at the confluence of the Nan-wan River and the Ruili River in western Yunnan. It is also known as Meng-mao Triangle because of its proximity to Meng-mao. It was historically a territory of China

and was occupied by British Myanmar [Burma] at the end of Qing Dynasty. On January 28, 1960, China and Myanmar signed the 'China-Myanmar Boundary Agreement' in Beijing, and China relinquished its sovereignty over the Meng-mao Triangle.

32 One of the 'Eight Passes' of Teng-yue. The original site was outside the western border of Long-chuan County, Yunnan, and in the south of the old border between China and Burma during the Ming and Qing dynasties. In the late Qing Dynasty, when China and Britain demarcated the border of Yunnan and Burma [Myanmar], it belonged to the latter. In the 22nd year of Wanli in the Ming Dynasty (1594), eight passes were built on the main road of the China–Myanmar border, namely Hen-hu Pass, Wan-ren Pass, Ju-shi Pass, Tong-bi Pass, Tie-bi Pass, Hu-zhu Pass, Han-long Pass, and Tian-ma-guan. In the 45th year of Qianlong's reign (1780), the 'Nine Passes' were set up. From north to South, they were Gu-yong Pass, Dian-tan Pass, Ming-guang Pass, Da-tang Pass, Zhi-na Pass, Meng-bao Pass, Ba-zhu Pass, Shan-mu-long Pass, and Shi-po-po Pass. The establishment of 'eight passes and nine passes' played an important role in the stability of the frontier of Yunnan from the Ming and Qing dynasties to the Republic of China.

33 Man-yun also known as Man-wen-ji in Burmese is said to be inhabited by many people. It is located at the end of Rui-li Dam in Yunnan. A winding highway passes here from Nan-kan and with many twists and twirls crosses mountain, and reaches Bhamo, an important town in northern Myanmar on the banks of the Irrawaddy River (also known as the Great Jin-sha River).

34 This area is inhabited by ferocious southern tribes.

35 Jin-sha River, emanates from upper reaches of Yangzi River [Chang-jiang] and flows through Qinghai, Sichuan and Yunnan to finally merge with Min River in Yibin, Sichuan and form the Yangzi River.

36 Gang-di-se in southwest Tibet is revered by Tibetans as the center of the universe.

37 Famous in India as Brahmaputra River, it flows from Tibet to Assam and Bangladesh.

38 The Nu people are one of the ethnic groups with a small population mainly distributed in Fu-gong and Gong-shan in Nujiang prefecture, Yunnan, and in Kachin state, Myanmar. They speak various languages of the Tibeto-Burman family. They are called Nu because they live along Nujiang [Salween River].

39 They are located in the valley area of the Dulong River in Gongshan, Dulong and Nu Autonomous County, Yunnan.

40 Also known as Luoyu/ Luo-ba/ Lhoba [tr. Southerners], these are a diverse amalgamation of Sino-Tibetan speaking people. These are located in areas starting from the east of China–Bhutan border and stretching to the west to Men-yu and Luo-yu in Myanmar passing through southern Tibet and Arunachal Pradesh.

41 Many of these tribes/ethnic groups are distributed around the area of Er-cha-shan (Two Tea Mountains) and outside the jurisdiction of Ma-li's senior Commanding Officer. They have red hair and yellow eyes, wear tree bark as clothing, and sleep on the tree at night.

42 This is a town in the present Kachin state in northern Myanmar.

43 Also a town in the present Kachin state in north Myanmar it is located at the confluence of Da-ying and Irrawady Rivers. It is one of the major trading centers for gems and cotton between China and Myanmar. It produces sugar and now manufactures diesel oil engines.

44 The Awa Dynasty (1364–1555) was established by the ancestors of Shan nationality in the middle and lower reaches of the Irrawaddy River. The present city is in De-da-wu County, Myanmar. It was established in 1527 by Lu-chuan royal family who were also Shan, and was destroyed by the Burmese Dongyu Dynasty in 1555.

45 Known as Bhamo, this military town in northern Myanmar belongs to the Kachin State.

46 Between 1824 and 1885, three major Anglo-Myanmarese Wars took place: the first one was from 1824 to 1826, the second was between 1852 and 1853, and the final one was in 1885 which finally led to the British annexation of Myanmar.

47 The Qianlong Emperor (September 25, 1711–February 7, 1799) was the fifth Emperor of the Qing dynasty and the fourth Qing emperor to rule over 'China proper', reigning from 1735 to 1796.

48 This appears to be a short form of E-na-te-he [厄纳特赫 United Provinces or mainland India].

49 Chinese characters used by Huang for the ancient names of India are different from those normally used.

50 Faxian's period of journey to India and back is from 400 to 413 CE.

51 Northern Wei Dynasty is referred to in Chinese sources as ruled by 'plaited barbarians' who introduced many foreign ideas including Buddhism. Song Yun (from Dunhuang) and Hui Sheng were sent to India in 518 CE by the Dowager Empress of the Wei. They returned with 175 books.

52 Xuanzang journeyed to India from 629 to 645 CE.

53 Chinese often uses Meng-gu [Mongolian] or Mughals and Persian as Mongolian.

54 Nan-yang [lit. South Seas] was the name given to Southeast Asia during the Ming and Qing Dynasties as per a concept centered on China. This included Malay, Philippine, and Indonesian Archipelago as well as the coastal areas of Indo-China and the Malay Peninsula.

III

RECORDS OF TRAVEL TO THE WESTERN REGION

[Xi-you ri-ji 西輶日记]

VOL. 1: FROM CHENG-DU TO BA-TANG

[CONG CHENG-DU DAO BA-TANG 从成都到巴塘]

In the fifth month of 1878, complying with the orders of the Imperial Court, Sichuan Governor Ding Baozhen deputed me to Tibet and India for exploration. This matter was already reported to the Military Intelligence. The Imperial memorial with the statement and explanation to the Emperor (Guangxu) was filed in the Department of Military Intelligence. The office of the Foreign Minister issued me a Chinese and English bilingual passport and arranged for my visa from the British Consular Office in Beijing. Setting off from Cheng-du on the seventh month of 1878, I was accompanied by Zhang Hongjun, a martial art expert from Gaoan County [Jiangxi], Nie Zhensheng from Changsha [Hunan], Qiu Zuyin from Cixi [Jiangxi], and one servant and a cook.

On the seventh day of the beginning of the seventh month [in 1878], we started our journey from the South Gate of Cheng-du. After travelling for about 20 *li* and passing through Cu-qiao [Cluster Bridge], we moved another 20 *li* and rested in Shuang-Liu district. The thermometer displayed a 92° temperature at 12 noon. (The temperature was recorded at 12 pm and afterwards it was always noted at the same time.)

By the eighth day at the beginning of the seventh month, we had journeyed about 50 *li* and arrived at Xin-jian district. Before arriving at the district town we crossed three rivers one after another. The road was covered with sand, stones, and reeds. Reaching there we realized how inconvenient it was to travel with heavy luggage.

DOI: 10.4324/9781003505396-4

After traveling for another five *li* we entered the boundary of Qiong-lai district. We then proceeded further for another five *li* and rested at Yang-chang. It rained heavily in the evening.

On the ninth day of the beginning of the seventh month, we traveled four *li*, crossed a river, and then moved sixty *li* further and rested at the Qiong-lai district city [in Western Sichuan in the Qiong-lai mountain region]. The vast area from the provincial capital Chengdu to Qiong-lai was plain, and the land was fertile. Thick and lush rice could be seen everywhere. Crops were sown on all available land areas even in the city. Faraway in the distant southwest looming mountains could be seen.

On the tenth day of the seventh month, at the beginning of Autumn [in 1878], we set off again from the East Gate of the city and traveled to about 90 *li* towards the southbound road. We lodged at the provincial government office at the district town of Bai-zhang-ri in Ming-shan district. Two to three hundred families resided there. They were dependent upon the mountains to survive. From there, we entered boundaries of Ming-shan district. Roads were low to high, slippery, and covered with cobblestones. The temperature recorded 88°F (31.1°C).

On the 11th day, we journeyed 45 *li* on the road passing through the Ming-shan county town. The town was very small with only a half *li* of road connected its east and west ends. After proceeding further 10 *li*, we crossed the Dian-an Bridge and climbed up the mountainous road for 5 *li* to reach Jin-ji-guan [Jin-ji Pass].[1] On the road side, there was a stone monument with a poem inscribed over that.

> Two narrow passes of Mount Qionglai,
> Cliffs standing high and erect hide Cai Dukedom,[2]
> Like a set of scrolls vertically hung from the four sides,
> They wrap Mt. E-mei like clouds.
> Below moon rises and rolls over River Chang-jiang,
> Calming and rehabilitating the Qiangs.[3]

We traveled further for 30 *li* and crossed a river. The current was swift. Just before the sun set in the mountains, we arrived at Ya'an Prefecture[4].

On the 12th day, we started from the South Gate. The mountain road was rugged and very difficult to walk on. Traveling forty *li* along the crooked winding river we moved towards south after crossing it. We stayed in Guan-yin-chang [Guanyin Buddha/Avalokitesvara market] and transferred our luggage once again to porters.

On the 13th day, we got up very early, climbed ten *li* uphill, and then traveled downhill for about ten *li* and reached Gao-qiao [high bridge]. Entering the boundaries of Ying-jing county,[5] we proceeded ten more *li* and had our meal at Shi-jia-qiao [Shijia bridge]. After covering another ten *li* and passing over a ferry crossing, we went 20 *li* uphill and over another ferry crossing, traveling a total distance of 60 *li* [in a day].

On the 14th day, we traveled 30 *li* and arrived at the boundary of Qing-xi[6] County. We then walked over ten *li* to Huang-ni-pu [name of a small hamlet], climbed uphill and followed the road along the stream. The road was narrow and difficult to walk on. Piles of stones and wood were scattered everywhere. We crossed two bridges made of wooden-planks connected with iron cables, and proceeded ten *li* towards Xiao-guan[7] village for rest and stay. The section of the road near Xiao-guan was particularly difficult and steep, with a slope slanting to more than 70°. The mountain pass, transiting amidst two hills standing opposite to each other like walls, was so narrow that only two horses could pass side by side. Xiao-guan had about ten or so thatched huts and shops. Although the scorching afternoon sun was shining above, the people still felt gloomy and cold. In the evening, it rained heavily.

On the 15th day, we traveled ten *li* to reach Da-guan[8] village. After another twenty *li* from there, we noticed three crookedly winding streams completely surrounding the deep valley. We walked further for five *li* and reached Cao-xie-ping[9] which was near the top of a mountain. Local residents wore leather clothes to protect themselves from the cold. The top of the mountain was called Da-xiang-lin [Great Elephant Peak]. Starting from Huang-ni-pu, we climbed up the stone steps one by one, and covered about 45 *li*. Mountains in this range stood side by side. They were low but steep and rose pointedly from under one's feet to truly straight into the clouds. Passing travelers held their breath and were left almost speechless. The mountain tops were bare and not even an inch of grass grew. After that, we carefully descended walking through the winding ridges. The road tortuously moved back and forth. It was very steep and totally dangerous. In the local sayings, this area was referred to as 'jiu zhe ban' [90 percent hillside], the five *li* ride on the horseback as 'er shi si pan' [24 coil/plate like rounds], and traveling again to the next five *li* as entering in to 'sheep-fold/sheep-pen'. Our porters split here as taking the route in the direction of the Ni-tou Courier Relay [horse] Station could save about 15 *li* of distance by road. We walked five *li* down the mountain and stayed in Qing-xi County. Very few people resided in Qing-xi which was surrounded by four wall-like mountains. Two streams flowed from the top to the bottom and appeared like dashing from mountains with their heads down and feet up. The mountains were planted with hundreds of acres of rice in fields arranged like steps. All the way from Rong-jing County, residents cooked highland barley/rice for their meal. These grains are thicker and their ends are shorter and round. Besides that, the only other thing that you could eat were cakes made of corn and buckwheat.

On the 16th day, we walked 70 *li* and stayed at the Ni-tou post. All day long, we walked up and down the peak and valley of the mountains and along the riverside. Although peaks were not very steep, but rocks falling from the towering cliffs and precipitous river bank were almost everywhere. They piled up and cluttered the road and mountain streams. Consequently, the water flow was very turbulent, and the road was almost blocked. It was difficult for the horse to find a place to step on, and the sedan to move backwards or turn around. This was an extremely difficult and longest rough patch for travel on the road. We were finally able to reach the lodging site just before the sun was to set. Both the men and the horses were extremely exhausted. Many a time we barely escaped falling to the ground. Whenever they encountered a dangerous place, we had to step down from the sedan chair and walk. All along the way the mountains were completely bare and rocky with no way to grow food and vegetables there. According to the thermometer, the outside temperature was 88° (or 31.1°C).

On the 17th day, we covered 25 *li*, passed the Que-lai Bridge [Magpie Bridge], and then climbing another 25 *li* on the mountainous road crossed the Fu-long Temple [Temple of Vanquishing Dragon/Hidden Genius] and ascended the Fei- yue [Soaring] Ridge. The height of this mountain was second only to the Da-xiang [Elephant] Ridge. When the sun was just to set in the west behind the top ranges of the mountains, dark clouds suddenly rolled down. A heavy thunderstorm hit the area; hails as big as shirt buttons fell from the sky; and the weather became freezing cold. All the men and livestock were so cold that their legs trembled. The temperature on the meter at once fell down from 86°F (30°C) to 64 (17.7°C). Ascending to the top of the mountain we came across a small temple enshrining the statue of Guandi [Daoist God of War]. Looking to the southwest, we saw green forest-covered mountain peaks towering into the clouds. The white snow accumulated for the past thousands of years radiated dazzling five-color light under the sun. Looking down at the Hua-lin-ping [colorful forest valley], it was like looking at Qing-xi County from Da-xiang-ling. It appeared right in front of us but required walking down 15 *li* to reach. Tai-ning Du-si [Tai-ning's highest military garrison] was stationed at Hua-lin-ping with a total of 500 soldiers.

On the 18th day, we walked downhill for 30 *li* and stayed in Leng-qi Town.[10] There were dozens of households in the town, facing the Da-du River. An official with the surname of Zhou was stationed here all year round. But it was just a token government office.

On the 19th day, we walked 50 *li* towards northwest along the bank of the Da-du River and stayed at a place called Lu-ding Bridge. There were about 300 shops on both sides of the bank. On the east bank of the river, there were offices of inspection (xun-jian[11]) and flood control (xun-fang -ba[12]). The Lu-ding Bridge was built in the 34th year of Kangxi [1965] during the period of the Qing Dynasty. It was 31 feet long and 9 feet wide. Two sides of the bank were connected by nine iron cables, laid on which were wooden boards. Two thick iron cables were used as handrails on each side and were fixed with four iron stakes at each end. The iron stakes weighed more than 1,800 kilograms. On the east bank of the river was a stone stele pavilion with words 'Confucian Temple erected on the order of Kangxi at the Luding Bridge' inscribed on it. On the west bank of the river, there was a Guanyin [Avalokiteshvara] Pavilion with an inscription saying, Da-du River originated from the barren hills of Song-pan County. On its way, it merged into the big Xiao-jin-chuan[13] [Xiao-jin river] and flowed south through the upper and lower Yu-tong[14], streaming down more than 2,000 *li* till reaching Lu-ding. It again meandered south to Shen-bian[15] and then turned east, passing through the northern border of E-bian-ting[16] in the south of Qing-xi County to reach Jia-ding Fu (now Le-shan City). It then merged in the west with the Ya-long[17] River, which streamed eastward and joined with the Min-jiang [Min river].[18] According to legends, Emperor Song Taizu (960–976 CE) demarcated the boundary with Tubo[19] (Tibet) and sketched this river with a jade axe. All the territory to the west of the river then lost the jurisdiction of the Song Dynasty. Today's temperature on the thermometer was 86° (30°C).

On the 20th day, we crossed the Lu-ding Bridge and traveled northward along the west bank of the [Da-du] river for 70 *li*. We stayed at Wa-si-gou [Tiled temple gully] at the point of its union with the Lu River from the west. The temperature at the thermometer displayed 80° (27.4°C).

On the 21st, we turned to the west and traveled 70 *li* along the south bank of the Lu-he [Lu River] to Da-jian-lu (place name – Shooting Arrow Furnace). After crossing the bridge, we came across surprisingly steep and frightening mountains and rivers. Strangely shaped rocks suspended in the air from peaks. The river here surged at a much faster speed than earlier ones. The water colliding with stones turned into breakers and made heavy and loud sounds. It resembled a powerful and energetic white dragon, believed by the people to be residing at the edge of the Milky Way observing all the wonders of the universe and rushing straight from the sky into the water. At noon, it was 85° (29.4°C) on the thermometer. After arriving in Lucheng, the temperature turned down drastically. I thought it would have been better to bring an extra piece of clothing. The terrain also sharply began to turn into upslopes, rising more than ten feet a *li*. From Luding Bridge to Lu-cheng, it rose to several thousand feet in height. From the provincial capital Cheng-du to Da-jian-lu, we traveled a total of 975 *li*.

Lu-cheng[20] market town was sandwiched between two rivers and was securely surrounded by three mountains. It was very breezy in the morning and evening. The mountains were covered with snow all year round. Not everybody wore thick fur clothes in the midsummer. Han and ethnic minorities lived together. People of ethnic minorities had strange features. They were distinguished by their eagle like nose, dark skin, difficult and different spoken languages, disheveled hair, bare feet, and the red-brown dress/robes.

Monks of western region [from India] and lamas were everywhere on the road. Lu-cheng is the key entry-point to southwest China. It is the throat of Tibet. A security officer and his assistants were stationed there.

The Ming administration instituted a system of hereditary tribal head-men[21]. One was stationed in Lu-cheng city. Under his jurisdiction was one Zhang-guan-si [senior official][22] and 49 local officials controlling 100–1000 ethnic households[23]. They were spread in the east to the boundary of Leng-bian Tu-si,[24] which was more than 120 miles from Lu-ding Bridge, in the west to the boundary of Li-tang Tu-si,[25] which was 280 miles from Zhong-du Xun-di, in the south to the boundary of Mian-ning[26] county, which was 600 *li* from Le-xiang, and in the north to the boundary of Zhang-gu-tun which was 450 *li* from Xiao-jin-chuan.

Da-jian-lu [War-arrow Furnace] was also the ancient country of yak. According to a folklore, when Wu Xiang-hou and Zhuge Liang marched south, they sent General Guo Da ahead to build an iron furnace to make bows and arrows. Of course, it was an unfounded description without a source[27]. It appeared that in the period of Tang and Song dynasties, the invading Tubo [Tibetans] from the Central Plains must have passed through this main route, and might have made bows and arrows here. As far as Zhuge Liang's journey from here to Cheng-du during his southern expedi-tion was concerned, the route was completely different. It was impossible to pass through this place.

On the first of the eighth month, the temperature was 64°F (17.7°C

On the second of the eighth month, I met French Missionary Father Bi.[28]

On the third, I had a meeting with Kuo-er-ka [Gurkha/Nepali] Country's tribute envoy, Ge Ji. He had set off from his home country in the fifth month of the previous year [1877] and was finally able to arrive in Lu-cheng in the sixth month of the present year [1878].

On the eighth day, we left Da-jian-lu from the south gate of the city at 9 A.M. and traveled to 20 *li*. I tried riding on the horseback for the first time. From this place, the road bifurcated following the two streams of the river. One of the roads turned to the south, and passing through a large snow capped mountain reached Mian-ning [in South Sichuan]. From here, we traveled on a gentle sloping road towards the southwest for about 20 *li*, and stayed in Zhe-duo.[29] There were two cave houses,[30] which faced south with the Da-xue [heavily snow capped] Mountain visible at a far away dis-tance. Shining in the setting sun, it resembled like a silver barrier. It was a beautiful and magical landscape. Boiling hot springs gushed out from the depression of the mountain. Passing pedestrians came here to take a bath. The temperature was 64° (17.7°C).

On the ninth day, we got up early and started climbing up the mountain. It was quite large but not very steep. We walked through the slopes and over scattered rocks for 50 *li* to reach the top. The mountain peak then appeared suddenly. There were odd shaped stones all along the slope, and the place was filled up with dense fog. Not even a household or a person could be seen. Our eyes observed a very desolate scene and traveling up here made us worry about robbers. Most of the rocks in this area were ironstone. More than a dozen *li* down the mountain, there was a cave house. We stopped there for a little rest and some food. After that, the terrain gradually became flat and more and more local residents began to be visible. We walked 30 *li* and stayed at the A-Niang-ba (also called An-liang-ba). We traveled a total of 90 *li*, It was 58°F (14.4°C) in the thermometer.

On the tenth day, we replaced our Wu-la [Tibetans serving as forced labor] and traveled 25 *li* past a lower government official post. This place was at a strategic location with considerable military importance. After trekking for another 25 *li*, we halted at Dong-e-luo [lit. trans. Eastern Russian Luo River]. On this route, the terrain was flat, hills were beautiful, and water and plants were in abundance with highland barley growing luxuriantly. The whole place appeared prosperous. Any time somebody passed by ethnic minority village hamlets, hospitable locals came out to greet and treat Wu-la [Tibetan labor] with butter tea. The temperature here was 64°F (17.7°C).

On the 11th day, we again changed our Wula, traveled 20 *li*, ate something at the foot of the mountain, climbed upslope riding the horse, and covered a total of 30 *li* from up to down. There was a Gao-ri [High Sun] Temple at the top of the mountain and over a 100 lamas (some were even from places several *li* far away by road that passed through the front of the temple). Medicinal plants like Chong-cao [caterpillar fungus] and Bei-mu [the bulb of fitellart] were produced on the hills. We trekked 20 *li* through an old pine forest where trees stood beside the road like weird dragon claws. The huge ones are several meters thick and grow in the wild. Once they die they are left on both sides of the road in the deep mountains as no master carpenter could reach here. We stayed at Wo-long-shi for the night, where two scouts were stationed. We covered a total of 75 *li* today. The temperature was 64°F (17.7°C).

On the 12th day, I got up watching sunlight brightening up the sky. The road was flat and wide, and the terrain was downslope. We descended for about 50 *li* and ate food in a Ba-jiao-lou [the octagonal building]. The scouts [border soldiers] came out to welcome us. We then walked westward along the small river, passed four bridges on the left and right sides, and covered a total of 50 *li*. Our party stayed in Zhong-du which was then under the seasonal flood. It was the estuary of the Ya-long River. The place had a flood prevention office that also took care of managing the ferry. The east bank of the river was under the boundary of Ming-zheng Tu-si, and the west bank of the river belonged to the territory of Li-tang Tu-si. On both sides were sharp and unexpected rock barriers. The current was turbulent, and the temperature was 80°F (26.6°C).

On the 13th day, there was rain. Because no arrangements for the Wu-la labors could be made, we stayed put there for a day. The temperature was 65°F (18.3°C).

On the 14th day, we crossed the river under continuous rain, replaced our Wu-la labor, walked 40 *li* on hilly roads, and stayed in Ma-gai-zong [place name?].

On the 15th day, the weather was fine. We again got up early to cross the snowcapped mountains, and using yak to transport luggage, reached the top. The snow was falling heavily, and the cold was biting. The temperature in our meter dropped down to 48°F (10°C). Crawling up and down for 40 *li*, we reached Jian-zi-wan [The Scissor Bay]. There was a cave house stationed by the scouts [border patrol]. It was full of sweat and filth. We sat down on a straw mat, rested for a while, and then rode for another 30 *li* to reach Bo-lang-gong [place name?]. Flood Control Officers were positioned here on the cross-roads to protect from robberies by the local raiders. After walking down the mountain for 20 *li* we lodged at Xi-e-Luo[31] where there were seven to eight cave houses which housed the scouts. The stream flowed eastward and the terrain was flat. At ten o'clock in the evening, a bright moon appeared on the horizon. When one climbed the watchtower, the arc of the star Gou Cheng[32] was measured to be at 30° and 20°. The first arc of Nan-dou was 30°.

On the 16th day, because Wu-la laborers were not arranged we stayed there for the day. I measured the sun's high arc/curvature/radian right at noon to be 64.30°.

On the 17th day, it was overcast and raining that consequently delayed our departure until almost noon. We walked up and down through the slope for 40 *li* in deep valley and dense forest. I stayed in Za-ma-la-dong[33] [a place name] in a narrow, small, and damp shop, and curled up on my bed like a turtle. Constantly billowing smoke there kept piercing people's eyes and bringing tears. Tight clothes, bed nets, and bedding remained damp and cold. I was unable to sleep.

On the 18th day early morning, the rain continued. We walked 20 *li*, passed a Man-ka[34] [the ethnic minority check-post], and went over the snow-capped mountains riding the horse. I trotted up and down for 30 *li*. It was extremely cold and the temperature dropped to 0.4°F (4.4°C). In the afternoon, the snow fall stopped and the sky became clear. We descended for 20 *li* from the mountain and reached Huo-zhu-ka[35] [checkpost], There was an official residence that served as a resting place. This place was, however, surrounded all around by bandits and robbers. A Flood Control Officer and 17 soldiers were stationed there for protection.

On the 19th day, the weather was clear. While crossing the river, we were hit by a flash flood that broke the bridge. The water rose up to one meter high. I waded through the water on horseback. My clothes and shoes were all soaked. We had to take a circuitous bypass of about 20 *li* along the river-bank. After passing a Man-ka [the ethnic minority check-post], we walked another twenty *li* on the gently downsloping road. After the downhill, there was an endless plain, and then another 20 *li* to Li-tang.

The total distance from Da-jian-lu to Li-tang was 665 *li*.

At 11 o'clock that night, the high arc of Gou-chen Star [North Star] was measured at 31.30°. I discovered that on that day, the sun's right ascension changed in 22 hours and 31 minutes. Subtracting the error of visual height by four points from the average arc of Gouchen star [North Star], and subtracting the error of fog refraction by one point, the actual arc of Gouchen star [North Star] was 30.25°. After the changed figure, taking into account minus three points of earlier error, the latitude of Li-tang was calculated to be 31.32°.

At the same time, the highest arc of Beiluo Shimen Star [South Star] at noon measured at 28.15°, subtracting the visual error of four points, and the fog refraction error by one point, we got the maximum degree of Beiluo Shimen Star minus the quadrant. The remaining arc was 61.50°, this was the height from the highest point at the noon. I checked the star table. The Bei-luo-shi-men Star in southern latitude was 30.22°. Subtracting the remaining radian/arc/curvature, I calculated the latitude of the place to be 31.28° which was exactly in line with the number measured earlier.

Li-tang was at a high altitude and had a cold climate. It was surrounded by snow-capped mountains. Its terrain was open and flat for several tens of *li* in length and breadth. The stream here flowed slowly. If the Han people were allowed to cultivate, tens of thousands of hectares of fertile land could have been opened up. Accustomed to the ease and comfort of herding life, ethnic minority people were unfortunately not adapted to the hard work of farming life. In addition, there were thousands of lamas who devoured but did not do any work. Therefore, the land had been fallow and the region sparsely populated, which was very different from the places under the jurisdiction of Ming-zheng Tu-si. After the sun set in the west, lamas went to the Da- zhao Temple and found pleasure in extolling merits and virtues of Buddha's good deeds. 3,600 lamas lived in the temple. There were four huge copper pots for making tea, which could hold hundreds and hundreds *dan* [liters] of tea.[36] Next to the temple was a Wu Wang Hall, and at the back was an earthen mound/moat that surrounded the temple with water from the stream encircling it. The range of snowcapped mountains in the front resembled silver screens, and the sharp mountain peak in the middle appeared particularly beautiful and grand. Under the foundation of the temple and in the nearby mountains there were rich goldfield, but the lamas forbade people from digging and mining.

Li-tang's Xuan-fu-shi-si[37] [ethnic chieftain at the prefecture] was called Da-ying-guan, [chief administrator] and the Fu-shi-si [deputy chieftain] was called Xiao-ying-guan [deputy administrator]. Under them were four senior administrative officers: Wa-shu-Mao-ya[38], Wa-shu-chong-xi[39], Wa-shu-qu-deng[40], and Wa-shu-guo-long[41] and two eldermen of local 'hundred-families' households: Wa-shu-mao-mao-ya[42] and Wa-shu-ma-li.[43] Their territory in the east reached 320 *li* up to the river boundary of Ming-zheng Tu-si, in the west 240 *li* up to the Er-lang bay boundary of Ba-tang Tu-si, in the south 580 *li* up to Lakong Ling dammed water pass of Yunnan's Zhong-dian[44] County boundary, and in the north 440 *li* up to Chu Mu river territory of Zhan-dui Tu-si.

On the 22nd day, we traveled for 15 *li* and reached Re-shui-tang [hot spring pond]. There were bearded central Asian barbarian natives settled there on pieces of land rewarded by the emperor. They wore peach-colored hats over their ears and yellow Chinese lama's long gowns with Buddhist motifs. They were called Na-da-ji. They completely followed Han culture, proficiently communicated in Han [Chinese] language, and were skilled in the method of divination. They presented me seven yellow colored medicinal pills and a clay statue of Buddha which was about one inch long. Here, the hot spring water steamed out of the pores of the stone, split, and flowed into several places. A square pool was built to bathe in it. The temperature of the water as per our thermometer reached 110°F (43.3°C). We then rode for more than 10 *li* and crossed a river. While walking upslope, we were suddenly hit by heavy rain. Hail fell from the sky, soaked us all over; and people and horses trembled with cold. We stayed at Tou-tang (also known as Gong-sa [Public convenience]) that day. There was a public bathroom, which was very low and narrow. The total trip was of 60 *li*.

On the 23rd day, we woke up early to cross the snowcapped mountains. The wind was so cold that my skin began drying and cracking. After walking 40 *li* to Gan-hai-zi, there was a man-tang [barbarian convenience store] that could provide a meal. We then passed through a mud dam and a tiger-skin [narrow] ravine, and circled up and down the mountains five times. The road was often interrupted by huge boulders and was completely gloomy, deserted, and uninhabited. After walking 40 *li* we reached La-er-tang village, where soldiers were stationed. Following the ravine downhill for 25 *li* we reached La-ma-ya. We traveled a total of 150 *li*. The weather here was warm and sunny. The river flowed towards the southeast. Barley was planted on both sides of the river. There were dozens of cave houses. The local people even with the unruly heads were also very respectful and obedient to us.

On the 24th day, the weather was fine. On the rocky hills and over the ridges, the road was full of twists and turns. After passing the mountain ranges, there were deep woods and dense grass everywhere, and the winding pathways disappeared at a distance. Walking along the riverbank, the scene was fresh and beautiful, and scores of dancing butterflies fluttered around the front of our horses' head. We walked a total of 50 *li* and stayed at Er-lang-wan [place at a river bend] where there was a shop. From Li-tang to this place, we walked towards the southwest, as the Da-xue Mountain stood in front of us, and we had to pass through a detour. I heard from the locals that there was another shortcut from Gong-sa to the west, taking only three days to reach Batang. This, however, passed through a meadow with no place to stay, and was very inconvenient for travelers.

On the 25th day, the weather was again fine. We entered the ravine from the foot of the mountain and turned to the northwest. The road was fairly flat. We walked a total of 60 *li* and stayed at Li-deng-san-ba [a place name] because Er-lang-wan [river bend] was in front of the snowcapped mountains and San-ba [Li-deng-san-ba] was behind it. Although walking by these snowcapped mountains for the past few days, the weather was sunny and warm, but the wind on the top of the mountain was very strong, often causing headaches and breathlessness to the travelers.

On the 27th day, it was the Autumn Equinox. We went into the ravine and climbed the snowcapped mountain for 30 *li* to reach the top of the mountain. Monstrous rocks towering aloft were steep and dangerous which made people very scared. I decided to dismount and walk. We had not found a place to eat for the last few days. On the meadowland, I just had boiled tea and ate *tsampa* [roasted Qingke barley bread – a staple Tibetan food] to fill the belly. We later walked about 40 *li* down the mountain through the woodlands and stayed in Bang-yi-mu. The Han and ethnic minority soldiers stationed in this village produced abundant Qingke [highland] barley.

On the 28th day, we followed the ravine and descended down to Xiao-ba-chong [a place name]. There were cave houses where meals were provided. We then went further downslope for 40 *li* to reach Ba-tang. Along the way, there were cliffs and scattered rocks everywhere. The water here streamed as swift as the Lu-he[45] River [i.e., Lu-shui River/Nu-jiang River]. The weather was just mild and warm, and the heat and the temperature on the thermometer rose to 84°F (29°C).

At noon on the 29th day, the sun's high arc was measured to be close to 59° (this time the sun was at 45 minutes south latitude).

There were seven stations from Li-tang to Ba-tang, covering a total distance of 545 *li*.

More than 300 households of Han and ethnic minorities resided in Ba-tang. There was not a single official to manage grain procurements. The weather was warm, and the soil was fertile. Highland barley could be grown twice a year, and many varieties of vegetables could also be sown. There was a Ding-lin Temple with more than 3,000 lamas. It is said that Ding Lin was a descendant of the ancient Ding-lin-qiang tribe. It is also said that Ba-tang is the hometown of the White Wolf King, Tang Zou. This was, however, only an unverifiable legend.

The Ba-tang Xuan-fu Chieftain and the deputy chieftain governed six places: Yu-zong, E-bo, De-long [jie-ao], and several other Jie-ao [stubborn and intractable region]. These were spread over both south and west sides of the region. There were also seven Tu-si spread to: Gang-li, Sang-long, Guo-bu, upper and lower sections of Su River, area overlooking upper and lower Ka-shi, and the expanse near the both banks in the northwest side of the Jin-sha River. These included the territory in the east up to the Li-tang boundary of Er-lang Bay/bend, in the west to the Ning-jing mountain's Jiang-ka's boundary, in the south from Geng-zhong-qiao [Geng-zhong Bridge] to Zhong-dian-ting[46] [Gyeltang/Gyalthang], and in the north to Sang-ang [sang ang] barabarian region to De-ge Tu-si boundary. The total length from the east to west was more than 700 *li*, and from the south to north was more than 1000 *li*.

The first day of the ninth month - no entry.

On the tenth day of the ninth month, the high arc of Pleiades was measured to be at 59.10° to the meridian. After subtracting the visual error and fog error by 5 points, the local star's latitude was detected at 53° south, and the latitude of Ba-tang was calculated to be 30.2 °.

On the 13th day, (ji-wei-you-zheng) of the ninth month at a quarter past six, the solar term was Cold Dew (referring to October 8, 1886).

At 12 o'clock at night on the 14th day, the Gouchen star was measured to be close to 30°.

VOL. 2: FROM BA-TANG TO TENG-YUE

[CONG BA-TANG DAO TENG-YUE 从巴塘到腾越]

On the first day of the 11th month of the Bingxwu year [1889] the temperature was 10° on the thermometer.

In recent years, several western countries often sent people to Tibet
on explorative missions. But they were blocked by the local Tibetans and
finally diverted to Yunnan. Similarly, when our party arrived in Ba-tang,
the local Tibetans became suspicious when they heard that someone was
going to India. They gathered locals to obstruct us in every way and were
not amenable to listen to our reasonable explanations. Finding no other
way out, we sought help from the Grain officer Zhao Mu to explain the
situation to the Governor and obtain the approval to divert via Zhong-
dian, Yun-nan, to India. There were two roads in this place. One went
west from Ba-tang to Ba-long. It was a nine-station road which passed
through A-dun-zi after crossing the Jin-sha river, and then went along
the other side of the river, to arrive at a ten station-stops at Wei-xi-ting.
It was the same route that Zhao Mu had taken to escort the British official Ji-wei-li (See Margary Affair in Chapter I) earlier. The other road
was from Ba-tang to the south. It passed through Liu-yu and Zhou-dui to
Zhong-dian Bridge and went all along the inner side of the Jin-sha River
with just a few stops in between. Considering that this road was relatively
remote and desolate with only a few people traveling, it was necessary
to carry enough dry food and a felt tent to sleep in the wild. Natives and
bandits both frequently roamed there, so Zhao Mu and his two officers
assigned soldiers to escort us.

On the 20th day, we turned from Ba-tang towards Xiao-ba [eastern
Sichuan] and dashed to 30 *li*.

On the 21st day, we set off before dawn, and turned south and traveled
upslope along the ravines of the river. The road was narrow and difficult
to negotiate, with messy twined deadwood branches and scattered rocks
everywhere. Further, the road was icy and it was very easy to slip and fall.
After the sun rise, I abandoned sedan and rode on horse for 50 *li*. We ate
something after exiting the forest and then started scaling the snowcapped
mountain. Its peaks were very high; I was dizzy and panting. Finally at dusk
we reached our camp-house. We walked a total of 120 *li* that day. Because
there was no water and grass for horses to drink and eat, and no place
to stop and rest along the way, people and horses were exhausted. It was
extremely cold to sleep in a black tent at the night, and we only pretended to
be asleep by the fire.

On the 22nd day, we went downhill along the ravine and passed the virgin forest and wild grass, turned to the southeast and crossed Er-ban-qiao

[Er-ban bridge] (the stream under its left flowed from Bang-yi-mu). Walking further 50 *li*, we stayed in Dong-la-duo, where there were six to seven rock houses.

On the 23rd day, we went south along the stream, the forest was dense, the weather was relatively warm, and there were residents along the way. We walked 60 *li* to Zhu-wa-gen. The Tibetan Buddhist Red Sect Monastery[47] especially welcomed us to stay there. More than 300 lamas resided there. They performed for us with sounds of drums and golden cymbals in hands, and led us all the way up the mountain. Animals were slaughtered for a feast for our party. The main temple hall was very majestic and magnificent.

We traveled downhill for 50 *li* on the 24th day and stayed in Liu-yu. The weather in this place was warm and the land fertile like Ba-tang. More than 300 households were scattered in several nearby villages. They were known for their proud and overbearing nature. Their settlement could be regarded as the most prosperous place on the outer side of the Jin-sha River. From here, a stream flowed southwest to the Jin-sha River, and there was another small stream that converged to it from the south. Going to the left we reached A-dun-zi after eight stops, and then arrived at De-rong after two stops. Turning right to the south and traveling along the ravine was the road to Zhong-dian.

On the 25th day, we took a day off.

On the 26th day, we walked along the ravines of the local river. There were several rock houses on the way where people set off fire on green grass for smoke as a mark of respect for us. After walking 30 *li,* we stayed at Ren-dui.

On the 27th day, we traveled towards the east. The densely forested valley was deep and extremely cold. The mercury on the surface of the thermometer was frozen and condensed. Riding on the horse we crossed the mountain gorge. After climbing high over the mountain, there was a piece of open land which was flat. The weather there began to warm up. After going downhill and resting for a while in the pine forest, we turned to the southeast and went down the ravine, and stayed in Zou-dui. In total, we walked about 100 *li*. There were several rockhouses, and 60 houses were scattered on the vast fertile fields.

On the 28th day, we walked along the cliff to the south. The road was very remote and narrow. After arriving in Ka-sha we had a short rest. Riding on the horse, we then crossed the opening point of the narrow waterway and saw the Ba-long-da river converging here from the northeast. Its current was turbulent. Walking for a few more miles, we passed through Ban-qiao, and then turning south traveled for more than ten *li* to the turn of Ban-qiao along the west bank of the river. At the time of sunset, we stayed in Ka-gong. There were several rock houses built on high slopes. We walked for about 90 *li* in total.

On the 29th day, it was the winter solstice. We journeyed down the river to the south. The road was steep and difficult to navigate. After walking 40 *li*, we stayed at Qiu-mai [place name].

On the first day of the 12th month of 1889 (i.e., 13th year of Bingzi), we walked along the river for 30 *li* towards the south to Gong-pai-xi [place name]. There were several watchtowers here. We had originally planned to stay here, but because it was still early, we decided to continue traveling on the road and walked another 30 *li* before halting at Tu-ma-tong [place name]. Nobody lived nearby this place, all the people resided about 50 *li* away. Traveling all the way from Zuo-dui on a narrow and difficult road and tall and dangerous mountains, I often had to get off the sedan chair and ride on either the horseback or leave the horse to hike on foot because at many places we had to use hands to climb up like apes. In this remote hinterland not even a shadow of human figure could be seen, what to say of the majestic figure of an official. Even the two Ba-tang officials who accompanied us had never visited these places.

On the second day of the 12th month, we got up early in the morning and hurriedly set off on the road to the south-east. We passed through the cliff and crossed the La-zhu River at the place of Litang's Er-lang Bend. Several rivers converged there. When passing through the Ban-qiao (wooden bridge), we could see a turbulent river. Its location was dangerous and indeed greatly frightening. We then went over the steep upslope to arrive at Jia-zhu [place-name]. Dozens of ethnic minority households lived among the cliffs and precipice, and planted below wheat in step formation like neatly arranged fields.

On the third day of the 12th month, the wind was pretty strong and we traveled south along the river. Going up and down the slopes and ridges, we passed through a Xiao-man [barbarian/ethnic tribal] Village where there were several watchtowers. To reach Ca-la [place-name], it was necessary to climb stone cliffs, half of which were connected by slanted/crooked bridges where two drum-like structures (gu cao) were placed for support in walking. Passing through these stone cliffs, we viewed the Jin-sha River and found that the orientation of all the mountains and the flow of the water turned east from here. In the north of the Jin-sha River was the territorial boundary of Wei-xi County[48]. In the distant east, visible were numerous snow peaks standing tall amidst strong winds. We slowly and carefully walked along bends of the mountains. Cliffs and precipices here appeared like 1000 knives stuck in the mountains. The force of the turbulent Jin-sha River was so breathtaking that I dared not look down. By the time of sunset, we reached A-lu-gong [place-name] covering about only 60 *li* in total. All of us and horses were so exhausted that none wanted to proceed further.

On the fourth day, we walked along the Jin-sha River through the winding mountain road towards the southeast, and then went down the steep slope for 30 *li* to reach Ben-zi-nan [place-name]. Ferry boats were available here. Many stone houses were scattered on the southern bank side of the river. The sight reflected a little prosperity. A flood control official was posted there. From here, a three-stops road went to A-dun-zi in the west, and a two-stops road to Tacheng in the east. On the north bank of the river, there was only one household which was under the jurisdiction of Ba-tang. After walking for another 20 *li*, we came down to Tu-zhao-bi [place-name]. From here, the road started to widen. The major profession of the local aboriginal people here was to mine gold from the sand [of Jin-sha river]. Citrus and pears were produced locally and were very sweet and delicious.

On the fifth day, we walked southeast along the river, and climbed up and down the slope for 35 *li* to reach Qiao-tou-xun (also known as Geng-zhong Bridge), which was the boundary between Sichuan and Yunnan where a one-official manned border-post was set up. After reaching here, the two guards from Ba-tang returned to their place. The river-water here flowed from the east. It was as deep and wide as the Ba-long-da River. Its source must be above the distant Li-tang. As we traveled from here towards the east, the Jin-sha River became invisible. After walking another five *li*, we lodged in Nong-ba-me-duo [place-name]. There were dozens of households here. Two streams, one from the east and the other from the northeast, converged here and flowed as a river to later join the Jin-sha River in the south.

On the sixth day, we traveled east on the steep slope for 30 *li* to Zhi-fang-tang [place name] and another 20 *li* to Nixi [place name].

On the seventh day of the first lunar month, we ate food in the middle of the night, then sat down to wait for the sun to rise. By the time the sky began to lighten up at dawn we had walked for about 20 *li* in the torch light. After traveling to another 20 *li*, we reached Chang-duo [place name] and ate something. The residents here used wooden planks to build their houses. The eaves were in the shape of Chinese *"ren"* [人 = people] character, which was more like the scene on the mainland. From this place onward, the air started getting chillier, and the terrain turned flat. After walking for another 40 *li*, we reached a lake. It was tens of *li* wide and covered with thick ice as bright as mirror. By the time of sunset, we arrived in Zhong-dian. The city was densely populated by Han people and ethnic minorities, and its customs appered similar to those of Ba-tang and Li-tang. From Ba-tang to Zhong-dian, it took us a total of 18 days to walk, it was a journey of more than 1000 *li*.

The area under the jurisdiction of Zhong-dian Fu-yi Tong-zhi[49] [Zong-dian Barbarian Pacification Deputy Governor] was more than 300 square miles. The area attached to it was called Zhong-dian Fu-guo[50]. Its jurisdiction was in the west up to Geng-zhong-qiao of Ba-tang's territorial boundary, known as Ni-xi-jing; in the south up to A-xi-xun at the border of

Li-jiang, called the Jiang-bian-jing [river border]; in the east up to the border of Yong-shun[51] Tu-zhou [native tribal/barbarian prefecture], also called the Xiao-zhong-dian-jing; and in the north to Weng-shui Guan [mountain pass] at the boundary of Li-tang, called the Ge-za-jing [Zhong-dian] which was provided with two Tu-bao-zhang[52] [Deputy Guard-Officer], and 16 Tu-ba-zong[53] [lowest level field officers] from the army. These official positions were not hereditary. The native language of people in this area was different from that of the Tibetan areas, and they believed in either red or yellow religious sect[54]. They had a large temple outside the city which had more than 2,000 lamas. We stayed in Zhong-dian for five days. It was extremely cold at night here. The leather robes and bedding froze as hard as ice. It was impossible to sleep at night, and we could only get out of bed and sit around the fire-heater to keep ourselves warm. My wristwatch and other glass utensils cracked, and the sliding-pole of the sedan chair became unusable. After that, the whole journey was on horseback.

On the 13th day, Zhao Mu, who was still accompanying us on the journey, returned to Batang. We walked 80 *li* from Zhongdian and stayed in Xiao-zhong-dian. The road was level and the area was densely populated. It was no longer as desolate as it was at Kou-chu [the gateway of the Great Wall].[55]

On the 14th day, we traveled 25 *li* on the south-east road and stayed at Qing-xiang-shu.

On the 15th day, we got up early in the morning and rode under the moonlight. After journeying 30 *li*, the sky gradually lightened up. When we reached the top of the mountain, a strong cold wave of wind suddenly started to blow. The fog piled up and became dense. The ice on the ground turned hard. Soon fine snowflakes began to heavily fall on us. We got off from horses and made tea to warm our bodies. When our frozen hands and feet relaxed, we proceeded to descend the mountain. The downhill road was steep and dangerous. The stone pathway was very narrow and covered with deadwood twigs and hedges. Around the time of sunset, we reached Ge-liu-wan, which was close to the bank of the Jin-sha River. In total, we walked about 100 *li*, 40 *li* uphill and 60 *li* downhill. When streams swelled in spring and summer, it was necessary to take the road from Xiao-zhong-dian through Jin-sha to this place. The distance was about 30 *li* longer, but it was relatively wide and flat.

On the 16th day, we walked along the Jin-sha River to the southeast. The weather was warm, and the land was fertile and broad. This place was called Jiang-bian-jing. It was the rice producing area. We walked 90 *li* up to Wu-zhu and lodged there. There were several hundred households of residents.

On the 17th day, we again traveled 60 *li* in the southeast along the Jin-sha River and stayed in Leng-du. Hills were beautiful here, and the river flowed quietly. On both sides of the river, there were continuous rows of tiled houses, which were very similar to the scenery in the south of the Yangtze River. With ornamental fruit trees [plum] blooming with buds, and the willows growing twigs in early spring, it was like a literati living in seclusion in the mountains and coming across a good friend in the remotest corner of the world surrounded by faint floral fragrance. How could one not be ecstatic!

On the 18th day, we journeyed 50 *li* in the east-south direction and reached Mu-bi-wan. After crossing the river, we stayed in A-xi-xun, which was at the boundary of Li-jiang County. One Bai-zong [lowest army officer] was installed here.

On the 19th day, we went downslope to 30 *li* and reached Ci-shi-ba. There was a lake there with a radius of several tens of *li*. We again crossed two depressions while going downslope and passed through a huge embankment. By dusk, we reached Li-jiang city. We covered a distance of 70 *li* in total by the road.

The city of Li-jiang was known as Me-xie-zhao[56] in ancient times as mentioned in one of the six imperial edicts.[57] In its north was the Yu-Long [Jade-Dragon] snow mountain, sparkling clean and serene it stood like a silver-colored screen. The Mongol clan of the Nanzhao kingdom[58] [c. 738–902 CE] was enfeoffed in Bei-yue. Even today the local temple preserved a Ming Hongwu year's proclamation ordering Deputy Envoy A De to take charge of the local people and manage them to submit to the authority. He was later rewarded with a 'Mu' surname and the post of local Prefect, and the proclamation was recorded on inscription. Descendants of the Mongol clan continued to hold this position until the First Year of Emperor Yong Zheng [1678]. After the reorganization of the post of Tu-gui-liu,[59] the position was demoted to Tu-tong-ban.[60] There were nine ethnic minorities in Li-jiang, namely, Me-xie,[61] Li-li,[62] Guo-guo,[63] Gu-zong,[64] Xi-fan,[65] Ba-ju,[66] Ci-mao,[67] as well as Qiu-zu[68] and Nu-zu living in the area of Lan-cang[69]River.

On the 25th day, we departed from Li-cheng, returned to Ci-shi embankment/dyke, and continued to walk along the Lake. We later turned southwest and went over the downslope of the valley. The road was particularly steep here. We traveled a total of 70 *li*. We stayed at the foot of the mountain where there were two earthen houses.

On the 26th day, we walked south to 30 *li* and arrived at Jiu-he-jie [Nine River Market]. Many small shops were there. A checkpost was installed to collect taxes. This was the boundary between Li-jiang and Jian-chuan.[70] We walked another 30 *li* and arrived at Jian-chuan. The land was flat and wide all the way. A stream flowed eastward to Jian-hai. The city of Jian-chuan was three *li* wide. It was densely populated and full of shops. It appeared more prosperous and better than Li-chang. Most of the buyers and sellers were women who wore grass sandals on their bare feet and carried hanging bamboo baskets on their backs with a string tied to their foreheads. Their attire was no different from the other ethnic minority people.

This was the first day of the first lunar month on the fifth year of Emperor Guangxu (1879).

On the second day of the first lunar month, we started from the South Gate and walked 20 *li* across a bridge (over the stream flowing southeast) to Dian-wei ei. We then passed a lake that had a radius of more than ten *li*, and then turning to the southeast upsloped more than 20 *li* reached Ye-ye-tang to lodge. There were only a few thatched shops there.

On the third day, we downsloped 30 *li* and arrived at Guanyin Mountain, which was located under the boundary of He-qing-zhou.

Traveling further for about 15 *li*, we passed Jiu-jie-xun, and after 10 *li* entered the boundary of Lang-qiong, and walked further about 15 *li* to stop at Ying-shan-pu. Along the way, the road was flat, and the land was open and densely populated.

On the fourth day, we journeyed towards the southeast for 15 *li* and passed Jin-shui Temple. The mountain road was narrow. We walked southward along the river bank for 15 *li* to Zhong-suo, and then crossed a bridge and reached Deng-chuan-zhou[71] after 20 *li*. The city walls there were crumbling, and inhabitants were few. After another 15 *li*, we reached Shang-guan and lodged there. On its left was Er-hai (e-hai) Lake, and on the right was Cang Mountain. The entire city was three *li* in diameter. It was a strategic pass for the movement of the people, and it had a checkpoint for the custom tax collection and an office for the flood control.

On the fifth day [of the first lunar month], we walked south along the foot of the mountain. The road was flat, the land was fertile, and there were continuous rows of villages everywhere. The Er-hai Lake was full of waves, the Cang-shan Mountain was snowy, the weather was warm and pleasant, and the scenery was beautiful.

From Li-jiang to Da-li, the distance by road was 860 *li* with a total of 13 stations.

Da-li was the most prosperous city in southern Yunnan. Its economy was well developed. Shops were numerous, and people moved freely. Du Wen-xiu, a rebel leader of the Hui ethnic group, once controlled this place for 18 years. In the 12th year of Tongzhi (1873), the imperial court sent troops to retake Da-li and fought fiercely with Du Wenxiu. Almost 90 percent of the region was then destroyed by the war.

The ancient city wall surrounding Da-li county seat Tai-he was more than 100 *li* long, with a width ranging from 30 to 40 *li*. It was flanked on one side by mountains and the other faced a lake. The terrain was firm. One could reach here only through Shang-guan and Xia-guan townships. Here, all the four seasons were warm, and there were often strong winds in the morning and evening. It was among the most beautiful places in Yunnan Province.

The 14th day marked the beginning of the first solar term, i.e., the Spring.

On the 22nd day, we traveled 30 *li* from the South Gate and passed through the Xia-guan township. It had a tax collection checkpoint and was more prosperous than the Shang-guan. Several check-posts in the city wall guarded the most important custom points. The outer Xia-guan was divided by three highways (that belonged to the territorial boundary of Zhao-zhou): One was for the entry and exit to Yunnan Province that went 30 *li* left towards Zhao-zhou, the second was in the south 90 *li* ahead to Menghua, and the third one was on the right to Teng-yong. The water of Er-hai-ke flowed from the front of Xia-guan to the southwest encircling Cang-shan Mountain from the back. There was a huge stone bridge, called Tian-sheng Bridge, that spawned across the river, Bu-xie-mei. The water under the bridge flowed swiftly, surged high, and broke into white snow like waves. After rushing 60 *li* to He-jiang-pu, the stream of water merged with Yang-bi[72] River.

On the 23rd day, we turned northwest along the river bank, and walked up and down through the depressed slope. The mountain road was narrow and difficult to negotiate. The water flowed with a gush. Only a few people could be seen outside in the area. The place was no different from the Tibetan area. With constant wind and rain accompanied with frequent bursts of spring thunder made it even more desolate. After walking 60 *li* along the Yang-bi River, we camped. This place belonged to the administrative jurisdiction of Menghua and an inspection department was stationed there. Across the river, three miles further away was Yong-ping's local administration, flood control and numerous other offices. This place faced Shang-guan from east to west, with Cang-shan in the middle, so the road after branching out from Jianchuan passed through two and a half stops to get here.

On the 24th day, we walked northward for about two miles and passed a stone bridge. There was a stream gushing out from the foot of Cang-shan Mountain. Its winding and crisscrossing movement made it appear like holding a bow and taking a shot at the Yang-bi River from the south. This was the demarcation point between Meng-hua and Yong-ping counties. After passing the flood control office again, we went over a 60 steps long iron chain bridge, turned towards the west, crossed a small stream flowing to south Vietnam, climbed an upslope, and walked through a totally ruined stone road for about 30 *li* to the top of the slope. Dyke protection officials were stationed there for observation. We then walked 30 *li* downhill and settled down at Tai-ping. A stream from the southwest rolled out there. Tai-ping had one office each for the Flood Control and the Foreign Affairs.

On the 25th day, we traveled in the southwest direction, climbed up the slope, and walked 45 *li* across a chain bridge of about 50 paces over the Sheng-bei River. The river originated in Jian-han Tu-si and flowed south from there. The Tai-ping Stream here converged with it from the east, the Huang-lian Stream joined it from the west, the river then turned south and then merged with the Yang-bi River. Crossing the bridge and tackling the mountain curves through twists and turns of the road, we walked for 15 *li* and camped in Huang-lian-pu, where a Flood Control Officer was also stationed.

On the 26th day, we set off before dawn, climbed up and down the slope, and reached Yong-ping County by sunset. We covered a total of 120 *li*. Yong-ping county town had no more than ten *li* of fields and only about a dozen of households on its outskirts. Yong-ping was called Bo-nan County in ancient times. The old city was on the east bank of the Yin-long River. It was washed away and destroyed by the flood. During the reign of Qianlong, the county city was moved to the foot of the mountain on the west bank of the river and was thus located about 15 miles away from the old city. Most of local inhabitants however still lived in the old city.

On the 27th day, traveling towards southwest, we climbed and came down steep slopes. The road there was curved like the character '之[zhi]' and had a dozen twists and turns. After traveling for 20 *li*, we passed the Ji-hong Bridge and reached the mainstream of the Lan-cang [Mekong] River. Two mountains stood there opposite to each other like walls, towering more than thousands meters high. The bridge built with a stone foundation was about 75 steps long, over which 16 iron cables were covered with wooden boards. These were very stable. On the mountain cliff, large characters were inscribed. They were post-Ming dynasty inscriptions. After crossing the bridge, we went up the mountain range. The stone road was steep and slippery, and appeared towering into the clouds. Its degree of difficulty was no less than that of the Elephant Ridge/cliff. There was a Shui-yun [water-cloud] temple on the top of the mountain. After walking 20 *li*, we halted to stay in Shui-zhai. There were dozens of villages located in the land area shaped like the bottom of a pot.

On the 29th day, we traveled downhill for 60 *li* to Ban-qiao, and then walked further 20 *li* to close to Yong-chang Fu's [prefecture] Bao-shan County town. In the west of the town was the outer Bao-shan and in the east was Qing Hua-hai [place name] which was a flat area stretching for several tens of *li* from north to south, very similar to Dali.

Yong-chang was once the ancient country of Ai-lao.[73] Since the Han Dynasty, it is known as Yong-chang Fu Prefecture. During the Yuan Dynasty, an office of a metropolis level military marshall was set up in this silver producing field mine area at the foot of unruly Yi tribe's Meng-le Mountain, and was about a 1000 *li* south of the present seat of prefectural government at Jin-chi. Later, it was renamed Wei-yi-zhi / Yongchang when defense administration was moved there. During the early Ming Dynasty, 2000 households resided side by side in Yong-chang. The imperial officials/eunuchs dispatched to guard the place were too exploitative and that caused a rebellion. In the first year of Jiajing (1522) in the Ming Dynasty, the governor He Mengchun sent successive petition to restore its military and civilian government. After the suppression of San-Fan Rebellion,[74] Youngcheng was, however, still set up again as prefecture with jurisdiction over Bao-shan and Yong-ping counties, and Teng-yue and Long-ling provincial administrative divisions.

Today was the first day of the second month.

On the fourth day of the second lunar month, we went first south for seven to eight *li*, turned west, and crossed a slope. We stopped and stayed at Pu-piao-yang station, after covering a total distance of 70 *li*. A Flood Control Officer was stationed here.

On the fifth day, we traveled more than ten *li* towards the northwest. After going round the mountain, we turned to the southeast, and then moved again in northwest direction to the Lu-jiang Bridge. The distance was about 60 *li* in total. The Lujiang[75] [Nu-jiang] River was about 20 *zhang* wide. A stone pier was erected in the middle of the river to build a two-section iron cable bridge. On the 23rd of the previous month, a strong windstorm had blown away its three iron cables, and on the 28th, five cables were broken. Bamboo rafts then carried people across the river. Each raft could hold only three to four people. There was a small market at Qiaotou, which was held every five days. It was filled with thatched stalls mostly of the Han people. That day, because of the delay in crossing the river, I couldn't make it to market in time, so I stayed here only. The local weather in early spring was already warm enough for the people; it was just like midsummer in the interior. After the fourth month, the plague begins to spread here, and the Han people start to leave the place one after another. At that time, all those who passed by here did not even dare to stop for a while and swiftly moved forward riding their horses. On about 20 *li* of the flat land on both sides of the river bank, the rice was grown and cultivated by the Bai-yi people. It belonged to one Mr. Xian – the Pacification Officer of the Lujiang river, whose family had jurisdiction over it. Women of the Bai-yi[76] tribe wrapped their heads with black/blue head dress, wore black/blue dress on their body with a red square cloth hanging at their back. Most of the men and monks dressed in yellow clothes, but what they believed was not the Yellow Sect, but the Burmese [Thervada] Buddhism. Their language was also different.

On the sixth day, we walked westward on a steep mountain slope for 30 *li*. All along the road wooden logs were fallen. People lived on cliffs and percipices because the ground got very hot and muggy. Summer and autumn were the only two seasons compatible with living. The road going uphill in the southwest direction was particularly precipitous. After walking 35 *li* to the top of the mountain, we felt like being close to the sky. After crossing the top of the mountain, the winding road going around the mountain was lined with thin bamboos and dense grass. The weather there was gloomy and the air cold and threatening. After traveling 15 more *li*, we camped at

Tai-ping Tang [dyke/embankment]. There were only a few soldiers stationed at the dyke. We walked 80 *li* in total. At night, the weather turned very cold.

On the seventh day of the first lunar month, we walked downhill for 30 *li* and crossed the iron chain bridge over the Long-chuan River. There was a Flood Protection Officer here. We walked five more *li* and stayed in Gan-lan-zhai [place-name], where there was a custom tax collection office.

On the eighth day, we headed westward and climbed up and down the slope for 60 *li* to reach Teng-yue. It was surrounded by the mountains, and there was about 20–30 *li* wide open flat area in the middle. The land was fertile. The outer city wall was divided into 18 sections. The city itself was densely populated, and sounds of chickens and dogs could be heard everywhere. Its size was about eight square *li* and was located at the foot of the northwest mountain. The whole area was vast and under the jurisdiction of seven chieftains. It was a frontier area with numerous guarded mountains and narrow passes and provided a vital communication link between China and Myanmar.

The road from Da-li to Teng-yue had a total of 13 stops, and the distance was 870 *li*.

VOL. 3: FROM TENG-YUE TO MIAN-DIAN

[CONG TENG-YUE DAO MIAN-DIAN 从腾越到缅甸]

On the 16th day [of the first lunar month], we set off from Teng-yue at nine o'clock by the South Gate and headed westward. After passing through Ping-gang, we walked 30 *li* to the end of a small river, traveled along the Da-ying[77] River for another 30 *li,* and passed the Song-guan Pass where a small river flowed from the northwest. After walking for another 30 *li* to Zuo-ying [place-name], where one Tu-cheng [local administrator?] and one Du-shou [metropolis security officer] were stationed, we walked another five *li* to Nan-dian, and stayed at the Tu-si Ya-men [government office]. All along the way, the road was smooth, the land fertile, and the population large.

On the 17th day, the Nan-dian Xuan-fu[78] Office sent ten local soldiers to escort us to the south. After climbing and descending the slope, we turned to the west, and traveled along the river for 80 *li* to reach Gan-ya [place-name]. It was more convenient to go to the west bank of the Da-ying River from Nan-dian via Lan-zhuan Bridge, but the mountain road was very difficult and dangerous. Native savages/bandits regularly prowled to rob, and made movement unsafe. The water outlet of the Da-ying River was spread wide and all over, and at the first glance appeared full of sand and gravel with no sight of its banks. Divided into numerous small tributaries, this river flowed westward into Bing-liang River. The old city was on the south side of the river where there was a tax collection checkpoint, attached to which was the only pathway available for merchants and tourists. Xin-cheng [new city] was located to the east of the Bing-liang River and at the foot of the mountains in the north of Daying River. The Tu-si Xuan-fu [chieftain] was also surnamed 'Diao'. He was so named by Ming Emperor Hongwu in his third reign year (1370) to commemorate his military exploits. This surname continued for 23 generations till today.

The Bing-liang River originated in Tibet and flowed through the wild and deserted mountainous country. The size of its area could not be verified. Its entrance point in the northwest (China) was at Yong-ai, and after passing through Zhan-xi-lian, it stretched uninterrupted for a long distance and turned into a clean and vast river. Along its bank, there were about 70 active checkposts. The river streamed south through Gan-ya and joined the Daying River. The terrain was open and flat. The river water-flow was gentle, and its width was wide, reaching several tens to hundreds of feet. The locals called it the Hai-po River or the Xi-pa River.

On the 18th day, Gan-ya Xuan-fu Tu-si [chieftain office] spared 50 local militiamen to escort us to cross the Da-ying River. We walked 30 *li* south along the bank of the river to Man-zhang Market, where there were 20 thatched family shops. After walking further for a few *li*, we passed a ferry crossing. The river was very shallow and wide. It was necessary to use a local boat made of hollowed tree-trunk to cross the river. The boat could accommodate a dozen people. Crossing the river and then turning to the northwest we traveled more than 20 *li* of flatland to Zhan-da Xuan-fu Tu-si [chieftain's office]. The Tu-si chieftain's surname was 'Su'; his family had occupied this position for the last 19 generations. Businessmen and tourists while passing through the old city of Gan-ya stayed in Long-zhang Market Street without any need to cross the river. The territories of all the three minority chieftains constituted of fertile flat land, which appeared flourishing and prosperous unlike those in inland prefectures and counties in Yunnan Province. All the local people were of the Yi ethnic group, and their appearance was no different from that of the Han people. Their dress was mainly blue. Silk was not there, and not a single person could be seen wearing tattered patches for hundreds of *li*. Local women used blue head dress which rose more than a foot high to wrap their heads. They put silver rings on their ears with a length of three inches and width of six or seven inches. Two kinds of rice were available, one was hard rice and the other was soft rice which was worth 15 cents per catty. The cooked rice was crystal clear and translucent, much like the Guan-yin Indica rice in my hometown of Jiangxi. Most of the shops along the way were opened by the Han people.

On the 19th day, Zhan-da's chieftain sent 30 militiamen to escort us 30 *li* south to Tai-ping Street. There were shops run by Han people as well as by native barbarians [ethnic minorities]. The latter brought firewood and vegetables to sell along the street. Men and women kept their hair loose and covered their foreheads. They dressed like the Yi people. After another 20 *li* along the riverside, we turned to the west and walked more than 20 *li* on flatland to reach Man-yun, which belonged to the territory of Nan-dian Tu-si. A group of us stayed at the Guan-shen [Frontier God] Temple. There were 30–40 small shops here, which constituted the remotest area of China. Neither Han officials nor chieftains and ethnic minorities were present. It was a place where fugitives and sinners gathered and savages hunted. If we had not have been walking together as a group of people, we could not have dared to come here. Our group stopped here for more than ten days to wait for the right time to set off.

Huang Maocai's Random Notes

The Land of San-xuan

In the Ming Dynasty, areas of three Xuan-wei [designated Pacification] chieftains – Nan-dian, Lu-chuan, and Mu-bang – were known as the Land of San-xuan [Three Pacification Commisioners].[79] These land areas were fertile, the local people were strong and belligerent, and the Myanmarese [Burmese] often violated the border. Two generals from my native Jiangxi,

Deng Zilong and Liu Yan, had been guarding this area for a long time. Later, Mu-bang was taken over by the Burmese. Then, only two Xuan-wei Tu-si remained. The southern road divided areas of three Xuan-wei chieftains, Nan-dian, Gan-ya, and Zhan-da. The northwest road was demarcated by the Hu-song River, and the southwest road was separated by the Long-chuan River. Their seven Xuan-wei [chieftains] were under the jurisdiction of Teng-yue sub-prefect.

The 'Eight Passes and Nine Trails' were distinctly set up to foster or exterminate thousands of housholds of barbarians. The militia garrisoned here controlled the Myanmarese [Burmese] and the indigenous barbarians [ethnic minorities]. The northwest passes were called Tong-bi-guan [Copper Cliff Pass], Ju-shi-guan [Hard Rock Pass], and Wan-ren-guan [Ten Thousand People [80]Pass]. They covered the road leading to Meng-gong [81] and Bin-jing. The official north pass was called Shen-hu-guan [Protecting Pass] and linked to Meng-bao Pass [or Ai = narrow pass/trail], Zhi-na Pass, Gu-yong Pass that led to Cha-shan [Tea Mountain], and Ma-li [Hemp neghbourhood]). The northeast passes were famously known as Dian-tan Pass [Yunnan shoals and rapids trail], Ming-guang Pass with roads leading to the areas of Nu and Qiu [the Drung or Tulung] ethnic groups. The southwest passes were identified as Tie-bi-guan, Hu-ju-guan, and Tian-ma-guan and overlooked the ancient tributary highway from Myanmar. The southern pass were called Han-long-guan and Bang-zhang Pass, and were connected with the road leading to Mu-bang. The road lying more than ten miles west of Man-yun was called Ba-zhu Pass; it followed the river. During the last 20 years with steamship reaching directly to Xin-jie, businessmen and tourists traveling further passed through here. The remaining two trails were submerged in the river water and could not now be verified. Tian-ma Pass and Han-long Pass were also classified as Myanmar's territory a long time ago. The hinterland of China was prosperous and peaceful, while Myanmar increasingly became poor and weak. The border management was slack and urgently needed to be organized afresh to restore the past system to both recruit and recapture the local barbarians. At the larger level, such measures would consolidate our country's border defense, and at the local level would protect the businessmen and tourists from harassment and harm. All these are matters that border management experts must pay attention to.

The Savage Mountain had three roads: the upper road was the Huo-yan-shan [Flaming Mountain] Road, the middle road was the Shi-ti [stone steps] Road, and the lower road was the He-bian [riverside] Road. The middle and lower roads were comparatively convenient, where, unlike the upper road, it was easy to find firewood for fuel to cook food. All the three roads had Bao-tou [Turbaned ethnic groups], and each stockaded village had its own king and did not interfere with each other's affairs. A father protected his son, and / or committed robbery together with him. The barbarians/ ethnic minorities lived in thatched houses, and the big ones can accommodate dozens of families. One can enter and exit only through the front door; there was a ghost door in the back that could not be accessed casually. More than one *li* away from the stockaded village, there was a wooden stake at the intersection called the stockade gate. Passing pedestrians must dismount there. Our traveling group disguised and mixed with the groups of merchants. We had to be extra careful because we carried a good amount of cash for our travel expenses. We had, therefore, also recruited 20 hotshots/shooters and 20 polemen to escort us through the stockaded mountain villages. Dozens of barbarians with ferocious and frightening faces often swarmed the road to loot money. My other companions were afraid to move forward. I comforted them with encouraging words and mustered up their courage to proceed further.

xxxxx

On the 29th day, we departed at ten o'clock with a huge team of 300 people and more than a 1000 mules and horses. We marched northwestward up the mountain slope for more than 30 *li*, and camped in the wild open area with neither sleeper-tents nor wooden planks. Cold wind in the night blew over our skin and we felt desolate and miserable.

On the 30th day, we set off before dawn, passed the Hu-song River, walked 30 *li,* and stayed at the exit of the Huo-yan [Flaming mountain] Valley. We passed through San-ye stockaded village the next day.

On the first day of the third month, we got up early, crossed the Huo-yan [Flaming] Mountain, scaling up and down steep slopes for about 40 *li*. The road was narrow and only one horse could pass at a time. In dense virgin forests, screeching sounds of monkeys could be heard everywhere. Entrenched in the mountainside was a stockaded barbarian village.

On the second day [of the third month], we went downhill, passed by San-ye stockaded village, crossed three times the trickling water of Hong-ben River, walked 30 li to Ping-ba, then turned south, and covered more than 30 *li* among the reeds to reach Man-mu.

Notes on Man-mu

Man-mu had a hereditary position of tribal/barbarian chieftain under the jurisdiction of Myanmar. About a few hundred inhabitants lived in this place in the stilted bamboo-made buildings over three feet above the ground. The barbarian chief barely covered his body and had only a piece of cloth wrapped around. The terrain was relatively low and flat, and the land was fertile. They planted seedlings in February, and the rice could be harvested in April. The rice grains were very long, and the cooked rice was particularly fragrant. Each catty of rice was worth about one cent in silver. All financial transactions were made with silver coins. A silver coin weighed three *qian*[82] and two fen[83]. A crane was cast on it. Everydayuse materials were traded with rice. Timber was available everywhere, and anyone could take it for firewood. These timbers were washed down from the wild mountains during the high flood season in summer. There were 20–30 houses of Han Chinese on the market street at the river bank, all of which were used by Teng-yue people to store their goods for use in emergency.

On the third day, officials from Myanmar came to beg for an audience. They wore upper clothes and skirt and had white fur tied over their heads. They handed over the letter [of welcome] written on a palm leaf paper. Yunnanese merchant of Xin-jie and the official tourist representatives also visited to greet and take care of us.

Man-yun and Man-mu both had no toilets or cesspools. Cow urine and horse feces were everywhere. The ground was dirty. In hot weather, the evaporating stink of the ground spread everywhere and easily people succumbed to such contagious diseases as falciparum malaria. Flies and mosquitoes abounded. Bites of a kind of insect called biting midge [meng mie] left a black spot that was very itchy and uncomfortable.

On the fifth day, we hired a local boat. The first boat was a hollowed out central portion of a huge log, which was tied together with two other logs. Bamboo strips were laid on them to carry 50 bundles of cotton and nine sailors. There were three oars each in front and rear. It had a hut-like cabin where I could sleep alone. The rest of the people slept in the open on the boat. The Myanmarese officials sent one or two soldiers to escort us along the way. Wherever we arrived and stopped these soldiers were replaced by others, just like a 'pool store' in Tibet. At noon, the cable of the boat was untied, and we sailed for more than 30 *li* along the bank and anchored.

On the sixth day, we traveled the distance of about 60 *li*, and arrived at Xin-jie in the afternoon. We stayed there at the Guan-shen Temple. A letter of request sent ten days ago from the Protocol Office of Teng-yue Town was already in the hands of the Myanmar officials in Xin-jie. We also brought a copy of this letter from Minister Chen to the local senior officer, requesting that concerned Myanmarese officials be conveyed to grant all travel permissions to the chief visitor. At night, local officials sent five people to guard us.

Notes on Xin-jie

Xin-jie[84] was located at the exit of Bing-lang River with a very convenient land and water transportation. All the ships engaged in business and trade assembled here. An Yun-ji [Officer] was posted here by the Myanmar state. He was a first-class official with five security guards. The British had set up a consul here. It was known as 'Ya-ye-ban' and guarded by 30 English soldiers. Burmese people lived in wooden houses, or simple houses built with bamboo in two to three days. Only the Han people had tile-roofed houses in Xin-jie; 40–50 households of Yunnanese lived there. Few hundred people visited the place for business purposes. They built a richly ornamental

Guan-di Temple in Xin-jie with a hall, a corridor, and a stage adorned with carved beams and painted rafters. It looked very large and spacious.

The Great Jin-sha [Golden Sand] River flowed from the northeast to Meng-gong. Its source was Yalu Zangbu [Yarlung Zangbo or Yalu Tsangpo, Tibet] River, which flowed 5000 or 6000 *li* from its birthplace to here. Myanmarese called it Yi-li-wa-di (Irrawadi) river. Bin-lang, Da-ying, and other rivers merged with it from the east. The terrain was flat, the rolling waves were massive, and the width was six to seven *li*. With the rise of water level during the flood, it expanded to more than ten *li*. Ships therefore could ply over it. British ships regularly sailed here every month. Irrawaddy River was about the same length as Yangtze [Chang-jiang] River of our country [China] – about 10,000 or so *li*. Yangzi River originated from Mu-lu Wu-su in Qinghai, streamed 3000 *li* to Xu-zhou Fu [present Yi-bin prefecture] in Sichuan, where it merged with the Min River, and then flowed 2000 *li* to Hubei's Yi-chang Fu [prefecture]. Ships could operate over it. Irrawady River originated from the A-li area of Tibet, flowed through the inner and the outer Tibet for more than 3000 *li*, then turned south, passed through Mo-yu's barbarian area, and then rushed to another 2000 *li* to Man-mu and reached Xin-jie. Above Meng-gong were boulder canyons and turbulent waters, so boats could not maneuver here. From Xin-jie to Ba-san Port, the boat sailed for about ten days, which was equidistant in *li* from Yi-chang to Shanghai over the Yangtze River. It was also the first large river in the southwest border, which could be compared with the Hei-long River in the northeast border.

According to the Myanmarese custom, all males should be tattooed before they reach ten years in age. The waist and thighs were tattooed with patterns of flowers, plants, birds, and beasts. These were dyed with indigo. They used a red headscarf to hold their hair in a bun, wore iron rings in their ears. Their upper body was naked, and the lower body was wrapped around with a cloth with flower- prints and designs. It was difficult to distinguish between men and women at a glance. All Myanmarese routinely went to Irrawaddy River in the morning or the evening to take a bath. While returning home, they carried home water in an earthen waterpot kept on their heads. Myanmarese took off shoes at the entrance door of the house. Meeting older people, they squatted down on the ground to show respect. They ate with their hands, did not use chopsticks and other tableware, drank cold water when thirsty, did not know how to make tea, and did not kill livestock. Seeing blood on the ground, they definitely take a detour. Father and son did not live together. Women were hardworking and men were lethargic. All the work was done by women, so the Han people living here liked very much to marry and keep Myanmarese women.

All the land in Myanmar was owned by the royal family. The farmers paid rent and taxes to the royal family. The common people did not own any private property. Myanmarese believed in Buddhism. All their savings were donated to Buddhist monks and they themselves did not keep any extra money. Myanmarese people liked to build temples and pagodas [stupas], all of which were splendid. There were dozens of pagodas in every village and town. They called their temples '冢 [Zhong=tomb]' and monks '绷几 [beng ji=wrapped in swaddling clothes]'. Monks holding earthen alms-bowls begged from house to house for sustenance. People with male child obligatorily initiated the boy into monkhood in order to study Buddhist scriptures. They prepared palm leaves for use as a paper substitute for Buddhist sutra-books which were inscribed with iron cones. Fonts of their Myanmarese script looked like a continuous series of circles at the first glance. There were 26 letters in the Myanmarese language.

As one went all the way from Gan-ya to deeper in south Myanmar, the temperature increased higher and higher. By the time one reached Man-mu and Xin-jie, the temperature turned scorching hot. In late spring, the weather was as unbearable as the midsummer in mainland China. After April, it rained heavily and the sunshine became rarer. It was also the high season for malaria and other epidemics. On the road, pedestrians were then hardly found. One must wait until the high autumn season in September to travel again. In Myanmar, the months of February, March, April, and May were the hottest, and the months of June and July the weather turned cooler due to rains almost every day. Lands along the banks of the Irrawaddy River were plentiful and fertile. Harvesters and rice planters were visible everywhere because plants could be sown all year round. Rice and grain were cheap. Women did the work of cultivating the fields. Land was tilled by two bulls with horns tied together. Traders did the business of buying and selling only in their own region and rarely went abroad. A large amount of cotton was produced locally. More than 100,000 camels were sold and bought in Yunnan every year. The barbarian mountain ranges in Meng-gong and Meng-yang in the northwest were rich in jade. Rough precious stones were piled up in the capital city of Awa. However, there were few skilled craftsmen in Myanmar who could carve jade out of stone for various luxury uses. In recent years, due to the gradual expansion of quiet sea routes, exquisite jade was regularly shipped to Yunnan.

[In Xin-jie], on the night of the seventh day, we saw a drama performed on the street. A woman and two men sang and danced. Singing was beautiful and skillful; it was like the flower drum opera and tea picking opera sung and performed in countryside. The musical instruments included clapboards, gongs and drums, suonas, iron clangs, and cymbals, etc. The audience sat around to watch, and from time to time they made loud applauses.

On the eighth day, I met two French priests there and showed them my maps.

On the 14th day I met with two British gentlemen, Mr. Fan and Mr. Si. Fan had taught in Ningbo and Shaoxing for many years and could converse in Chinese, while Si had never been to China and could understand only little Chinese.

On the 16th day, Mr Fan and Mr. Si helped us buy the steamer-tickets. The Master of the ship, Jia-bi-dan[85] [Ka-pi-tan = Captain], was a Swedish. We booked 15 upper deck cabins, and the seven-person ticket cost a total of 212 *dun*. In addition, we paid 3000 silver *qiao* as well as a fee of 50 dun for insurance.

After dinner on the 17th day, we boarded the steamer.

On the 18th day, the two British gentlemen, Fan and Si, came to the steamer to see us off. They also wrote a letter for us to the minister stationed in Wa-cheng. The steamer set sail at eight o'clock. As the river was wide and shallow, it did not sail very smoothly. The steamer was 16 *zhang*[86] long, two *zhang* four *chi* wide, and had two steam boilers. It towed two small boats attached to its left and right sides. It sailed west first, then turned south, and arrived at Mo-tai at about four o'clock. As there was more firewood to be bought, it docked here.

On the 19th day, the ship sailed southward, and passed by Ge-sha at the lunch time. The Long-chuan River merged with Irrawaddy from the left. At noon we passed Lai-dong, where Myanmar collected taxes. On the west of the river, there was a terrrain of hills.

On the 20th day evening, we arrived at Awa City. The Irrawaddy River turned to the west from here. Many ships were docked there. There was a dragon-shaped boat with two dragon heads and two dragon tails. Several decks for compartments were built in the middle. We heard that it was specially designed for the King of Myanmar. Awa was originally an old city. Five *li* away from the river, and a few *li* to the southeast of the city was a place called Meng-de-li[87] [Mandalay]. The King of Myanmar lived there in a palace surrounded by the wooden fence-wall. A few miles to the east was the city of An-la-pu-na[88] [Amarpura], where more than 3000 Yunnanese lived.

On the 21st day, I sent the official introduction letter from Teng-yue office to the Foreign Business Representative at the Han-ren [Chinese people] Street, and requested him to forward my profile [name-sticker] to the Government of Myanmar.

After having breakfast on the 22nd day, I hired a horse-carriage to go on the eight-*li* road to Ju-yong to visit the British minister. Incidentally, I took along a Yunnanese to translate from Myanmarese. The British Minister was in his 40s, gentle and elegant, and had been to the A-li region of the Tibetan hinterland. The envoy from Xin-jie, Yayeban, was also present there at the same time. We went back to the ship and returned again to pay respects to them. The King of Myanmar also sent two people to our ship to welcome us to the city, but we politely declined because we had to travel early the next day.

The King of Burma was 21 years old. He ascended the throne only in September last year [1878]. Four ministers assisted him in the administration of the government. They were called ‘Men-ji’ [扪几= *Mantri* =Minister???]. Gengwen Menji was now in charge of the government.

The area up above Xin-jie usually turned cool in the evening, but going down southward the weather got hotter day by day, with the temperature rising to more than 110°. The heat was unbearable. Our cabin [in the ship] was full of small ants which bite us using their pliers like jaws and pincers [mandibles and mouth] making skin extremely itchy. In addition, swarms of mosquitoes and flies surrounded us, and red scars covered our skin. We kept itching all night long, and could not sleep at all. The pier in Awa City exuded a strong pungent stench which kept irritating our nostrils.

On the 23rd day, we got up early. The passing steamer and the boat in front of us appeared the same. The steamer was pulled from the right side, and we set off at nine o'clock. After anchoring at Men-jia in the evening, it was further towed from the left.

The ship ran aground on the 24th day, and it could not be started until the high noon sun moved down westward on the 25th day.

On the 26th day, we arrived at Men-na by the time of sunset. Men-na was at the border of Myanmar and had a large population. After passing the city, we entered the boundary under the jurisdiction of the United Kingdom.

A senior official [Yunji] of Men-na, along with ten or so family members, was returning from Awa city to resume his post. The Yunji traveling with me on the same boat was the highest-ranking official and was also in charge of culture and military affairs. He could use the ‘Golden Umbrella’ while other civilian officials could only use oilpaper umbrellas. People coming to seek appointment with him had to take off their shoes and prostrate on the ground outside his house. His descendants had to get down on their knees when delivering and receiving things. People, while asking questions, also knelt down.

On the 27th day, we stopped at Bie-mou [Bhamo, also called Bie-luo-mo]. This was under the jurisdiction of the British. Many British style buildings were constructed here. It also had trains and railway tracks. From here, one could reach Yang-gong [Yangon] within a day.

On the 28th day, the steamer sailed at 10 o'clock. On the 29th day, we stopped at Ya-dong. Midway downstream, some English officials boarded the ship to deport ten or so Myanmarese convicts. Their hands and feet were all tied with iron chains.

From downward Bie-mou, the steamer turned southeast and plied. The terrain was low and flat. No mountains were in sight. Both sides of the river had many towns with small shops. Encountering passenger and cargo-laden boats the steamer stopped for several minutes to allow them board and load the stuff. In addition, the river was wide and the current quiet but was heavy with silt and shoals. The ship often ran aground, so no one dared to sail at night. We daily covered not more than a total distance of 300–400 *li*.

Notes on Mian-dian [Myanmar/Burma] on the First day of the Third Leap month

Mian-dian [Myanmar] was also known as Bie-er-ma [Burma]. In its east were Xian-luo [Siam = Tai-guo = Thailand] and Lao-wo [(or Zhua)= Laos], in the west were countries of Yin-du [India] and Meng-jia-la [Bengal], in the south was the ocean, in the west was Ya-shan [Assam] province, and in the northeast was Teng-yue Division of Yunnan. The line of latitude was north of the equator from 16° to 27.10°. The longitudinal line moving towards west was from 19.10° to 21.10°. In the past, this area was shared by three countries. They were distinguished by the name A-wa, A-la-gan [Arakan], and Mi-gu. Each had its own administration and fought among themselves. During the period of Qing Emperor Qianlong [1736–1795], Mi-gu in league with armies of two Western countries, Holland and Portugal, captured the capital of Myanmar. Meanwhile, suddenly, a lowly officer from the A-luo-ban gathered a number of people and rebelled. He restored the Myanmarese dynasty and installed himself as the King. His son Shan Ba-ling continued the kingship and later destroyed the Mi-gu. Moreover, he formed alliance with Vietnam in the east, and acknowledged allegiance with Xian-luo [Siam = Thailand] in the south. His army was very strong; no one could win him in the warfare. He also invaded China at this time. After Shan Ba-ling, his younger brother Min Di-la continued as the king. He followed up the streak of victory by occupying Arakan's Jia-Zha-er [Kachar] and Jia-bao region.

In the early years of Qing Emperor Daoguang (1821), the Myanmarese coveted riches of India, so they used their entire military force to invade the British state of Bengal. The Myanmarese army was, however, poorly disciplined. It attacked fiercely and retreated quickly. The battle on the ground relied on surrounding the battlefield with a hard and sharp wooden fence. Britain fought them hard for two years, winning once and losing once. However, due to difficult local conditions, the British army suffered from rampant malaria and other infectious diseases. The army originally planned to retreat but spread the rumor that they would attack by both water and land routes and directly strike at the city of Awa. The King of Myanmar was very frightened; he immediately surrendered and ceded the land. For reconciliation, he compensated 9 million yuan for the military expenses. Since then, the British little by little annexed and occupied the most fertile lands along the coast. Earlier during the Yuan and Ming dynasties, China had sent troops to Myanmar many times, but they were not able to conquer it. But, the British, on the other hand, occupied it very easily. How? It was because China sent troops from Teng-yue in Yunnan, where the mountain road was rough and difficult to travel, and the transport of military supply and ration was very hard. In addition, the weather was hot, the rain poured heavily, and the epidemics were terrifying. Man-yun, Man-mu, and other places even during the time of our visit were like that. There were basically no pedestrians in sight, and one had to wait until the weather turned cooler in September before proceeding further. British and Indian places were adjacent to Myanmar, and navigating steamships was certainly not as difficult as crossing over mountain after mountain from China. Warships and artillery of Myanmar were no match at all to those of the British. The British occupied the port of Yanggong, which was equivalent to strangling the throat of transportation of Myanmar. The merchant ships in the inland river directly arrived at Xin-jie and controlled the economic power. British ministers and important officials were stationed in Awa City. They interfered in the affairs of the state. Moreover, Myanmar had traditional feud with Siam, and it was isolated and in helpless situation. The British deliberately made friends with Siam and successfully used the military strategy of 'making distant friends and attacking near enemies'. Simultaneously, the Arakan, Mi-gu, Ma-ta-ban, Ti-ni-se-ling, and other tribes were all incorporated into the British territory. From the northwest to Bengal and from the southeast to Malacca (Ma-liu-jia), their territory stretched to 5000–6000 *li*. Important officials and heavy troops were sent to guard it, and wires and cables that could quickly transmit and receive messages were placed everywhere. Therefore, the Chinese only knew that the British occupied India as a colony to gather fiscal revenue. They, however, did not know that the British had invaded and occupied Myanmar and occupied its important ports, all because they were not able to transmit information quickly.

The position of Foreign officials in Myanmar was acquired through inheritance from generation to generation. It was said that there were more than 4600 chieftains. The officials were well-off and the masses were poverty-stricken. The officials received no salary, and they accumulated wealth by exploiting the people. Yet, they could confiscate the property of the common people at will. The king controlled all the power. His name and position could not be violated at will, and anybody doing so was beheaded. All appointed officials pledged allegiance to the king. Officials from highest to the lowest absolutely obeyed the king's orders without even the slightest variance. The present king was a successor to the throne. He was very young and vigorous, and once coronated replaced all the former officials of the old dynasty. He killed more than 60 relatives and brothers. Two of them escaped to the British embassy and escaped death by sheer luck. The British sent them to India to be kept under strict close guard and waited for an opportunity to exchange them for securing benefits. Initially, the British envoy suspected that the treacherous villains under the Government of Myanmar themselves provoked and created conflicts ignoring the original intention of the king. He then found an excuse to see the king to advise/admonish him. But, who knew that the king himself was very angry with the British envoy and reprimanded him for meddling in the internal affairs of Myanmar! The king called the envoy to tell the [British] Empress to return their two fugitives princes hiding in India to Myanmar after the latter's return to the country. When the British heard about this incident, they were all shocked and angry. The conflict and animosity between the two countries emanated from this incident. (Incidentally, the place where I [Huang] lived in the country of Bengal was very close to the residence of a Myanmarese prince. One day, the prince and his family came to visit me. He was about 30 years old and very friendly to me. The next day I went back to visit him and walked into his mansion. His wives, concubines and children all came to meet. When he recalled the family disaster, they could not help crying. Since the new king had succeeded to the throne, most of the former ministers and officials had been killed, and hundreds of descendants of officials had fled to India and now lived with the prince. The government of United Kingdom strictly protected them and provided them adequate funds and materials. It used them to blackmail the king of Myanmar, threatening to install a fugitive prince to take over the government there. Since spring, the United Kingdom and Myanmar had been in hot dispute. Local newspapers [of both the countries] admonished each other. Water and other materials were secretly mobilized and the army was moved to defend important passes. The British envoy stationed in Ava was ridiculed and shamed by the Myanmarese. He died of humiliation and anger. Artilleries, ammunitions, and guns were then strictly banned to enter the port.

On the second day of the third lunar month the ship arrived at Yang-gong at 5 o'clock in the evening.

On the third day, in the early morning, the British envoy/minister sent his subordinate officer Dun Wen [?] to the ship to welcome us. After our meal, we rode four *li* on the horse-drawn carriage to reach our hotel. It was well equipped with all the crockeries and clothes and everything was exquisite. [Dun Wen] then invited us for specially prepared food. We declined again and again. At 3 o'clock in the afternoon, we called on the British Ge-wen-na [Governor], whose position was equivalent to Chinese Governor-General or Imperial Inspector General. In Myanmarese Language, he was addressed as 'Yunji'. He was about 50 years old and was exceptionally warm and kind. While there were many Fujianese and Cantonese there, they all spoke in very different dialects. Fortunately, there were still people from Teng-yue who could act as translators for us.

On the fourth day, we presented the Governor items like Sichuan brocade, Huzhou silk fabric, and rhubarbs.

On the fifth day, we went to visit the Zoo which housed bears, leopards, wolves, scorpions, apes, gibbons and other beasts of prey like gorillas – that looked like five or six-year-old child with big heads and small legs. Besides these, there were many exotic animals with difficult to remember names. At the upstairs specimens of dead animals were placed in glass boxes. Their feathers and eyes, however, looked as real as when they were alive. These included animals such as snakes, worms, birds, beasts, animals with scales or shells, as well as rarely seen gold stones and other vegetation found beneath the sea surface. They had strange appearances as described in such classic books as *Er-ya [Literary Expositor], Shan-hai-jing [Classics of Mountain and River], Bo-wu-zhi [Annals of Natural Sciences]*. It was a pity that because of my very busy travel schedule, I did not have time to read all these in detail.

On the seventh day, we went to visit Rui-de-gong [Jade Heart Palace-Temple], which was a Myanmarese Buddhist Temple. Many Buddha statues and small pagodas were displayed there. People bathe them every morning. Both men and women bow down to worship. People enter and exited in an endless stream. Buddhist devotees take off their shoes at the gate of the temple before entering. Myanmarese culture and customs are based on Buddhism. All national affairs are conducted by monks. Therefore, the status of the highest-ranked monks were no less that of the Tibetan Lamas.

Notes on Yang-gong [Leng-gong] and Connected Region

Yang-gong was also known as Leng-gong or Lang-kun. It was orginally a mysterious ancient country. The width of Yang-gong was about 1000 *li* and all of which was covered by vast and fertile flat land. Its products were abundant and rich. People living were mostly cultured and vegetarian. Chinese people called them 'vegetarian shaman'. Believers in Islam had darker skin than the Mynamarese people. They cut their hair and did not tie their hair in a bun. They also did not have tattoos on their bodies. But in all other things and dress, they were no different from other Myanmarese people. More than 10,000 businessmen from Fujian and Guangdong lived here while only ten or so people were from Yunnan. Having no contact with mainland women, most of the Han merchants married Myanmarese women.

Yangong is located 16.20° latitude in north and 20.15° longitude in the west. It was hot all year around and rainy in the summer. In the west was Ba-san [Bassein] and in the east was Mo-er-mian [Moulmein], and they traded among each other. Merchants and goods gathered on the dock; wood produced here could be used for building ships, and the annual value of the total export of wood was 200,000 silver taels. In addition, rice and cotton were two major items for export. The Irrawaddy divided into several tributaries below Bie-mu [Bhamo]. The left tributary flowed southward through the Yang-gong for about 50 *li* before merging with the sea. The main trunk went southward through Ba-san and joined the sea. It was called Ba-san River, and in Mo-er-mian was known as Lu-jiang River.

The A-la-kan [Arakan] division was located in the northwest of Ba-san. From north to south it was more than 2000 *li,* and 200–300 *li* from east to west. The region was covered by huge continuous mountain ranges. There were few roads to go there. Inside the mountain ranges were the territories belonging to Myanmar, and outside these ranges were the British borders. Inhabitants belonged to mostly cultured and vegetarian tribes. The southern exit-port to the sea was called Ai-jia [?], and the northern one was known as Che-ti-gang [Chittagong]. There were roads from here leading to Bengal. Both the sea-ports had many Chinese people engaged in trade and business. Since last 20 years, the British were opening up these places in a big way by encouraging immigrants to construct buildings. These places had gradually prospered.

The Ma-ta-ban division was connected with Siam in the east, touched the Bay of Bengal on the west, the Jie-ye at the east, and the Mi-gu kingdom in the north. The mountains are endless and the fields are fertile. Originally it belonged to Myanmarese territory, now it has been ceded to the United Kingdom. Its trading port is called Mo-er-men [Moulmein]. It is a prosperous area, where many Fujianese and Cantonese people live. In the past, Siam and Myanmar were at war. This place was then a battlefield for a long time. It was barren for nearly 20 years. The British worked hard here and widely recruited people from neighboring countries to reclaim wasteland and plant opium. The number of opium growers gradually increased. It is said that a few years ago, the British specially went to the remote mountainous areas of Yunnan to recruit people from the Bai-yi and other indigenous ethnic groups. They were paid travel and other expenses to grow opium and had tax exemption for five years. I [Huang] also heard that the United Kingdom specially set up consular officers in Manmu, Xin-jie. They offered generous rewards to win over indigenous people who came from the mountains. At the same time, several missionaries proficient in Chinese or aboriginal languages, too rode alone in deep mountainous regions, their intentions obviously required no imagination.

The Da-wei division was adjacent to the Siam Mountains in the east, the Bay of Bengal in the west, the Ba-zhan River in the south, and the Ma-ta-ban in the north. Its area from the north to south was more than 1200 *li,* and from the east to west stretched from 200 *li* to tens of *li.* Inhabitants were divided into three tribal groups, namely, the Ye, the Da-wei, and the Ni-se-ling. There are archipelagos near the sea, most of the residents were cultured and vegetarian.There were also many Chinese. The mountains along the coast produced bird's nests[89], sea cucumbers, and timber. The provincial capital city was called Mo-ni, where the British stationed more than 1500 soldiers and three naval warships, all of which were under the command of the British Consul Ge-wen-na [General/Governor?] in Yangon.

Yang-gong is rich in products. Annually, after paying for all the local expenses, about 400,000 yuan in taxes could be saved. I once personally visited the silver treasury and found it to be exceptionally prosperous. After decades of British operations here, its degree of prosperity had reached to the level of the large Indian cities.

Myanmar is a large coastal country with an area of 3000 *li*. During the time of Yuan and Ming dynasties, it repeatedly invaded China's borders and sent troops many a times, but they were unsuccessful because they were unfamiliar with the road, the weather was hot, and infectious diseases were prevalent. Today, with Myanmar's national strength weakened, Siam sliced off its land in the east, and the British occupied the land in the west. The national situation was already in precarious state and the country was in imminent danger. The British had long treated Myanmar as something in their pocket, which could be used anytime. They had once planned to build a direct railway from Myanmar to Yunnan as an important land link to conduct trade and commerce. If this link-road would have been built, the British would alone have enjoyed its benefits and interests. Other countries could then have only helplessly looked for their share, or could trade along with others at various ports in the southeast where all the merchant ships plied. Presently, Britain had built a railway line from Yang-gong to Bie-mu covering more than 1000 *li*, and another one of about 2,000 *li* long from Bie-mu to Man-mu and Xin-jie along the Irrawaddy River and through Awa City was in preparation. Consequently, a journey from India to the Yunnan border through water and land route takes only a little more than ten days. Compared to the time required to bypass Nanyang to the east of Guangdong, it took only one-third of the time. Speaking of this route, it was good not only for Britain, but also for China. Chinese traders frequently come to Myanmar for trade. Most of them who came to Myanmar on foot from the north were from Yunnan, and those who traveled to this place by the coastal route were from Fujian and Guangdong. It was proposed that China must set up a consulate in Awa City, which could protect Chinese businessmen and travelers, and could also develop contacts with various inland border tribes. Some people were worried about building of railways. They were afraid that the surrounding area would then not be peaceful, but they did not realize that business exchanges could actually consolidate and strengthen the border defense, and the self-defense alone was not a foolproof strategy for the border defense. If envoys could have been dispatched to the isolated Ryukyu islands before, Japan would definitely have some scruples about its strategy of encroaching on China. Myanmar was under the eyes of its powerful neighbors. In the past, it was suppressed because of its tyranny, but now it was being supported due to pity for its weakness. The *Yi-jing [Book of Changes]* says: 'Tread on frost, Remember hard ice is to come' [Know how things will develop from the very beginning, Be vigilant and prepared]. Is it really a good idea to build a barrier fence and put yourself in a dilemma?

VOL. 4: INDIA AND THE HOMEWARD JOURNEY
[YIN-DU JI QI GUI-TU 印度及其归途]

On the 21st day of the third lunar month, we boarded the Yang-gong Fu-xing Mei-li-ya steamship. The first-class cabins were gorgeous and tidy. Walls of its rooms were made of birch wood, its grainy texture was marble-like, and the deep and shallow ripples appeared like a natural landscape painting. Vessels on the inland river were paddle boats, and those plying on the sea were dark steamships.

On the 22nd day at six o'clock in the morning, the steamship set off and went more than 50 *li* towards the east. After exiting the seaport, it turned to the southwest. On the way, the wind was quiet and waves were calm. Just after noon, however, huge waves began to surge and fall.

In the early morning of the 23rd day, we saw a Buddhist pagoda from the middle of the sea. We then turned to the northwest, and aided by favorable winds, the ship opened its sails and accelerated. However, the ship rocked so terribly that the whole crew was sea-sick.

On the evening of the 25th day, we arrived at the estuary of the east Indian port and waited for the high tide.

On the 26th day, we entered the mouth of Hu-zhi Li-jiang [the great Ganga–Brahmaputra River delta] and sailed towards the northeast. After a tortuous journey of more than 100 *li*, we arrived at Kolkata [Ka-li-ge-da] at two o'clock. It was the capital of Bengal in East India.

On the morning of the 27th day, we disembarked and stayed at Yong-feng Foreign Trade Co, Ltd. After eating lunch, we went to pay respects to the British officials Jia-mei Shen-na [Commissioner], (called bi-jue [?]), who was in charge of finance, Xi-ge-li-de-la [Secretary] (also called Ji-bao [Chief?]), which is similar to the post of Hong Kong's Chief Administrative Secretary, Bo-li-si jia-mei-shen-na [Police Commissioner] (similar to Hong Kong's Chief Inspector).

On the 29th day, the Ji-bao [Chief Secretary] dispatched his subordinate officials to my room to help in renting a mansion for our stay. The monthly rent was Rupees 300 only, and the monthly cost of a carriage was Rupees 120 only. He also sent four servants for assistance.

On the first day of the fourth month, we moved to a mansion. All the cost of our rent, carriage, and candle lights was paid by the company. We very resolutely declined this offer but they humbly persisted. Finally, it was agreed that after half a month of hospitality, we would start bearing all the expenses.

On the fifth day of the sixth month, we reserved a [coach] in train from Xie-li [Hoogaly?], which departed at one o'clock in the afternoon and arrived at Ge-nan-da [Ranaghat ?] at five o'clock. This branched in right to Gu-si-ti [Kushtia ?], and then turned left to pass through a branch of Dan-mu-de [Damodar ?] River (from Ka-li-ke-da [Kolikata/Calcutta] to here, the total distance was 115 mai [miles]. Three-quarter of a mai [mile] was equivalent to a *li*, each mile was thus about three *li* in China.) At six o'clock, we took the steam-boat to cross the river [Padma ?], which was also the name of the Ganges there. The river was swelling with broad and high waves, its breadth at some places was more than ten *li*. After traveling for more than three quarters of an hour, we disembarked at Sha-da [Sai-ghat?] and changed the ship. The steamer set sail at nine o'clock and arrived at Xi-li Ge-li [Siliguri ?] at nine o'clock in the next morning. (The total distance from Sha-da to here [Siliguri] was 196 miles.) Early on the seventh day, we hired a horse-cart to travel more than 80 miles to Du-ji-lin [Darjeeling]. After staying here for three days, we took the train back. The route was flat and wide. The railway track was built over the paddy fields and filled up ponds. Instead of following the old road, the straightest path was used to lay the track. Now finding the opportune time, repair and renovations were being carried out. In near future, one would be able to go directly to Darjeeling. There were thatched huts on both sides of the railway track, and the roof-top was covered with a circular canopy. This was similar to the Chinese Wu-peng boat [Gondola or 'black awning boat' of Shaoxing]. Further, seedlings had just been planted, and that provided people with some impression of traveling in the south of the Yangtze River in China. Many small rivers criss-crossed, iron bridges wre erected over them.

In the past, I was always worried that building the iron railway tracks would require huge funds. But now after actually seeing them here, it seemed to be easy and not as difficult as imagined. The railway track was about six feet in width, and two iron bars with a diameter of more than one inch were laid on it. A wood sleeper was nailed more than two feet apart, and the earth and stone were pressed to keep the two railroad bars parallel. Hence there was no difference in the width all along. The railway track and the train wheels were thus perfectly set. Each carriage had four wheels. Carriages were divided into three classes. Upper-class carriages were beautifully arranged and tidy, and soft seats and beds were available. The fare was also five times that of the middle/interclass carriages. Half of the carriages belonged to the lower class. These were more spacious and could accommodate hundreds of people. There was a steam-powered locomotive in the front, and the dozens of freight cars and passenger cars were connected end to end. It could travel 200 *hua-li* [one *hua-li* = ½ of *li*] per hour. Because of the huge resistance of the water, an engine of the steam-ship required power of more than 2000 horses, while a train that plied on flat land and on smooth railway tracks did not encounter the road resistance. Thirty horse-power could pull sixty carriages. As soon as the steam locomotive started, it sped because its weight generated speed, and the speed increased power. Power and speed are interrelated. As a result, excessive production was contained without any danger of bursting, and people sitting on the train did not lose balance, escaped suffering of bumps, remained safe, and endured bursts or explosions. Generally, commercial goods were easy to transport, and its movement time could be regulated, which were most unlikely to be delayed for too long. In recent years, Western countries could be said to be making rapid advances in the area of science and technology. They all regarded the development of railways as the first priority. Further, when two countries were fighting, the temporary construction of railways facilitated the transportation of armaments, which was quite different from the time-consuming and labor-intensive transportation by people and carriages.

On the 24th day [of the sixth month], I booked a coach to go to Gu-si-ti [Kushtia], and then again took a steamer to Ya-shan [Assam], and went back and forth for 20 days. Every time I traveled, I had to tell the Assistant Secretary Jibao in advance, by writing a handwritten letter, and sending it to his office-destination by telegram. I traveled with one or two people as well as translators. Other nearby places like Da-ka [Dhaka], Ma-li pu-er [Barrackpore], and Yin-zhi-li, were the same as places in Fujian and Guangdong. I went there together with a few friends for holiday for a day or two only and returned.

On the sixth day of the eighth lunar month, a group of us took a train to travel to the central part of India. Along the Ganges, we traveled up to A-la-ha-ba [Allahabad], Ya-jia-la [Agra], Dexi [Delhi?], Meng-mai [Mumbai], etc. Reaching at a place, we usually stayed for a few days, and also lived in a mansion or a hotel. The local people were all courteous and hospitable, but the language was different. Unaccustomed to the soil and water, I could not understand the local language, which was a major regret of our tour.

After returning to Bengal, I stayed there for a long time and traveled to various cities in northwest India thus spending about six months. Details were all recorded in the 'Miscellaneous/Reading Notes on India', so I would not say more here.

On the 13th of the ninth month, we took a steamer from Bengal to return to China. After three days of sailing, we arrived at Ai-jia-yu (Kyaukpyu/ Akyab?). In the port city of A-la-kan [Arakan], there were many Chinese engaged in business activities. Three days later, we reached Yang-gong [Rangoon] and stayed at the Teng Mao Hotel for five days. Then boarded the 'bi-ba-de-li' [Piccadilli ?] steamship. At the helm were five Westerners, and the rest of the staff were Chinese. It was much more convenient to eat and talk here than on the Western ships. After exiting from the seaport, we sailed south towards the Indian Ocean. The wind and waves at sea were so violent that everyone on the board suffered from sea-sickness. Such a weather condition were annual phenomena. After three days, everyone became accustomed to it and started to take food little by little. Looking to the southeast from afar, chains of mountains became indistinct and faded. Five days later, the ship arrived in Penang, and we stayed at the Yong-yu Hotel. The owner's surname was Yan. He was from Fujian. Penang spread in an area of 50–60 *li*. Its inhabitants were from the Wu Lai-yu race (also known as Ma-la [Malay]). They originally belonged to the borders of Xian-luo [Siam/Thailand] and were now under the jurisdiction of the United Kingdom. With green hills and clear waters, the area was beautiful and scenic. Its luscious streams and all weather like spring attracted wealthy businessmen from Yang-gong, Bengal, and other places to come and settle here. It was truly an overseas wonderland. Most of the people in Guangzhou and Chaoshan farmed in the valleys. Coconut, betel nut, and cardamom were produced abundantly. There were more than 100,000 Chinese people in the whole island. The street scene and people were no different from those in mainland China. We hurried to offer sacrifices to the God of Land in the temple fair. The local people called Tai-bo-gong as the the God of Land, and acted in plays on Taige's story, used colorful lanterns, ribbons, flowers, etc., and dressed up as Taige seated on a gorgeous sedan chair meant for the god. There was a theater building, and all men and women performers came from the eastern Guangdong's Cantonese opera school.

On the first day of tenth month, we boarded a British steamship at sunset and set sail to travel southward. The ship moved smoothly and easily, the wind was peaceful and the waves were calm. A chain of mountains located not far from the shore on the coast of Ma-liu-jia [Melaka/Malacca] were visible now and then. On the beginning of the third day, I saw the island of Su-men-da-la [Sumatra] lying in our front. Then the steamship turned and sailed towards east. By the evening the ship stopped. The next day at 9 o''clock in the morning, we arrived at Singapore. We went ashore and stayed at Heng-guang-he Inn.

Notes on Singapore

Singapore was also called Ze/Jie/Xi-le-po,[90] which was linked to the king-dom of Rou-fo [Johor] in the past. The name Singapore originated because of the influence of a large tribe of samana-residents. This place was captured by the British during the last years of Qing Emperor Daoguang [1820–1850]. It gradually began to flourish, became rich and prosperous, and turned into an important transit route on the sea. Merchant ships had to pass through here to collect telegraphic messages and other information gathered from all over the world. Naturally, it acquired a significant status in the South China Sea. The British placed a Ge-wen-na [Governor][91] to administer three ports of Singapore, Melakka, and Penang. China also recently sent a consul to Singapore. His name was Hu Xuanze. He was from Guangzhou. The

British presented him with a precious star shaped jewel. He also simultaneously served as the consul for Russians. When we went there, the Governor was absent due to some administrative work elsewhere. Consul Hu and I [Huang] then met with the Additional Administrator and the French consul.

On the 15th day, we boarded the Zhen Ma steamer to sail towards the northwest. On the sea, the wind was smooth and waves were calm. Five days later, we landed in Xi-gong [Saigon], An-nan [Vietnam], and stayed at the Hong Tai Hao Hotel. The owner's name was Zhang Pei-Lin. He was a native of Xiang-shan County from Guangdong Province. He was also the representative of the local merchants. I went with him to visit the highest French administrative chief in Annam.

Notes on Saigon

Saigon (also known as Chai-gun), was called Nan-jun or Zhan-cheng in ancient times. It was a part of Jiading province in Annam. Saigon was bordered by the sea from three sides, and the north side was adjacent to Shun-hua (which was Guang-nan) and Zhen-la (which was Jian-pu-sai [Cambodia], also known as Gan-bei-zhi). From east to west, and north to south, it was spread in an area of 600–700 *li*. Six cities under the jurisdiction of Saigon were recently ceded to France. Divided into several tributaries the Lancang [Mekong] River flowed into the sea here. Saigon's weather was very hot, and even the winter was like midsummer. The local produce included five grains and silk-cotton/kapok. More than 300,000 Chinese resided in the area. Every year each individual was forced to pay a personal tax of five silver yuan. At the same time, the import and export taxes were also levied. It could be said that tax liabilities were heavy and harsh. More than ten *li* away from Saigon was a place called Di-an [embankment], also called Zhu-quan. Many Chinese shops were opened there, and the trade was prosperous and lively. Two opera theaters operated there. Boats plying on the domestic river route could only go up to Jian-pu-zai [Cambodia] to do business. The two countries of Annam and Siam were separated by mountains. As for as maritime trade traffic was concerned, it was difficult and dangerous to ply rubber boats in the shallow water of Guang-nan Bay in the northeast; the heavy silt obstructed Siam Bay in the southwest. These made it totally unsuitable for the movement of ships. Those ships which wanted to proceed to Xian-luo's [Siam's] Bin-jue must detour to Singapore, and those which desired to sail to Annam's Dong-jing must divert to Dan-ya. There was a small island several tens of *li* away in the sea in southwest, it was called Kun-lun Mountain, where criminals from Saigon were held.

This year, more than 300 poor people were to be sent to prison on account of nonpayment of their personal taxes. Fortunately, (Chinese) businessmen's representative, Zhang Peilin, helped them pay redemption of personal taxes to get back to their native places.

Notes on Encountering A Hurricane

On the second day of the 11th Month, we boarded the Ji-li-lun steamship which left at the dusk and headed northeast on the so-called Qi-zhou-yang [sea]. In the middle of the night, a hurricane suddenly hit the sea. The ship jolted violently. The sea water poured in from the gaps in the ship's windows and completely drenched us. I had to change clothes more than ten times. The next day, a strong north wind again struck. Mighty waves simply overwhelmed [toppling the mountains and overturning the seas]. Both sides of the ship were battered by more than 100 meters high wall like waves. The luggage and clothes were all soaked. All the people on the boat began to loudly scream for help and cried. We and all other passengers turned numb and endured this without being able to move our body and stayed dumb-struck for five days and nights. Totally sunk into a state of uncociousness/stupor, we didn't eat a single bite of food. Later, the force of wind gradually weakened and then we increasingly felt the pang of unbearable hunger. The food on board was already almost finished, and everyday only a small bowl of gruel could be served. There was not enough coal to burn, and all the wooden utensils on the ship were used to keep fire burning. Finally, cotton was instead used as fuel. Fortunately, the wind stopped. In the morning we saw swallows flying around the bow of the ship and realized that we were not far from the shore. At noon, we saw the outline of the mountains. Everyone on the ship put their hands on their foreheads to rejoice and congratulate. For all of them it was like a happy re-birth. The ship arrived in Hong Kong at nine o'clock in the evening. Usually, the journey between the two ports did not exceed four or five days. This time, encountering a rare massive sea wind, we sailed for twelve days! We did not anticipate experiencing such an extreme stage of suffering in maritime journey. Further, passengers occupying space at the top of the cabin-room sought help from foreigners staying inside the cabin to take shelter from the wind and waves. Foreigners however found ways to extort money from them and amassed a good fortune. Therefore, whenever overseas tourists heard the news that Chinese Merchants' ships were going to sea, they would crane their necks and stand on tiptoe to wait. I traveled for the two whole years, and I went together with six people and returned with them. I was fortunate that there was no disease or disaster in the journey. It was all due to the dignity and blessings of our emperor. I [Huang], as before, took a steamer to Guangzhou, then hired a small boat for inland travel to Ji'an, and Jiangxi to participate in funeral of my grandmother who had passed away at the age of 92 years. After attending the ceremony, I set off from my home on the fifth day of the third month and passed through Hubei to arrive in Chengdu, Sichuan on the fourth day of the sixth month to report to Governor Ding Baozhen.

Notes

1 Jin-ji Pass was the first awe-inspiring border pass of China's southwest in Western Shu kingdom of the ancient Zhou state. It was between present Ming-shan and Ya'an counties [Chengdu, Sichuan].

2 Cai was an ancient Chinese state during the Zhou period and was destroyed during the Warring States period. It however never remained as a kingdom in its own rights and was considered primarily to be a county of the borderlands.

3 They lived mainly in a mountainous region in the northwestern part of Sichuan on the eastern edge of the Tibetan plateau. They are one of the officially recognized ethnic groups in China with a history traced to about 3000 years back in oracle bone texts. Their territory lies between Historical Tibet and China.

4 Present Ya'an city in Ya'an Prefecture in Sichuan Province.

5 Present Yingjing district/county in Ya'an Prefecture [Sichuan].

6 Present Hanyuan district/county of Ya'an Prefecture.

7 Present Xiao-gan village in Hanyuan district, Ya'an Prefecture.

8 Present Daguan village near Ya'an city, Hanyuan county [Sichuan].

9 In present Da-xiang-ling in Hanyuan county.

10 Now a town under the jurisdiction of Luding County, Ganzi Tibetan Autonomous Prefecture, Sichuan Province.

11 In the Qing Dynasty, inspection stations or check-posts were established along the borders, rivers, and the coastline as well as in every town, city, and key point of the pass. These were managed by the lowest rank officials [official of the ninth grade] and were under the jurisdiction of the County Government.

12 Name of the low ranking military official of the basic military unit during Ming and Qing period.

13 Xiao-jin and Jin-chuan counties of A-ba prefecture of present Sichuan province.

14 Yu-tong is both a place name and a group name. As a place name, it historically refers to the territory of Yu-tong Tu-si, which roughly includes the eastern part of Kang-ding County and the western part of Lu-ding County along the Dadu River. The current Yu-tong area refers to the Yu-tong area in Kang-ding County. Yu-tong people historically lived here. The Yutong group is divided into upper and lower parts. Shang-yu-tong refers to those in the area of Jin-tang in today's Kang-ding County; while Xia-yu-tong is identified with those in the area of Mai-beng Township of Kang-ding.

15 The present Shen Village in Lu-ding County.

16 The name of the administrative division in the Qing Dynasty is now E-bian-yi Autonomous County in Sichuan Province.

17 This is the largest tributary of the Jin-sha River.

18 An important tributary merging from left to the upper reaches of the Yangtze River, also known as Wen-jiang and Du-jiang.

19 Tubo is the medieval Chinese name of Tibet originating from the Tubo Kingdom of the illustrious Tibetan leader Songtsan Gambo (618–650) who brought together more than ten separate tribes during the Tang Dynasty (618–907).

20 This is in the present Kang-ding county.

21 During the period of Ming administration, Jia-rong was one of the 18 government-appointed hereditary tribal headmen. Today it belongs to Kang-ding County of Garze Tibetan Autonomous Prefecture and Ya-jiang, Dao-fu as well as a small part of Mian-ning County of Liang-shan Prefecture.

22 Name of the Local administrative head. It was instituted during the Yuan dynasty for the south-western minority areas and was also known as Man-yi Zhang-guan-si [Barbarian/Non-Han Senior Officer].

23 Under the Tu-si [local ethnic official/ chieftain] were hundreds to thousand local ethnic households. During the 40 years of Kangxi, all the surrendered minority

groups were scattered into present Sichuan's Kang-ding, Lu-ding, Ya-jiang, Jiu-long, Dao-fu, and Dan-ba county territories.

24 The Leng-bian Zhang-guan-si was one of the 18 Tu-si of Jia-rong which is under the territory of today's Lu-ding county and Ya'an terrritory's Tian-chuan county.

25 Li-tang Tu-si and Li-tang Xuan fu-si were stationed in Li-tang.

26 It belongs to the southwest of Sichuan Province and is located in the northern part of Liang-shan-yi Autonomous Prefecture.

27 Huang Maocai appears to be referring to stories about Zhuge Liang and his southern expeditions in *Romance of the Three Kingdom*. Their veracity are however, contested by historians.

28 French Catholic Missionaries were active in the region.

29 This is present Tang-cun split from Kang-ding county.

30 Cave houses [Diao-ang] are a common housing type in the Qinghai-Tibet Plateau in southwestern China and parts of Inner Mongolia. This is a kind of house built with rubble or earth. It is usually three to four stories high. Because it looks like a pillbox/ bunker, it is called a cave house.

31 Xi-e-luo village is located in Ya-jiang County, Ganzi Tibetan Autonomous Prefecture, Sichuan province and is 63 miles southwest of the county seat.

32 It is the ancient Chinese name of the 'Ordinal Crape Myrtle' constellation and is known now as the 'North Star' in astronomy.

33 The ancient name of Garze or Kandze, Tibetan autonomous prefecture, formerly in Kham province of Tibet, present Sichuan.

34 Ethnic minorities in Southwest China were traditionally called as '*Man*' in Chinese and many '*ka*' [check points] were established to isolate, control, and conquer them.

35 A place/checkpost name in Garze or Kandze, Tibetan autonomous prefecture.

36 This was in the memory of probably Wu [state] King, He Lu (514–496 BC).

37 Traditional title of chieftains among the frontier tribes of Yunnan.

38 According to Li-tang District Gazetteer, ancestors of the officer Wa-shu-mao-ya moved from Ba-yan-ka-la mountains in Qinghai to reside in the plains of Li-tang-mao-ya-ba. Local people called them 'Yong-zhu-ben' meaning 'left side officers'. They belonged to a nomadic tribe.

39 According to Li-tang District Gazetteer, ancestors of the officer Wa-shu-chong-xi were the same as those from Qu-den Tu-si. Their main grazing land was in present Ya-jiang County's Xi-e-luo region. Local people called them 'Wo-tuo-ben', i.e., the 'right side officers', who originally had jurisdiction over 308 herdsmen.

40 According to Li-tang district Gazetteer, ancestors of the officer Wa-shu-qu-deng also came also from the Ba-yan-ka-la mountains in Qinghai. Their main pasture land area was in the northwest of Mao-ya Tu-si. Local people called them 'De-wu-ma-ben-bo' which meant the 'middle officers'. They were part of a nomadic tribe.

41 According to Li-tang district Gazzetter, Officer Wa-shu-guo-long in the seventh year [1729] of Yongzheng submitted to the authority of the Qing Emperor. In the 12th year of Jiaxing [1807] he was awarded by a document with an Imperial seal that granted him control over 150 ethnic households and ten silver tales.

42 Wa-shu-mao--ya household received an unsealed but numbered imperial document in the seventh year [1729] of Youngzheng granting them hereditary right to control 98 household; this was popularly known as cha-lu-tu-pan [Examiner and Recorder of Local Barbarians/Tribes].

43 Wa-shu-ma-li household in the 12th year [1807] of Jiaxing received a document with an imperial seal to manage 140 households.

44 Gyeltang or Gyalthang town and county in Diqing Tibetan Autonomous Prefecture, northwest Yunnan. This is the present Shangri-La county.

45 Its former name was Lushui River, which was part of the Jin-sha River between Sichuan and Yunnan provinces.
46 Gyeltang/Gyalthang town and county in Deqen or Diqing Tibetan Autonomous Prefecture, northwest Yunnan.
47 This refers to the Nyingma Pa Sect which is the first and oldest sect in Tibetan Buddhism. Its monks wear red hats and it is therefore also popularly known as 'Red Hat Sect'.
48 Weixi Lisu Autonomous County was one of the known counties under the jurisdiction of Diqing Tibetan Autonomous Prefecture in the northwest of Yunnan Province. It was one of the significant trade pass connecting India, Myanmar, and Kangzang [Tibet]. It was also a famous market-place of the ancient 'Tea-Horse Market' in northwestern Yunnan.
49 Tong-zhi was an official administrative position during the Ming and Qing dynasties. It was the fifth-ranked official position of the Deputy to the Prefect, which was created mostly due to more workload in difficult or troubled regions. Each prefecture had one to two such officers with no fixed staff members.
50 Fu-guo referred to an administrative town which housed offices of the county, autonomous prefecture [for ethnic minority region], prefecture, provincial, and other such high level government administration and business.
51 Yong-shun County is in Xiang-xi Tu-jia and Miao Autonomous Prefecture.
52 A fourth or fifth ranked officer at the beginning of the Qing, he managed the military camp, provision, and funds for the troop. The post was established by the Qing to control the minority areas and was called Deputy Officer of the Guards.
53 They were also known as Bai-zong.
54 They were part of Gelug School of Tibetan Buddhism in China. The monks of this sect wore yellow hats, so it was called the Yellow Sect. Its founder was Tsongkhapa.
55 Kou-chu referred to the area north of the Great Wall, which included Inner Mongolia, most of Zhang-jia-kou, and Cheng-de in northern Hebei. It is also used to refer to the area north of the Great Wall in Xinjiang. Here it is used in reference to the ethnic minority areas in Tibet.
56 This is referred to in the Sixth Imperial Edict as Yue-xi-zhao and is located in present Bin-chuan County in Yunnan province.
57 In the early years of the Tang Dynasty, many ethnic minority tribes scattered in Er-hai area merged with each other and finally formed six major tribes, namely, Meng-si Zhao, Yue-xi Zhao, Lang-qiong Zhao, Beng Zhao, Shi-lang Zhao, and Meng-she Zhao. They were recognized as 'six edicts'. Among them Meng-si Zhao was located in the north of present Wei-shan and Yang-bi counties, Yue-xi Zhao in present Bin-chuan County, Lang-qiong Zhao in present Er-yuan County, Beng Zhao in present Deng-chuan in Er-yuan County, and Shi-lang Zhao also in present Er-yuan County. Because of Meng-she Zhao's location in the south of Zhu Zhao, it is also called 'Nan Zhao'.
58 It was formed when six local tribes inhabiting the area united in one powerful state with their own distinct culture system that withstood several Chinese invasions for long between eighth to the tenth century. It separated Tang China and the Tibetan Empire from Southeast Asian states.
59 Known as Tu-si and waste land reformation, it began in the middle and late Ming Dynasty. It led to the abolition of the original post of chieftain who ruled over ethnic minorities. In replacing this hereditary 'backward' post, the Imperial court sought to strengthen its centralized rule over ethnic minorities through promotion of the reformation of land and return to work.

60 The third class native official of the Tu-fu Administration in the Qing Dynasty was the chief civil servant of the Tu-si hereditary chieftain from the tribal leaders in the minority area.
61 Today's Naxi people.
62 Today's Lisu Tribe.
63 Today's Yi people.
64 That is Tibetan.
65 The Qiang people.
66 That is Pumi.
67 That is Maoshan people.
68 That is Dulong Tribe.
69 Flowed from Qinghai to Yunnan in China and became a part of the upper reaches of the Mekong River in Southeast Asia.
70 Jian-chuan County is located in the northwestern part of Yunnan Province and the northern part of Da-li Prefecture.
71 Present Deng-chuan County in the west Yunnan. It was a highland area with an average height between 2000 and 2500 meters.
72 The second largest tributary of Lan-cang [Mekong] River, and the largest tributary of the river in Yunnan Province.
73 Ai-lao was a non-Han/Chinese state in the southwest covering Yunnan and Laos in the Ai-lao mountain region. It flourished during the Han Period (206 BCE–220 CE) and was the abode of 'Southwestern Yi Barbarians/Tribes'. It disappeared in the third century. Presently it is inhabited by Dai and Jing-po tribes.
74 San Fan Rebellion [1673–1681] during the early period of Qing's Kangxi Emperor is also known as the Revolt of the Three Feudatories [fiefdoms of Yunnan, Guangdong, and Fujian] or the Rebellion of Wu Sangui [a Chinese Military leader]. Wu played an important role in the victory of Qing over the Ming, was rewarded governorship of Yunnan and Guizhou by the Qing, but later turned against the Qing and led a powerful rebellion.
75 Lu-jiang River, also known as Nu-jiang River of South Tibet and northwest Yunnan, belonged to the upper reaches of the Salween River forming the border between Myanmar and Thailand.
76 People of the Yi ethnic minority lived mostly in the southwest mountain regions of China's Sichuan, Yunnan, and Guizhou provinces. They are divided into three groups: White Bone Yi, Black Bone Yi, and Jia-nu, and their language belonged to the Tibeto-Burman group and is also spoken by some lesser minorities like Lisu, Naxi, Hani, Lahu, and Bai.
77 Da-ying River is an upper branch of the Irawaddy River which originated from the foot of high Gongshan mountain ranges located in Derung and Nu autonomous county in Nu-jiang-liu autonomous prefecture in northwest Yunnan.
78 This is the title of the chieftains of frontier tribes.
79 In the Ming Dynasty, Yunnan had the maximum Tu-si set up in the southwest region. Among them, the most significant were 'Three Proclamation and Six Pacification Tu-si Offices'. Three Proclamation offices were under Dian Xuan-fu, Ganya Xuan-fu, and Long-chuan Xuan-fu. Six Pacification offices were Che-li Xuan-wei, Myanmar Military and Civilian Xuan-wei, Mu-bang Xuan-wei, Ba-bai-da-dian Xuan-wei, Ming-yang Xuan-wei, and Laos Xuan-wei.
80 Measure of length, equal to seven or eight *chi*.
81 Also translated as 'Mo Gang', this is a town in Kachin state.
82 A traditional unit of weight, equal to 0.01 *jin*, and equivalent to 5 grams or 0.176 ounce.
83 A traditional unit of weight, equal to 0.001 *jin* and equivalent to 0.5 gram or 0.175 ounce.

84 In Myanmarese, Xinjie is Bhamo City in Kachin state, Myanmar.

85 The author Huang Maocai took the first word Captain as the surname.

86 One *zhang* is equivalent to 3.333 meters or 10 *chi*.

87 Mandalay replaced Amarpura as the capital in 1857 and remained so until 1948. Its name has perhaps the Pali origin from mandala.

88 A former capital of Myanmar, Amarapura is in the eastern neighborhood of Mandalay city. It is a Pali name meaning 'he Immortal City' and is bounded by the Irrawaddy River in the west, Chanmayathazi township in the north, and the ancient capital site of Ava (Inwa) in the south. It was the capital of Myanmar twice during the Konbaung period (1783–1821 and 1842–1859) before finally being supplanted by Mandalay 11 kilometers (6.8 mi) north in 1859.

89 The *Nidulariaceae* ('*nidulus*' – small nest) fungi are a favourite Chinese food item.

90 Among other Chinese names for Singapore, one was *shi-le* in (Chinese)/, the other was *Sitlat* in (Hokkien) which was transliteration of the Malay word *selat* that meant 'strait'. Its homophonic variations like *Shilebu* (Chinese)/*Sitlatpo* (Hokkien), written in Chinese characters as 石叻埠 or 实叻埠, were also used in early Chinese literature. See Jao Tsung-I's *The Chinese Sources for the History of Singapore* quoted in *Chinese names of Singapore* in https://singaporeccc.org .sg/chinese-names-of-singapore/.

91 In April 1867, Singapore became a Crown or Royal Colony administered usually by a Governor appointed by the English Crown.

IV

READING NOTES ON INDIA
[YIN-DU ZHA-JI 印度劄记]

VOL. 1: READING NOTES PART – I

Introduction

Since starting my half a year journey to India, I have traveled thousands of miles every day by ship and train and stayed in Bengal for the longest time. Now I have edited and organized into two volumes what I have seen and heard as Reading Notes. My humble descriptions of the ordinary trivial matters and everything else in these essays have been primarily based on my observation of geographical conditions. My approach is more focused and realistic without any attempt for careless and casual fabrication. As far as records of India's institutions with respect to politics, religion, and customs are concerned these are already noted by many European diplomatic officials visiting India from time to time, so I do not need to repeat that.

Text

Kolkata [also Ka-li-ge-ta / ka-ni-ge-ta / Jia-er-gu-ta /Calcutta] was the first big port in the south-west sea. It was constructed on the right side of Hu-zhi-li [Hooghly] River. From south to north, it stretched to eight miles (one mile is equivalent to three Chinese *li*), and from east to west four miles. High building, in the city stood like a forest. Roads crisscrossed the city, and it was difficult to count their numbers. On the waterways and roadways numerous types of vehicles plied in an endless stream. Bustling stores of all kinds filled up the street. Wealthy businessmen and the upper class people lived in luxurious and prodigal lifestyles. People from all over Europe

DOI: 10.4324/9781003505396-5

were gathered here. More than 1000 Cantonese households also inhabited here. They made a living mainly through their skilled craftsmanship. Most of them married local women. They also built Guandi Temple and Tianfei Temple and managed guild halls. Only Fujian people opened five well-capitalized family banks, namely, Yong-feng Bank, Zhen-feng Bank, Teng-mao Bank, Feng-bao Bank, and Wan-yi Bank, which had operated there for several decades.

The British instituted a post of Governor-General with full power to manage India. Accordingly, senior officials introduced appropriate measures following the situation. Every year in summer and autumn, the Governor-General moved to Xin-la [Shimla] (it is under the central India's De-lie [Delhi] division) for two seasons to avoid the summer heat. In case of any emergency, a telegram could be sent to get clear instructions. Although it [Simla] was more than 3000 *li* away from Kolkata, the communication exchange was very convenient, and it was not different from a face-to-face meeting. After the end of September, the Governor-General, as before returned to Kolkata. The Governor-General's palace was highly magnificent and beautiful. The officials and guards who moved in and out were very dignified, and their style was very different from people in other places. The Governor-General also had jurisdiction over the Yang-gong [Rangoon] in Myanmar and each archipelago in Nanyang. There was also a Deputy Governor-General[1] stationed in Du-ji-ling [Darjeeling][2]. Because of the war with Afghanistan this year, both the governors were commanding the mobilization of troops from Xin-la [Simla], so they have not returned to Kolkata by September.

Aspirants for the important official positions in India were first sent there from Britain to learn local languages at a young age. They were then posted to official positions and offered generous salaries. If there was no major fault in their work, they had permanent life-long positions. Native Indians would be hired only for low-level official positions and for those positions that required dealings with local people. These positions could also be obtained by wealthy families who donated a large amount of money.

The person in charge of the criminal law was called Wo-jue[3] [judge?], similar to the Chinese nie-si [law officer]. Civil lawsuits were first tried by bo-li-si [police]. If the case was is serious, the details were reported to the Wo-jue. If there was a dispute over the trial of the case, more than a dozen gentlemen and officials would be invited to supervise the trial. Both the plaintiff and the defendant would ask a lawyer to make a statement and debate on their behalf. Finally, all the gentlemen must sign and vote before setting conviction in the case. If one or two people did not sign, the trial must be withdrawn. Serious criminals would be sentenced to be kept chained, or be hanged. The rest of the criminals were mostly fined to redeem their crimes, and those who could not pay the fines were thrown into prison. In addition, there were officials who specialized in debt management. Anyone who owed debts would have their property confiscated and disposed to repay the debt. If you were so poor that you had nothing to pay your debts, you would also be thrown into prison. The time of imprisonment was determined according to the amount of debt owed, but the creditor must bear the food cost of the prisoner, and he would be released immediately if he was not paid even for one day. In short, if the debt was collected through officials, even after its recovery more than half got lost in the judicial process. Indians liked to litigate very much, and all the money went to the lawyers. Lawyers were proficient in law and eloquence. Many of them would go into politics; and officials after retirement would become practitioners of law. One could imagine power of those who became the national barristers.

Officials in each position had their special responsibilities. None of them was redundant. Important officials were exempt from trivial matters. They only looked after important instructions and arrangements. Officials of each ministry/ office did not overstep their power and authority. No official document ran around in circles. It did not require waiting for long and employing corrupt practices to reach before the highest officials. Therefore, officials could handle all kinds of daily affairs in person. If these affairs were onerous and complicated, they would inevitably be discussed and voted democratically, and no one person would make the decision. The salaries of officials were exceptionally generous, enough to keep them honest and clean. Officials cherished their reputations. Even small secretaries and prison guards were paid enough to support themselves without having to do other jobs at the same time. Promotions were made in the order of seniority. Because of the long tenure of the service, it was not easy to readily place trust in others. Rewards and punishments were clearly defined, everything was handled in accordance with the law, and national interests were the priority.

Iron pillar-boxes [mailboxes] were placed on the streets. They were hollow in the middle. If there was any dissatisfaction with government officials, the people were allowed to put their opinions in these boxes. Once in three years higher officials were dispatched for inspection. They investigated if each level of officials were performing their duties honestly, and if the people were satisfied with them.

Reporters of Xin-bao [Newspapers] went to the court every day to record the confidential trial documents and published them for the public to read. The truth and falsehood of a trial case thus first passed through the supervision and investigation of ten or so gentlemen, and then again circulated by Xin-bao for wide dissemination. All the matters thus came out very clearly and in detail, and it was difficult to deceive and confuse the public about right and wrong of both sides of the lawsuit.

City streets and alleys were installed with gas lamps for night-long illumination. The source of the city's tap water was located in Ma-li-po,[4] which was 40 *li* away. Hydraulic pumps of the size of more than ten *xun*[5] in length and three *chi* in width and with high lifting and pushing capacity were installed there. Several pools were dug next to it. The pumped water became clear and clean after being filtered by the sand and gravel in the pool. A thick iron pipe was used to push the water to the city of Kolkata, which was enough for several million people. Each family household used small iron pipes to connect the water to the kitchen or high-rise buildings. Iron pillars were installed all over the streets to provide the poor people with water to drink. Both tap water and lighting were managed by the local municipal corporation which collected taxes on a per-household basis. Toilet cleaning was also handled by the corporation. At the time of my living there, taxes for all the three were about a silver *lu-bi* [rupee] in 18 *duns* per month. These were collected together with the rent.

Goods transported by ships in the port were subject to tax. Taxes on tobacco and alcohol were the heaviest. Anybody found with smuggled tobacco and alcohol received severe punishment. Other taxes included the land tax, house tax, shop-signboard tax, livestock tax, fire and water tax, etc. Taxes were on all trades and professions. Every horse and cow were taxed. The common people did not complain about such heavy taxes. What was the reason? It was because in the past the officials and local tyrants ruthlessly fleeced the people. They did not care about welfare of the people and indulged in endless extortion. Compared to that the British were simply considerate, it was like coming out of the hot water and sleeping on the cold mat. The money they collected still returned to the local people. In addition to paying for the salaries of officials and soldiers, it was all used to build roads, bridges, ships, trains, generators, gas lamps, hospitals, schools, etc., which embellished lives of the masses.

A painting school usually had about 200 students, and the British were the main teachers. For those who studied painting, all the figures, birds and animals, flowers, plants, utensils, etc. were in ready-made patterns, either carved out of wood or made of clay. Carvers, clay sculptors, and painters were all assembled in one room. Beginning students learned to draw on the slate, and all the boundaries, rules, and guidelines followed the principles of geometry. After gradually learning to draw with a pen, a dozen or so people were asked to sit around an object in the middle of the studio, watch it thoroughly, and then to copy it. Or, one person sat in the middle as the model, and the other students drew his picture. Although the same person was simultaneously drawn by everybody, the final drawings were distinct as each person's direction, angle, light and shadow were different. The color symmetry was very delicate and detailed, and the one who drew the closest resemblance of the real person was the best. In the end, the ability to carefully depict all the details of the object, the aptitude to create size, composition, and layout of different parts of the whole painting, the application of bright vibrant or somber muted color, and the density and space of light and shadow from far and near, invariably offered to our eyes vivid physical and spiritual image of the object. Or, in drawing mountains, rivers, and the local scenery, or portraying places of historical interest and scenic beauty which were all part of objects of real life, images were not imagined but fresh and alive providing a satisfying feeling of being personally on the scene, on opening the painting scroll. As for copying the ancient famous paintings, it could be thoroughly redone and take on an entirely fresh look. Its size could be reduced or enlarged as per convenience. The calculation of scale of the boundary grid used in the painting was more or less same as that of the Chinese calligrapher's jiu-gong[6] [a calculation-method].

India teemed with good horses. They were six to seven *chi* in height and possessed a majestic and sturdy posture with shiny and thick hair. One to two horses were used to pull a cart or carriage, and they galloped as fast as wind and electricity. Roads were smooth and flat and were often sprinkled with water. Although they were crowded with pedestrians and vehicles, not even a little amount of dust rose. Carriages were delicate and beautiful and could seat four people. After sunset or in clear weather following the rain, the locals took their family members or invited friends to drive in their carriage all the way to the riverbank to enjoy the cool air or go to the stadium in the garden to watch the game; it can really be imagined as 'vehicles flowing like water and horses moving like dragons'. The Indian sedan chair was like a cabinet. It only used a piece of wood pole as a bar. One person sat inside, and four people together carried it forward. Compared with the Chinese sedan chair, it was more tiring and bad looking. The most convenient means of transport was, of course, the train. It traveled thousand *li* a day. If there were scenic spots and historical sites even hundreds of *li* apart, a train could be taken whenever one liked to enjoy, and one could leave in the morning and return in the evening. The weather in Kolkata was very warm, and only in the winter it was a little chillier when wearing two pieces of clothing was required. The other three seasons were hot and rainy. The locals covered the lower body with a white cloth, wrapping the back of the body, and a few *chi* cloth left in the front was used to cover the face. Some people wore white hats, some wrapped red cloth, and some people painted colored powder paste on their eyebrows, foreheads, the place between the eyebrows, nose bridge, chest, etc. Most of the people also had tattoo design on their body a legacy of the past. Indians ate with their hands and carried heavy objects on top of their heads. None of the people carried them on their shoulders or on their backs. Most of the businessmen and wealthy people wore British attire. All the Chinese living here usually wore short garments/jackets and put on a round hat with a long braid trailing behind half of their shaved hair; one could tell at a glance that the person was a Chinese.

In the southeast corner of the city was an area called Ya-li-po [Alipur].[7] There was a royal zoological garden, which was a few *li* wide. Rare and exotic animals were raised. There were four tigers, two leopards, and four lions, all in pairs. The lion was eight *chi* long. Its yellow-colored fur-skin had black decorative patterns. The male lion sported a curly thick mane, sharp hooked claws, and ferocious white teeth, which were no different from those seen in Chinese paintings. The lioness's name was Suan-ni [svamini?],[8] and her roar was like thunder. When other animals heard the roar, they trembled with fear. There was a large iron ball placed in the enclosure for the lion to play with all day long. The rhino was particularly huge. It had a horn growing at the top of its nose, and its skin was as thick as iron armor. Its strength was enormous and temperament fierce. No other animal matched as its counterpart. Rhinos most hated elephants and horses. As soon as they encountered them, they dashed to stab them to death with their sharp horns. Rhinos lived alone in ponds because they naturally liked to be close to water. Bears were like pigs, jackals were like dogs, and there was a giant ferocious and terrifying wolf, whose fur was like a donkey. Antelopes slept with their horns hooked on branches, flying squirrels flew with their tails erected. The most peculiar animal was called Geng-ge-lu [Kangaroo], which was a native of Australia. Its figure was short and the head small. Its feet were eight to ten *chi*, and the neck was eight *chi* to one *zhang*. It really possessed the mettle to hold its head up and reach out to the sky. There were many kinds of deer, several were like cows, and some were like horses; many had horns, and some were without horns. They were easier to tame. Deers often disturbed people, so people in northern India used them to pull carts, and so India is named as 'the country of deer'.[9] The most productive were only the families of monkeys. The big ones were as big as a child, and the small ones were as small as a mouse. The one with a tail was called *Yuan* [ordinary monkey/ langurs?], and the one without a tail was called *Nao* [barbary ape/gorilla/ chimpanzee?]. Some had furs in the neck and the others had that all over the body. Some while calling their companion made mournful miserable howling sound[10]. There was another type of monkey with a huge body and a loud voice, which maintained an unfathomable appearance all day long. It was said to be the Monkey-king, who often caught and ate those of the same kind [cannibals][11]. There were also those known as '*rong*' [marmo-set][12]. Chimpanzees possessed higher intelligence, and Westerners measured their brain capacity to be of 60 percent, which was almost the same as that of black Africans[13]. Two pillars in front of the big hall were used to make bird cages, with barbed wire meshes woven on all sides, and trees planted in the middle for birds to fly, drink, and peck. Although being in a cage, they appeared to enjoy the fun and frolic of being in the wild mountains. There were hundreds of species of precious birds; the names of all of them were difficult to identify. In another yard, there were small singing birds with melodious calls. It was full of bonsai and crystal-clear flowers and plants. Colorful flowers and plants dazzled the eyes. Everywhere strong fragrances filled the nose. Birdsong echoing like the ensemble of musical instruments provided pleasure to the ears. There were so many scenic attractions to come for at this place; it was overwhelming! The largest bird here was the ostrich, whose feet were like horseshoes. It could not fly high, but it was good at running. Arab countries used ostriches to transmit letters. In *Han Shu*, this is recorded as 'ma-jue'.[14] The Indian vulture was somewhat like a crane, with a mouth as long as one foot. It was gentle and kind, and liked to be quiet. It only lived on government buildings and temples, and the people respected them as gods. When vultures are sighted, they definitely attempted to feed them with meat. It is said that its mouth was worth dozens of taels of gold. It could dissolve hundreds of poisons. British officials strictly prohibited killing them, and those who violated it were severely punished. Other birds included parrots, peacocks, cranes, golden pheasants, egrets, blue birds, mandarin ducks, wild ducks, geese, thrushes, ribbon birds, quails, pheasants, etc., which were similar to those found in China. In addition, there were many kinds of aquatic and terrestrial animals such as giant pythons, big turtles, lizards, mussels, clams, etc. There was nothing more that I could tell here.

The translated/transliterated name of the museum was Yin-dan-miao-sun [Indian Museum]. It displayed cultural relics of India. Its galleries were very spacious. Hundreds and thousands kind of all jade and pearl jewels as well as rock gold were stored in glass cabinets for people to watch, study, and increase knowledge. There were also many unearthed animal skeletons, which had been fossils for a long time. Their shapes were very different from those of contemporary animals. It was conceivable that creatures had been naturally evolving and changing over time, or those present in ancient times had disappeared now, or those not seen in ancient times had appeared now. It is impossible to generalize all that. There was a map carved on wood, displaying the height of the terrain and twists and turns of the landscape making all that very comprehensible at a glance. There was also a map painted on porcelain. A naturally generated gold ore weighing more than ten pounds was on display.

The silver coin was called Lu-bi [Rupee]; it weighed 3.2 cents, and the smaller one is one-fourth or one-eighth in weight. Cast on its obverse side was the head image of the Queen of England. It earlier used to be an image without a crown, but in recent years, the head was adorned with a crown. This was because the royal crown of India was only worn at the gathering of the chieftains or kings of various areas and thus generated respect. The rupee circulating in Tibet was all along minted in arrow furnaces and then used in roadside shops. But these were mostly old coins minted before 1862; new coins had yet not circulated there. There were two kinds of copper coins: the big one is called ha-fu an-na [half anna], and each piece is worth 32 wen; the small one is called bai-shi [paisa], and each piece is worth 64 wen [copper cash]. Four bai-shi equalled one an [anna]. In addition, there were [East India] company's banknotes, which could be traded for general use. Their value ranged differently from ten rupees to several tens, hundreds, and thousands. Designs on these silver notes were extremely exquisite, and these must have been prepared by several hands before being printed. This was to prevent counterfeiting. The people of India are divided into four classes (castes). The top one was called Brahmin. All the leaders and officials in each settlement belonged to the Brahmin caste. People of all the castes below the Brahmins could serve as soldiers, do business, and work as coolies. Each person pursued their own [caste] jobs and was not permitted to marry one from the other caste. If one transcended the limits of their caste, he/she would be hollered for overlooking the caste origins and censured by the parents and the whole of his/ her caste society. Even if a Brahmin was extremely poor, a rich man from the lower caste must display extreme respect while meeting him, dared not disobey him, and even drank the water used for washing the Brahmin's foot [Foot-nectar]. A Brahmin would never sit and eat with a lower-caste person.

Government offices and prisons were often patrolled by the guards, parading with foreign guns on their shoulders, and uninterruptedly inspecting day and night. There were also soldiers patrolling the streets in parts under the command of Bo-li-si [police]. With the gas lights on all night, it was difficult for petty thieves to abscond, so thefts rarely happened. All homeless people were prohibited from begging, and special shelter-houses took care of the lonely, widowed, elderly, and disabled people.

The Chinese social system was considerate to the masses of the poor people, while the practices in Western countries only favored the rich, for poverty was shameful in their traditions. That made people eager to achieve success, do hard-work, and dare not slack off. Trade was considered most important for the development of a country. As most of the taxes were paid by the rich, there was no restriction on the expansion of each industry. The company monopolized the management to reap huge profits. With the help of the powerful country and the strong capital of the rich businessmen, the commodity trade expanded to all the corners. Although the company could be praised for its wealth and good management, the interests of ordinary people were overlooked.

Opium was a major industry in India. The state released land, recruited/licensed people to plant the opium, and paid them wages. It could continuously be produced throughout the four seasons. All the harvested opium was collected by the Company [EIC or East India Company] factories and sold every alternate year. Every bit of the profit so earned went to Company's coiffure only as it could not be sold privately. The production in Bengal was on Gong-ban da-tu [public managed large plantation], and the one produced in Mumbai was Bai-pi xiao-tu [white-skin small land].[15] Indians called the opium Bo-bi [poppy]. At first, Indians only knew about eating raw opium, but now they had learned to smoke it by imitating the Chinese. Most of them came to extremely love this method. In the next few decades, opium-consumption would certainly expand everywhere. Opium was originally produced in India and then circulated to China, and the method of its smoking was passed from China to India. Human beings could not control reciprocal movement of evil matters.

Five India-s had been known to the Chinese people since ancient times, but the historical origin of this name could not be verified. During the time of Jianwen Emperor [1398–1402] of the Ming Dynasty, the king of Sai-ma-er-han [Samarkand], Di-mu-er [Timur 1336–1405] (a descendent of Tie-mu-er [Temur/Taimur Khan 1294–1307 of Yuan [Mongol] Dynasty) annexed various Islamic kingdoms in the Western Regions, then invaded India in the south, and included India in his domain, named the Great Country of Mongolia (which was later displayed as the Mo-wo-er [Mughal] Kingdom in geography books, that actually originated from homophony/homonym of Meng-gu-li [Mongolia]). The Great Mongolian [Mughal] country was more than 20,000 *li* from east to west and from north to south; the annual tax collected was as high as 224 million and was the strongest empire in the eyes of all countries in the world. During the Zhengde years of the Ming Dynasty, there was a person from Pu-tao-ya [Portugal][16] who came to the west of India to engage in business activities, and then merchants from Ying-ji-li [English/England], Fa-lang-ji [French/France], Xi-ba-ni-ya [Spanish/Spain], and other countries came here one after another. However, the king of Great Mongolia [Mughals] was then strong and powerful and people were in awe of him. Later, several of his sons competed for the throne, which led to a continued civil strife in the country. The leaders of various kingdoms took this opportunity to strengthen their forces and became independent. The country became disintegrated, and the state power of the Great Mughals gradually declined. In the 20th year of Emperor Qianlong's reign in the Qing Dynasty (1755), the king of Bengal [Siraj-ud-daullah] secretly formed an alliance with the French and imprisoned all the British persons and army chief in the territory of the city [Kolkata] at Huo-wei-lian [Fort William][17], and killed more than half of them. The British were determined to avenge their sufferings, so they mobilized their troops. Led by the great British General Ji-li-fu [Clive][18], they pushed directly into the region of An-e [Bhagirathi–Hooghly?][19] River. The British took advantage of their victory and captured various other kingdoms in central and south India. In the 30th year of Qing Emperor Qianlong (1765), some kingdoms in central and southern India rebelled again and killed many Britishers the British. The British dispatched Yi-gu-di [Hector][20] to retake the territory. By the tenth year of

Qing Emperor Jiaqing [1806], the British[21] had driven out all the French and Dutch troops stationed in India and annexed their territories. Since then, the United Kingdom took full control of India and established several important towns such as Ya-jia-la [Agra], Meng-mai [Mumbai/Bombay], and Man-da-la-sa [Madras] to respectively manage divided parts of India. The highest civil and military power rested in the hands of Governor-General in Bengal. The British Army consisted of 30,000 soldiers who were divided and stationed in various important towns. More than half of them were identified as the Royal Army of London, which received double the military pay. There were more than 181,500 Indian Xu-bo [sipaahii] soldiers, half of whom were Hindu and the other half were Muslims. They belonged to different armies, were hostile to each other, and they were thus contained. This prevented their union and plotting against the state. There were also soldiers from Burma and the Nanyang Islands in the army. The number of soldiers stationed in each important town was probably not more than 2000 and more often less than a few hundred.

In the early years of Emperor Wanli [1572–1620] of the Ming Dynasty, the Dutch came to India, established a trading port, and gained huge profits. The British envied them, so in the 26th year of Emperor Wanli [1598], they asked their Queen [Elizabeth I] to grant a charter for a national company to engage in business in Southeast Asia. These traders raised 150,000 yuan,[22] which increased to 260,000 yuan in the second year, and their profit swelled to more than three times from before. British merchants repeatedly competed with Dutch merchants for power and profits in the port. In the 38th year of Emperor Wanli [1610], the British established a port in Su-la [Surat1619], and in the tenth year of Emperor Shunzhi [1653], they established a port in Man-da-la-sa [Madras1639]. In the second year of Emperor Kangxi [1663], the Portuguese handed over the port of Mumbai to the British [1668]. Other British businessmen then set up a new company in Mumbai. The two companies fought among themselves to suppress each other. In the 40th year of Emperor Kangxi [1701], the two companies merged into one [1708], borrowing 10 million yuan[23] from the state treasury at an annual interest rate of 800,000 yuan. Since then, the East India Company expanded greatly. During the Qianlong period [1736–1796], it several times dispatched troops to conquer the local kingdoms and expelled armies of the other countries from India. Almost the whole of India was now under the British rule. In the 13th year of Daoguang [1833], the British Company's [EIC] financial position became gloomy, and the national treasury consequently suffered from a huge loss of capital. Consequently, the Company was dissolved, and private merchants managed the trade and transportation of goods by themselves[24]. Everyone was very happy. The land in India came under the jurisdiction of the British crown, the name of the company was still preserved, and all property rights and taxes were owned by the state.

The Chinese recognized Hen-du-si-dan [Hindustan] as the full name of India. In fact, this name referred specifically to Central or Middle India [of Five India-s][25]. However, as in the Islamic language of the Western Regions [Persian] the place where the king/ emperor of the country was located was called Si-Dan [sthan= place]. In the past, in its [Central/ Middle Indian] city of De-xi [Delhi] the Great Mughal Emperor had established their capital. The Persianized name [Hindustan] was thus derived and has continued till today.

There are hundreds of large and small kingdoms and settlements in India. Some were identified with the same name as that of the capital, and some had names different from the capital. Historians, while recording history, either used the name of a tribe, or the name of a city, or the name of a region, it was erroneously divided into many countries. There were many contradictions and differences, and it was difficult to verify their authenticity and know the truth. To add to this, the language was not always the same, and the names passed through multiple language translations. Everyone spoke in different languages, and only in rare cases adopted similar pronunciations. Since there was no unified standard pronunciation from the beginning, the truth was difficult to ascertain.

All the Islamic states and settlements to the west of Cong-lin [Pamir plateau], such as Khanate of Bukhara, were annexed by Russia. They were only separated from northern India by the Xing-du-ke-shi [Hindukush] mountain. This mountain is in the territory of Ba-da-ke-shan [Badakhshan] country,[26] which was the region of cooler summer residence of Hu Bi-lie [Kublai Khan 1215–1294], the emperor of the Yuan Dynasty. The Russians coveted the richness of India and always maintained a wild desire to invade it. They sent people to India to poison and bewitch the local people by learning their language and cultivating their good will. They also planned to invade and occupy India through a secret alliance with countries like Saudi Arabia and Afghanistan. The British did their best to prevent crimes, stationed a strong military force to guard the main passes without daring even the slightest amount of slackness and sluggishness. It is said that last year Russian troops went on a hunting trip over the Fu-chu [Oxus] River, India's governor ordered chieftains in Ke-shi-mi-er [Kashmir] to take precautions. The Russians reprimanded the British for managing the state affairs of India. The two countries fought against each other fiercely, just like the war between Qin and Chu in the Warring States period whose fire never ceased. When the Russians attacked Tu-er-ji [Turkey], the British intervened, and when the British sent an expedition against the Afghans, Russia imposed obstructions. Although the two countries later formed friendly relations through marriage ties, they were suspicious of each other and secretly hostile.

Russia has clandestinely supported and encouraged Afghanistan to fight an everlasting war with Britain for decades. Last year, Russia stationed its diplomats in the city of Jia-bu [Kabul], and the British diplomats who came

here to seek an audience were turned away. After that, the British continued its war and launch attacks there. Because of the cold weather and difficult and dangerous roads, the British army was defeated many times. Yet,
eventually this army won a great victory when it directly attacked Jia-bu
[Kabul] city. The Afghan king [Amir][27] along with his family and property
fled to hide in Russia. His son A-gu-bai [Mohammad Yaqub Khan] managed
the country temporarily. Soon the Afghan king [Amir] died of illness, and
A-gu-bai [Yaqub] succeeded to the throne. He surrendered to the British and
sought peace with them. He ceded land to compensate losses to the British
army, and signed an armistice treaty, but the common people were unwilling
to accept defeat. In July of that year [1879][28], the Afghans killed a high-ranking British official. A-gu-bai's younger brother[29] then took advantage of the
popular sentiment against the British to fight for the throne. Caught in predicaments arising out of both internal and external troubles, A-gu-bai finally
abdicated the throne in favor of his younger brother. In fact, the British
did not have enough strength to destroy Afghanistan, but they were mostly
interested in raising Afghanistan as a buffer state to defend West [northwest]
India. Looking with cool detachment, one could see what Russia was fighting
for was not Afghanistan, but Kashmir. Its eastern border touched the A-li[30]
region of Tibet, and the northern border was adjacent to He-tian [Khotan]
and Ye-er-qiang [Yarkent/d][31] of the Xinjiang region. Therefore, for them
the matter of top priority was to strengthen and consolidate their country's
border defense. The British fought against Afghanistan for two years. At the
same time, they also marched into important areas of Africa. Their efforts
for the military victory were futile, and expenses for pay and provision of
the troops turned incalculable. The war continued for long without any
success. In the year 1852, a conflict started with Myanmar. Between May
and June, troops were sent there to get the compensation raised[32] on totally
bluffed up charges. The British military expenditures were sourced from the
Indian region alone; yet all the taxes collected were difficult to maintain the
power and strength of military. Not only did the wealthy have to pay taxes
per household, but even the common people's bullock carts were charged a
sum of five rupees. After protests and resistance by the people, it was finally
reduced to one rupee per vehicle. Places occupied by the people were not
many and the distance from east to west was tens of thousands of *li* apart.
Such fragmentary division could not defend all the fronts. This was unlike
Russia whose three sides had big oceans. Its settlements in each side could
unite into one slice. They could therefore seize the domain of other countries
without worrying about counter-pressures from the other. Because of that,
English, French, Prussia, Austria, and other countries could unite together
to form an alliance against Russia. But the original Black Sea alliance did
not pose a threat to Russia, and the several countries bound under the Paris
Agreement were afraid that this might not now last long.

The Xi-ke [Sikh] country, also known as Sai-ge [Sikh], was in northern India. It was an [independent] state established by King Lun Yasheng [Ranjit Singh] (also called Lin Rixing [Ranjit Singh] in the book *Ying-huan-zhi-lue*[33]*[Brief Records of the World]*) during the Jiaqing [1760–1820] period. The king's ancestors[34] had studied the teachings of Hinduism and Islam deeply and merged the two religions into one [Sikhism]. The Lord of everything in the universe is the only real God of all the countries and society[35]. All the leading gods of other religions and Buddhism were unreal and were to be abandoned, and only one religion stood on its feet. When King Lun Yasheng [Ranjit Singh] annexed Kashmir, his various chieftains crossed the Indus River to take control over several cities in Afghanistan. He recruited Europeans to train troops in the art of war. Neighboring countries were afraid of him. In the 19th year of Daoguang [1839], King Lun Yasheng [Ranjit Singh] died of a sudden illness. His grandson succeeded the throne. He was also a brave fighter who crossed the border many times to invade the British colonies. In the 22nd year of Daoguang [1842], he once again sent a large army to attack regions of the south. The British were completely unprepared, and they {Sikhs] won in a battle. Many British soldiers were killed. However, the British army valiantly resisted for a month and defeated the Sikh army. It drove into the capital city of La-he (also called Lao-er) [Lahore]. The Sikhs had to cede land and seek an alliance. The British had first conqured and occupied Bengal and exploiting the local situation later also subdued the surrounding kingdoms and settlements. [In Punjab], they encountered two generations of wise Sikh rulers under whose administration the country was peaceful, and the army was strong. They therefore stopped the war to seek peace and form an alliance with the Sikhs. They however unexpectedly found the [Sikh] successors to be gullible and incompetent. Taking advantage of such a situation, they launched wars year after year invading and dividing most of the Sikh territory.

The *Hou-han-shu*[36] *[Book of the Later Han Dynasty]* recorded that the country of Tian-zhu [India], was also known as Shen-du. It was thousands of miles southeast of Yuezhi[37] (also Yuedi) territory. Its natural condition and social custom were same as the Yuezhi. From the southwest of Yuezhi to the Kingdom of Gao-fu [Kabul] the eastern part of the Western Sea[38], and now the neighboring region of Pan-yue[39] (Vanga/Bengal) were the territory of Shen-du [India]. There were hundreds of independent cities, each with its own leaders, and several tens of independent countries, each with its own king. Although they were small in size and different in character, they all identified themselves with the name of Shendu [India]. In the past, they all belonged to the Yuezhi/Yuedi. The leader of Yuedi had killed the King of Shendu [India] and set up generals and governors to command the people and the area. When Zhang Qian was on his mission to Daxia [Tokhara/Bactria], he saw the bamboo stick of Qiong [Mount Qionglai], which was produced in Sichuan. People in Daxia informed that it was bought from Shendu [India]. Emperor Han He-di [88–126 CE] suspected that there was probably another trade route leading to India. He therefore sent envoys to check this route many times. After Emperor Han Xian-di [189–220 CE], the Western Regions rebelled, and no investigation were further pursued. During the second year [159 CE] and the fourth *yanxi* year [161 CE] of Emperor Han Huan-di [146–168 CE] and frequently since, many foreigners arrived at the frontiers of Rinan [commandery south of Jiaozhi] to present offerings.[40] According to a common legend Emperor Han Ming-di [57–75 CE] of Han once dreamt of a golden person with a long body and a halo around his head. He asked his officials to interpret the dream. Some of them told Emperor Han Ming-di that there was a god in the West named 'Buddha', his body was six *chi* tall, and he wore golden yellow clothes. Emperor Ming-di then sent envoys to Tianzhu [India] to look for Buddhist Scripture. The *Fa-hai-guo guo-zhi [Records of the White Snake country]*[41] believed that the Western Sea was the Mediterranean Sea, and the Tiaozhi [Characene and Susiana] and Anxi [Parthian] countries were the territory of India since ancient times. Today's Gaofu [Kabul] and Jia-pu [Kabul] in Afghanistan were similar transliterations, and the Western Sea should be today's Indian Ocean, not the Mediterranean Sea. Going down on the Indus River to the southwest was Gulf of Ke-man [Oman], which was the Western Sea. If the Mediterranean Sea is regarded as the Western Sea, it should have been recorded to be at the west and not the southwest of Yuedi [Bactria?] and Anxi [Parthia].

During the Three Kingdoms[42] period [220–280 CE], Wang Fan-chan of the Funan's[43] Wu state sent his relative Su Wu[44] to Tianzhu [India]. Starting from Funan, he was detained in Ju-li[45] [Kauri kingdom]. Then, moving along the coast of the Haida Bay towards the northwest direction, he passed through many countries on the border of the Gulf. It took him more than a year to reach Tianzhu [India]. It was 7000 *li* upstream from the exit point of the Tian-zhu River [Ganges]. However, it took him four years to return to China. At that time, Wu State dispatched Kang Tai[46], a Zhong-lang [middle level official?] as an envoy to Funan and Chen-Song countries to inquire about the customs of Tianzhu [India] in detail. He learned that Tianzhu [India] was a country where Buddhism originated. Its people were honest, sincere, and simple, and the land was fertile and rich. The king of Tianzhu [India] was called Mao-lun [Maurya?][47]. His capital city was surrounded and protected by stream and spring water channels and moats that finally flowed down into the river. On the left and right sides were 16 large states/countries [Mahajanpadas][48] like Jia-wei [Kapilvastu], She-wei [Shravsti], Ye-bo [Ashmaka/Assaka] were adjacent to each other, and were within about 2000–3000 *li* distance from Tianzhu. All of them adhered to Buddhism and believed that Tianzhu was in the center of heaven and earth.

During the reign years of Emperor Liang Wudi [502–549], a senior envoy was sent to King Qu-duo[49] [a Gupta King] of central Tianzhu [India]. His name was Zhu Luo-da[50] (also known as Biao Yu) and he came to India [in 502 or 503 CE]. His textual research revealed that Funan was today's Xian-luo [Siam/Thailand] country, which was originally founded over Ju-li [Kauri kingdom]. Some suspected it to be in Yanggong [Rangoon] and other neighboring places in Mo-er-Mian [Myanmar]. It could be reached along the Great [Haida] Bay towards the northwest direction, to the mouth where Ganga exited the Bay of Bengal. Countries such as Kezhi [Cochin], Pan Pan [Kelantan[51] or Amphoe Phunphim[52]], and big and small Gelan[53] [Quillon/Kollam] were all located in the area of A-la-gan [Arakan Mountains]. The ancient Tianzhu country was in Ya-la-ha-ba [Allahabad]. It was actually more than 3000 *li* away from Haikou.

Liang Shu [Book of Liang][54] records that the Western Tianzhu [India] country interacted with Da Qin [Imperial Rome] and An-xi [Parthian country] through trade. Treasures of the Da Qin[55] [Imperial Rome] were often transported by ships. Very few people from the southern territories of Tianzhu had ever visited the Da Qin country. According to my [Huang Maocai's] study, the Da Qin country was Europe's Roman Empire, while Anxi country probably rested between Persia and Turkey. Their mutual trade with India must be located in the area of Persian Gulf and the Red Sea, and it is absolutely impossible to cross Africa to reach the Zhong-hai [Mediterranean Sea]. Since ancient times, the Mediterranean Sea was remote and isolated from the world, and it was not a part of any suitable maritime route for the movement of ships. Only after more than a thousand years when the efforts made to dig the Suez Canal began, ships from Western countries could sail to the east.

According to the Ming Dynasty's *Zhi-fang-wai-ji*[56] *[Records of the Lands beyond the Imperial Administration]*, there were five 'Indias' in the Indian region, of which only South India still followed the traditions of the past, and the remaining four Indias were all annexed by the Islamic Mughal State. The Mughal state was vast and divided into 14 *Dao* [political divisions]. It had more than 3000 elephants and had annexed many neighboring countries in the past 100 years. It once invaded west India. The king of western India [Marathas?] commanded 50,000 soldiers, 15,000 war-horses, 200 elephants with each carrying a wooden howdah [saddle seat] that could accommodate 20 people, and a 1000 artillery pieces and 50 huge pots of gold and silver to resist the Mughal king. Yet he could not win. All were captured by the Mughals. According to my [Huang's] study, west India was actually the country of Afghanistan, and Mughal was a homonym of Mongols. The King of Sai-ma-er-gan [Samarkand] was originally a descendant of Yuan [Mongol] dynasty's cavalier Timur, who took over India and founded its capital in Delhi, and acquired the title the Great Mongols [Mughals]. In the early years of Qing Emperor Daoguang [1820–1850], the Mongol [Mughal]

King surrendered to the British and granted the EIC right to collect rents and taxes. He lived on the funds provided by the British people and was left only with a titular title of Emperor.

Both the *Hai-guo Tu-zhi [The Illustrated Treatise on the Maritime Kingdoms]*[57] and the *Ying-huan Zhi-Lue [A Brief Account of Maritime circuit]*[58] recorded that Russia and the Britain engaged in fierce battles in the snowy mountain range of Xin-du-ke-shi [Hindukush]. This was a wrong observation based on rumors. According to my [Huang's] studies and research, Britain and Russia clashed at the end of the reign of Qing Emperor Daoguang [1820–1850] and engaged in the naval battles over the Black and the Baltic seas. The land war took place in Turkey, and had nothing to do with India. In recent years, Russians and Khanates of Ji-wa [Khiva] and Bu-ha-er [Bukhara] gradually expanded their territory to the south. The British then invaded and occupied Ben-ruo-bi-shi-wa [Peshawar] and other tribal settlements, and gradually expanded their territory to the north. In the middle, they separated two independent countries Afghanistan and Kashmir, as well as Ba-da-Ke [Badshkhan], Shan-jia- bi-shi [Kapisa], Bian-da-ge [Panjdeh], and other small tribal states and settlements. The Hindukush Mountain is a strong barrier for India. Although the Russians coveted India they were not able to cross this border to invade. Even now when the British were at war with Afghanistan, it was on account of the dispute sparked by the Russians. The Afghan king begged Russia many times for help, and Russia did not send a single soldier to help. All the international critics thought Afghanistan was stupid and Russia was cunning. In the 18th year of the Daoguang reign of the Qing Dynasty (1838), Persia and Afghanistan competed for Xi-lie [Herat] (also known as Hei-lu [Herat] or Ya-jia- ye-tan), which in *Ming-shi* [History of the Ming Dynasty] is called Ha-lie [Hali River based] country. The Russians planned Persian policy while the British favored and sided with the defense of Xi-lie [Herat]. The British-Indian army and Persia were then actually engaged in fighting at the Hindukush Mountains. The false Chinese rumors might have originated from here, or from the so-called Sha-xu-ye [Shah Shujah].[59] It was suspected that it was a person's name and not a country's name. It could not be definitely ascertained if it was the name of the king of Herat, or the name of the king of Afghanistan.

The East India Company grew tea in Ya-shan [Assam] and employed tea masters from Fujian and Guangdong to train the local people. This proved to be considerably effective and successful. The Ya-shan [Assam] tea industry prospered day by day, and the annual production of tea turned into 100,000 taels worth of gold. Ya-shan [Assam] was adjacent to Tibet, so tea bags were made by imitating those of Da-jian-lu [Sichuan-China] tea[60] and transported from Du-ji-ling [Darjeeling] to Tibet, which not only saved the shipping cost but also lowered the labour cost. I [Huang] was very worried that Ya-shan tea would rob the profits of our country's Da-jian-lu tea merchants, so I tried to prevent it. (I was further worried when I accidentally browsed the Xin-bao [newspaper] and saw the report that Ya-shan tea merchants had jointly requested the Governor of India to build a railway, which was approved).

During the Tang and Song dynasties, Chinese monks continuously one after another traveled to India to seek and learn Buddhist scriptures and *dharma* [precepts]. Still today, Indians therefore called Chinese people Tang-sheng [Tang-born or the son of Tang] and Zhong-guo [Country of China] as Zhi-na (支那 with the pronunciation of 'zhi支' being 'ju 沮'). The English language adopted the sound as 'Qi-na 齐那', and for the Chinese people 'qi-li-shi' [齐利士]. (The Western alphabet had two sounds, one was called 'yi[伊]' and the other was called 'ai[唉]', so the combined sound for 'xi [西] yi[伊]' was 'zhi支-xi[西]-ai[唉]', and the sound in combination was 'Qi[齐]-ye[也]'[61].)

In the past, European merchant ships took a detour via the southern tip of Africa [Cape of Good Hope], making the journey long and winding. Alternatively, they took the other detour by landing at the Mediterranean city of A-le-sha [Alexandria, Egypt]. The cargo was then transferred by train to the Su-yi-shi [Suez] Canal and to the Red Sea. The '*Ying-huan-zhi-lue*' further notes that Asia and Africa are only connected by a narrow strip of land and it is wished that it could be cut off with a knife. It further notes that the place of Suez was under the jurisdiction of A-ji-guo [Egypt] [Meng-xi = Mamluk-Kingdom ?], which in Yuan History was referred to as Mi-xi-er [Misr = country in Arabic]). In the sixth year of Xianfeng in the Qing Dynasty (1856), a Frenchman Le-xi-bo-si [Linant Pasha][62] proposed a plan to dig a canal. After discussing with the Egyptian leader[63], he returned home to issue shares to raise funds, each of which was 500 francs (five francs was equivalent to one British pound). The construction started in the spring of 1858, with 70 dredging machines and an average of 20,000 porters per day. By the autumn of 1868, the construction was completed. It took 11 years, 20 million yuan in capital, and 287 *li* of the river route having a width of 200 *chi* and depth of 30 *chi*. Since then, the Mediterranean Sea and the Red Sea were connected to each other, and the movement of ships became shorter and convenient, saving 20,000 *li* on the travel. The toll tax was 2 yuan per ton (the size of the ship and the loaded goods were calculated in 'tons'), and each passenger on the ship only needed to pay 2 yuan tax to forever enjoy its benefits. The King of France commended Linant Pasha and bestowed on him the third-highest title of honor. When the French started work on this big project, the British laughed at them for being unreasonable and foolhardy. They thought that the gravel on both sides of the strait would be used again to refill the excavations, and it would be difficult to achieve success. Swaying rumors, however, could not shake the French king's full confidence in Linant. In fact, this strengthened and firmed the resolve of

Linant who did not give up and slacken his efforts that finally led to the successful accomplishment of such a great project. The British were not far behind in the trade competition in the Southwest Ocean, but they had no other way but to grant the rights of the Suez Canal to the French for exclusive use. When the British Crown Prince visited India in 1875, it was said that the King of Egypt wanted to rent out the Suez Canal and strengthen a relationship with Great Britain. The King also sent 400 shares [of Suez's project] to the prince on his birthday. The British then agreed to participate in the canal affairs. I [Huang] often thought that after the completion of the canal, the British would actually get good benefits out of it. Aden (in the mouth of the Red Sea), Maoli [Maldives] (in the Indian Ocean), Xi-lan [Sri Lanka/ Ceylon] islands, cities, and ports along the coasts in India and Burma, Penang, Ma-lu-jia [Malacca], and Singapore in the South Seas were places through which maritime movements took place. They were a must for the transportation of coal and other materials, as well as for the sale and purchase of goods. Thriving trade and business and earning by levying tax like the French brought in more income. Would not these facilitate more profits? Now the British again plan to build a railway from West India to the Mediterranean Sea via bi-lu-zhi [Baluchistan] and Turkey, while the Russians propose to lay a railway line from the Caucasus along the south bank of the Caspian Sea to India via Persia and Afghanistan. These are nothing but efforts to monopolize business, seek profits, and find ways and means that merchants all over the world employ.

VOL. 2: READING NOTES PART – II

Territory of Five India-s

The territory of "Five India-s" is vast. It extended in the east from Assam at 23˚ E latitude, moving west to Afghanistan at 48° W, and in the south from Cape Comorin at 7° N, to north to Cong-ling [Pamir high plateau] at 40° N. Between them, there were more than a dozen countries, large and small. Since ancient times, it was not a unified country. Today, the country's eight to nine parts out of ten are under direct British rule and jurisdiction, or under their installed officials administering local governments, or under settlements paying taxes to the British as their colony. The historical evolution of India witnessed constantly changing divisions and mergers of its various parts. In the Chinese Han and Tang dynastic history books, documented names of India were inconsistent with each other. In books like *Hai-guo Tu-zhi* [*Illustrated Treatise on the Maritime Kingdoms*] and *Ying-huan Zhi-lue* [*Brief Records of the World*], there were also differences in whatever was recorded. In my sketched whole map of India, I used names translated from English, and all of them were contemporary names. All hearsay narratives could only provide broad outlines. As for the construct of the legends and stories of the past dynasties and vestiges of Buddhism were concerned, there was not much time available to pursue detailed research, and I therefore sought advice from refined scholars and men of letters to make additions and corrections.

Eastern States and Region

The Province of Bengal (also known as Meng-jia-la, Ming-ya-hei, Bang-ge-la, Ben-gao-er) was in East India. In translation from English, it was also called Luo-wei-er [Lower-Bengal?] and Bo-luo-yun-si [Presidency of Bengal] – the province of the East [India]. From east to west and from north to south it stretched to about 1,500 *li* in each side, with jurisdiction over 18 districts. The land was flat and fertile, there were many trading ports, and the provincial capital was at Kolkata [Ka-ne-ge- da /jia-er-gu-ta]. The Governor/ Viceroy of India was stationed there. This was at 22°N, 32. (North Pole is 22° and 32 minutes). At more than 400 *li* to the north was the city called Ma-li-pu-er [Manipur], where the army was stationed, and again more than 400 *li* to the northeast was the city of Gu-si-ti [Kushtia district, in present Bangladesh], and it was close to the An-zhi-shi [Ganga] River. The business was flourishing, and the area was prosperous. This could be Gu-li-suo-li [Noakhali]? country mentioned in the *History of the Ming Dynasty*. Three hundred *li* to the east was Da-ka [Dhaka], which was also a big and important commercial city. All these were connected by railway lines and served by trains. In the east of the capital [Kolkata] was Shi-ta-jia[Shanipur?], where textile workers concentrated. Its southern port was called Gu-zhi-li (the exit of the Hu-zhi-li [Hooghly] River) where there were weaving factories. In addition to that, cities like Mo-er-shi-li de ba [Murshidabad], Miao-er-ta [Malda], Bu-li-ya [Phulia or Puruliya], Di-le-zhi-bu-er [Dinajpur], are all well-known.

Darjeeling's territory spanned more than 100 miles. It was overlooked by high mountains from three sides and had a cool climate. It was adjacent to Kuo-er-ka [Gorkha/Nepal] in the west, Zhe-meng-xiong[64] [Sikkim] in the north, and Bu-lu-ke-ba [Drukba = Dragon people/Bhutanese] in the east. It was on an important passageway into Tibet. The local tribal leader/king of the time had completely surrendered to the British. About a few hundred households were located here. The language and customs were similar to those of Tang-gu-te [Tangut] people[65]. The British built bunkers here, stationed the army, and set up an official named Xi-ge-li-de-la[66] [?], who was also the Lieutenant Governor of Bengal. He came here to work every summer and autumn. Most of the wealthy businessmen and big entrepreneurs built villas here to escape the summer. According to my observation, the British spent a good amount of money to lay a railway line here. They ordered people from Fujian and Guangdong to settle here, but they coveted huge business opportunities in Tibet (Tibetans call the British as Pi-leng [Firang], and Bengali people as Jia-ge-er [Chakar = Servicemen]).

Ya-shan [Assam] state, also known as A-sai-mi, is located in the northeast of Bengal. Its territory was spread from 1500 *li* in length to 3400 *li* in width and was full of mountains. Only the two sides of the Pu-lan-bu-da [Brahmaputra] River had flat terrain and fertile soil. Most of the residents came from China. All these migrants presumably belonged to the Yi tribe from Laos. They were simple and industrious, and believed in Buddhism. The British opened up land in Ya-shan to grow tea and raise silkworms, making this area rich day by day. The capital city was called Ruo-er-he-de [Jorhat[67]], a city where merchants gathered, and boats and ferries plied uninterruptedly. In the south, roads went to Burma and reached Teng-yue via Meng-gong and Meng-yang. The overseas journey took about 20 days. However, the mountains were steep and the hilly roads were difficult to travel. There was also a road in the northeast which passed through the Nu and Qi [the Drung] tribal areas to Jiang-ke and finally reached Ba-tang in Sichuan. This route was more gruelling and dangerous. For a majority of people, it was quite challenging to get out from there. The length of the journey could not be verified. On its north and east side barbaric and uncivilized tribal people lived. In the *Wei-zang-tuu-zhi* [*Defence Maps for Tibet*], they were mentioned as tribes with Chuo-ke niao-lu er-tu [with stupid tattoes of plants, birds and rabbit]. They were also known as lao-ka-zhi [old check-post guards]. They cut a few notches on the lips and painted them with bright colors, lived in caves or built nests, and ate raw snake meat and insects. The British bought them with money and gradually domesticated them.

There were several small states in the northwest of Assam, namely, Gu-zhi bi-ha-er [Cooch Behar], Ge-ya-er-ba-na [Goalpara?], and Lua-ya [Gola?], ranging in size from one to 200 *li*. In the south also, there were several small states, namely, the state of Ge-lu-shi [Cachar?], Ge-shi-ya [Cossya/ Khasi], and Di-bei-ya [Tipperah/ Tripura], Zheng-de-er [Jaintia], and Meng-nai-pu-er [Muneepoor/ Manipur], which were connected with the lofty mountains of Myanmar, and surrounded by virgin forests, high cliffs, and deep valleys. The folk customs were robust and valiant. All were under the administration of local kings and subject to the jurisdiction and control of the British.

The state of Bai-ha [Bihar] was adjacent to Bengal in the east, E-na-de [United Provinces] to the west, Gong-wa-na [Gondwana] to the south, and Ni-pao-er [Nepal] to the north. Its length was about 1000 *li* and width was more than 800 *li*. It had six cities under its jurisdiction. Tathagata Buddha preached here precepts of Buddhism for 50 years. He lived here for the longest time and left many relics. The city was close to the Dan-la [Dhadhar] River.[68] King A-du-shi [Ajatshatru] built a royal residence and a new city here. A place more than 100 *li* northwest from here was called Pa-te-na [Patna], also known as Ba-dan-na. In its east was the Ganges River. There was also an ancient small holy city which Indians called Ba-lian-fu-yi [Rajgir?]. Monk Faxian and Monk Xuanzang often lived here in course of their travel to India to study and copy Buddhist scriptures. It was also a place where a large amount of opium was collected.

Northeastern States and Region

Hen-du-si-tan [Hindustan], is also known as Wen/ Yun-du-si-tan, Xin-du-si-dan, referred to the Central/ Middle India of Five India-s of the Chinese texts of the past. It was well-situated in the middle of quadrilateral. The northeast was the place where Ganges and the five major rivers originated and converged. The land was flat and fertile, and the production was rich and flourishing. The people lived well. During the period of the Ming Dynasty [1368–1644], the Great Mongolian [Mughal] emperor established his capital here which remained functioning for more than 200 years. After the reign of Qing Emperor Jiaqing [1796–1820] and the English annexation of the city of Agra, a large number of heavy troops were placed to guard city-gates under a chief commander of the British Army. From being a part of the Bengal Presidency, it had turned into a northwest province.[69]

A-la-ha-ba [Allahabad] region bordered with Bai-ha [Bihar] in the east, Agra in the west, and two states of Ma-er-wa [Malwa] and Gong-wa-na [Gondwana] in the south, and Wu-de [Oudh] in the north. It was more than 1,000 *li* long and 500 *li* wide. It administered six cities. The capital was called

A-la-ha-ba-de [Allahabad], also known as E-na-te- ke-ke [United KK?]. It was the place where the Yan-na [Yamuna] river and the An'e [Ganga] river converged. A large troop of soldiers guarded its eastern side. Three hundred miles away there was the city of Pi-na-le [Benares/ Varanasi], in the south of which was the River Ganges. This was Bo na nai [Benaras/ Varanasi] of the ancient times. Indians considered it a holy city. In the northeast were the cities of Ya-xin-ge-er [Kushinagar ?] and Ge-lu-pu-er [Gorakhpur?], on the Gang-ge [Gandaka] River and border of Nepal.

Agra region was adjacent to Allahabad and Oudh State in the east, Ya-ri-mi [Ajmer-Merwara][70] in the west. Ma-er-wa [Malwa] in the south, and De-lie [Delhi] in the north. Agra was 900 *li* long and 600 *li* wide. It administered five cities. In the northeast of Agra City was Yan-na [Yamuna] River. The city was solidly built by the Mongol [Mughal] kings and their palaces and monuments still survive there. Towards 400 *li* in the north was the city of De-xi (another name was Tai-li [Delhi]) which was the old capital of the Mughals, many of their descendants still lived there and received yearly emoluments from the British.

De-lie [Delhi] region bordered in the east with Oudh, in the west was A-ri-mi [Ajmer-Merwara] province, the province of Agra was in the south, and that of Gu-er-wa-le [Garhwal] was in the north. Its length and width both were about 600 *li*. It has jurisdiction over six cities. Delhi, Bei-le-mei [Bareilly?], and Mu-na-de-ba [Moradabad] were all well-known and prosperous cities. The territory in the northeast was called Mo Yun [Kumayun], which is very close to Ngari [known as A-li in Chinese] Prefecture[71] in Tibet, with high mountains, dense forest, and few inhabitants. In the southeast, there was a city called Ba-le-li [Bareilly]. In the 19th year of Jiaqing (1814), it was occupied by Nepal and later ceded to Britain.

Gu-er-wa-le [Garhwal] region shared borders with Tibet's Ngari [A-li in Chinese] prefecture in the northeast, with Delhi in the south, and Xin-la [Shimla] in the west. It originally governed three cities. It was 500 *li* long and 300 *li* wide. Its capital city was called Xi-li-na [presently Srinagar, Uttarakhand], which was governed by the king of the native state, and the two cities in the east were then placed under the jurisdiction of the Delhi state.

Xin-la [Shimla] region was located in the northwest of Delhi. It was full of high mountains and beautiful scenery. The Governor-General stationed in Bengal built a mansion there for vacation and escape the summer heat. One could go there for mountaineering, hunting, horse-riding, and running.

The Wu-de [Awadh/ Oudh] States and Region

Wu-de [Oudh] (Ao-di-wu-na) [Awadhi-Unnao?] was also the ancient country of Yang-mo-luo [Mallas Mahajanpada]. Its city of She-wei [Shravasti] was ruled by King Bo-si-ni [Prasenjit]. In its east was Bihar, in the west was

Delhi, in the south was Allahabad, and in the north was Nepal. It was 900 *li* long and 500 *li* wide. Its capital was called Lu-jue-nao [Lucknow]. It was built on the bank of the Gan-de [Gomti] River. Adjacent to the north of Oudh city was Qing-jia [Ganga?] River. The city was in decline for a long time. In the southwest, outside the south gate existed ruins of Zhi-huan-jing [?] temple. Fifty miles away was a city called Fei-sa-ba [Faizabad] with many inhabitants. In addition, there were cities like Ji-na-ba [Ameenabad?], Bi-suo-ya [Baiswara], Ba-lai-zhi [Baharaich], and Dan-da [Gonda], all of which were places where merchants frequently assembled, and the local chieftains for generations carried out extortion raids. The British sent troops to guard them and sent high officials to manage finances.

Ben-Ruo [Punjab] States and Region

The province of Ben-ruo [Punjab], also known as Xi-lin-de [Sirhind ?] region belonged to the Kingdom of Sai-ge-guo [the Kingdom of Sikh] and was later annexed by the British. It bordered with Delhi from the east side, with Afghanistan from the west, with Ci-ri-bu [Rajputana] from the south, and with Kashmir from the north. Its length and width were more than 2000 *li*. Its capital was called Lao-er [Lahore]. It was, in fact the old capital of the Sikh King, Lun-ya-sheng [Ranjit Singh] and close to the north bank of La-wei-er [Ravi] River. Both sides of the river-bank were densely populated, and there were many trade fairs. Its cities of Ya-dao-ke [Attock] and Shi-wa [Peshawar] in the northwest corner, and Mu-er-dan [Multan] in the south-west corner were connected by railways.

The Ci-ri-bu-de [Rajputana] region also known as Ya-ri-mi-er [Ajmer-Merwara] state, bordered with the state of Agra in the east, Xin-di [Sind] in the west, and Gu-zhi-la-de [Gujrat] in the south, and the province of Ben-ruo [Punjab] in the north. It was 1500 *li* long and more than 700 *li* wide. The northern territory was mostly desert, and the southern was fertile and rich. Of the nine cities, only the capital, Ya-ri-mi [Ajmer-Merwara], was under the jurisdiction of the British, other cities were governed by the local kings and chieftains.

Nei-lu-zhi-sheng [Inland Provinces]

The inland provinces were called in English, Xian-de-ci [Central][72] Bo-luo-yun-si [Province]. Half of that region was under the jurisdiction of the British, and the other half was ruled by local kings of the states.

The region of Xin-de-ya [Scindia] was also known as Ha-na-ou-ti [Haaouti/ Amaraouti??]. It was at the center of India. Its land was scattered, disconnected, and interlocked like canine teeth with He-er-jia-er [Holkar] of Zhe-na-qi-er [?].

He-er-jia-er (Ge-er-jia-er) [Holkar]), Scindia, Ma-er-wa [Malwa], and other Maratha states were governed separately by local chieftains but were interconnected with each other.

Ma-er-wa (Ma-lu-wa [Malwa]) State was located in the south of the state of Scindia. It covered an area of 500–600 *li*, and its capital was Ying-duo--er [Indore].

Ben-de-le-kan state (Bang-de-er-gan [Bundelkhand]) was located in the east of the Scindia state. It was 600 *li* long and 500 *li* wide, and governed five cities. The name of its capital was Zha-de-pu-er [Chatarpur].

The state of Bo-bao-er [Bhopal] was located in the south of the Shen-er-pi-da [Shipra/Kshipra] River. It covered an area of 300 *li*, mainly in high mountains and dense forests, and its people were brave and resolute.

Lai-ge-pu-er (Na-ge-pu-er) [Nagpur]) state's eastern boundary touched E-li-sa [Orissa] in the east, Ma-er-wa [Malwa] in the west, Berar in the south, and A-la-ha-ba [Allahabad] in the north. It was 1500 *li* in the length and 900 li in the width. Its capital city was Lai-ge-pu-er [Nagpur] which was highly developed in trade and commerce.

The state of Gang-du-ya-na, also known as Gong-wa-na [Gondwana], was adjacent to the state of E-li-sa [Orissa] in the east, the state of Kan-dai-si [Khandesh] in the west, and the state of Ni-sang [Nissanputnam/Nizamaputnam[73]] in the south, and the state of Allahabad in the north. It was 1500 *li* long and 1800 *li* wide. Only its eastern and the northern territories were governed by the British, and the rest was administered by the kings of native states. The capital was called Wo-ba-er-bu [Jabalpur].

E-li-za [Orissa] State was next to the Gulf of Bengal in the east, Gondwana State in the west, Fei-sa-qian State in the south, and Baiha [Bihar] State in the north. Its capital, Ke-ta-ke [Cuttack] was a big and prosperous city, and its masses of people in the hill accepted only their own folk beliefs and rejected other customs and religion.

The above five states were all under the jurisdiction of the British Governor-General of Bengal. From the northwest to the southeast, their area stretched to more than 6000 *li* in length and 13000 *li* in width. This was roughly equivalent to more than half of the total area of India.

Man-da-la-sa [Madras] Region under the Administration of Army's Commander-in-Chief

The region of De-gan [Deccan], also known as Ni-sang [Nizam] was bordered with Lai-ge-pu-er [Nagpur] in the northeast, Bo-ri-pu-er [Bijapur?] in the west, and Jia-er-na-de [Karnataka] in the south. It was more than 2000 *li* long and 1300 *li* wide. It governed five cities. The capital was known as Hai-de-la-ba [Hyderabad] – Xi-da-ba [Secundarabad]. About 12,000 British soldiers were stationed here. Most of its territory was highland and produced abundant excellent wheat. Local kings were ruling the area for many generations, and cruelly exploited the people. During the Jiaqing period [1796–1820] of the Qing Dynasty, there were many wars with the British. Later, the British captured the state with resourcefulness. Although the British deployed a large contingent of army here, the area was still in turmoil and there was no peace.

The state of Jia-er-na-de [Karnataka/Carnatic] was extended to the sea in the southeast, to the states of Da-lai-fan-ke-er [Travancore?] and Mai-suo-er [Mysore] in the west, and the state of Nizam in the north. Its length was 2600 *li* and width 1300 *li*. It ruled over ten cities. The capital was at Man-da-la-sa [Madras], where the generals of the South Indian army were stationed. Although it was close to the sea, the area was inconvenient for docking the ships. Sand and mud blocked the water channels making it difficult for ships to reach the shore. The weather was extremely hot. The civil and military officials finished their business early in the morning and went back to their houses on the mountain or by the water to spend nights in cool places. The territory in the city of Pang-ya-luo [Bangalore] was guarded by the British. There was also the city of Xi-ling-ya-ba-tan [Seringapatam], which used to be the capital of the native state. It was at a strategic location with difficult access. In the early years of Jiaqing [1796–1820], the British fought many bloody wars year after year, and finally eliminated it.[74]. At the southern sea-coast, a Bu-luo-jia [Blue/Nilgiri?] mountain stood which was also referred to by Sakyamuni as Putuo Yan[75]. It was 1500 *zhang* high. The weather in its valley was extremely hot and difficult to endure but at the top the accumulated snow did not melt throughout the year. Walking from the bottom to the top of the mountain, one could personally experience all the four seasons of a year.

The state of Ge-ying-ba-du-er [Coimbatore] bordered with the state of Jia-er-na-de [Carnatic] in the east, the state of Me-le-ba-er [Malabar] in the west, and the state of Ma-du-la [Madurai] in the south, and the state of Sa-lin [Salem] in the north. It was 500 miles long and 300 miles wide. It governed over two cities.

The state of Ma-le-ba-er [Malabar] was adjacent to Coimbatore State in the east, the sea in the west, and Ke-qing [Cochin] State in the south, and Jia-na-la [Canara] State in the north. It was 700 *li* long and 200 *li* wide. It had three port cities namely, Ka-li-gu-de [Calicut], Dan-na [Tanur], and Bang-na-li [Ponnani].

The Da-lai-fan-ke-er [Travancore/Thiruvithamkoor] region was next to Ding-li-fei-li [Tinnevelly] state in the east, Ke-qing [Cochin] state in the north, and the ocean in the southwest. It was 500 *li* long and 200 *li* wide. Its capital city was called Te-lai-fan-de-lang [Thiruvananthapuram/Trivandrum], and it was under the jurisdiction of the king of the state. There were two commercial seaports, named Bo-er-jia [Parvur?] and Kui-lang [Quillon]. A piece of its land extended into the sea in the south. It was known as Ke-mo-lin-jue [Cape Comorin/Kanyakumari]. Ships at sea change their direction while passing through here. The wind and waves here were particularly violent. There was a small town called Mi-suo=ba [?][76] on Cape Comorin Island with green hills and clear water, beautiful landscape, and abundance of fruits. The leader of the town was earlier driven out from here by the Dutch, and residents migrated here from outside places. Now the town is under British jurisdiction.

Ke-qing [Cochin], also known as Gu-zhen and Ke-chen, covered an area of more than 100 *li*. It was located in the northwest of Da-lai-fan-ke-er [Travancore]. It used to be a colony of the Netherlands, but now it belonged to the British jurisdiction.

The state of Nan-jia-na-la [South Canara] was adjacent to Mysore in the east, to the sea in the west, and Ba-er [Berar?] in the south, and Mo-jia [Maratha] in the north. It was about 500 *li* long and 200 *li* wide, and had jurisdiction over five cities. Its capital was Meng-jia-luo-er [Mangalore], which was a coastal city, and the state of Bei-jia-na-la [North Canara] was under the jurisdiction of Mumbai.

In the east of the state of Mai-suo-er [Mysore] was Jia-er-na-de [Carnatic], in the west was Jia-na-la [Canara], in the south was Coimbatore, and in the north was Bo-ri-pu-er [Bijapur?]. It was 800 *li* long and 600 *li* wide. It governed over ten cities. The local king lived in the city of Mysore. There were important commercial cities here, namely, Bangalore, Se-lin-jia-dan [Seringpatnam], Gu-la [Kolar?], Ji-de-la [Chitaldurg/Chitradurga], with flourishing business.

The Ba-ci-jia region [area ceded to the British and a part of British Madras Presidency] was bordered by Jia-er-na-de [Carnatic] in the east, Jia-na-la [Canara] in the west, Sa-lin [Salem] in the south, and Ni-sang [Nizam/Hyderabad] in the north. It was 700 *li* long and 500 *li* wide. Its capital was called Bei-na-li [Bellary ?]. Railways passed through here and the transportation was very convenient.

The region of Bo-xi-er-jia [Northern Circars and Coromandel Coast][77], also known as Sa-ka-si [Sarkars], was adjacent to Bengal in the east, Karnataka to the southwest. It bordered E-li-sa [Orissa] in the north, and the sea in the south. It was more than 1500 *li* long and about 2–300 *li* wide. Qi-jia [Chilka] Lake was in the east and Ci-lin [Colain] Lake in the west. It governed four prefectures, namely, Han-sha [?], An-zhan [?], Fei-sa-qian/kan [?], and Na-zha-mian[?].

The above states were all in the territory of South India, and the whole terrain was like the tongue of a bucket extending into the sea. It was governed either by the kings of the local states ruling from generation to generation, or by local leaders jointly elected by the people. In the hills, people still followed the old traditions and Hinduism, and it was all under the rule and jurisdiction of the British army stationed in Man-da-la-sa [Madras].

Mumbai Military Governor district

Ao-long-jia-ba [Aurangabad] was bordered with the Deccan Plateau in the east, the sea in the west, Bo-ri-pu-er [Bijapur] in the south, and Kan-dai-si [Khandesh] in the north. The capital was Mumbai. Mumbai was surrounded by the sea from three sides. It was originally a Portuguese colony and was later ceded to the British. A consulate was built and a large contingent of troops was stationed here. This was unavoidable because of the movement of a large number of ships for business and trade. The people were rich, and merchants and traders came here from all over the world. They were what Cantonese called 'the white-headed [old] man at the foot of the port'. Chinese also come here to do business and trade. A shipyard was located here to build passenger and warships.

The state of Bo-ri-pu-er [Bijapur] was bordered on the east by the state of Delhi, on the west by the state of Kang-ken [Konkan], on the south by the state of Mysore, and on the north by the state of Aurangabad. It was 1300 *li* long and more than 700 *li* wide. It governed five cities.

The state of Kang-ken [Konkan] was located in the south of Mumbai, It was also known as Lu-na-za-li [Rutnagherry/Ratnagiri], which was mentioned as Ang-ji-li in the *Hai Lu*. The east side was close to the mountains and the west side was close to the sea. It is more than 500 *li* long and only a few dozen *li* wide. The capital was known as Le-la-zhi-li [Ratnagiri?]. Behind its southeastern mountains were two states, Gu-na-pu-er [Kolhapur] and Shao-wa-er [Savanur], parts of which were Portuguese administered colonies.

The state of Kan-dai-shi (or Gan-de-shi) [Khandesh] bordered on the east with the state of Bai-ci-er [Berar], on the west with the state of Gujarat, on the south with the state of Aurangabad, on the north with the state of Malwa. It was 150 *li* long and 500 *li* wide. It governed three cities, the capital of which was Gao-er-na [Burhanpur?].

Gujarat was bordered on the east by Malwa, on the west by Cambay, on the south by the state of Khandesh, and on the north by Ya-ri-mi [Ajmer-Merwar]. It was 1400 *li* long and more than 600 *li* wide. It had jurisdiction over four cities. The capital was called the port of Su-la-te-qi [Surat], and the important commercial city was known as Kai-bai, which was the homonym of Koman [Khaman/Cambay]. From this place to the west, it is called Koman Bay [Cambay]. To the northwest of the harbor was the state of Ya-mi-te-ba [Ahmedabad]. There were many people who robbed and stole. After the British conquered here, they set up troops to control them. There were many Buddhist relics in the territory.

Ru-gua-er [Guicowar] province, also known as Jia-de-di-wa [Kathiawar] state, was adjacent to the city of Ya-mi-te-ba [Ahmedabad] in the northeast, and the other three sides were close to the sea. The width of each was more than 500 *li*. The capital was called Bao-lai-dan-na [Bhavnagar?]. It was under the jurisdiction of the king of the native state. There were many cities by the sea.

The city of Kou-chi (also known as Jia-zhi gu-zhi) [Cutch/Kachha] was located in the northwest of Ri-gua-er [Guicowar/Kathiawar] State and the southeast of Xin-di [Sind] State. The ordinary people were poor, it was an earthquake-prone area, and the British army was stationed here.

The country of Xin-di [Sind] was next to the desert in the east, Kou-chi [Cutch] in the south, Bi-lu-zhi [Baluchistan] in the west, Afghanistan and Punjab in the north. It is 1000 *li* long and 600 *li* wide. Its capital is called Hai-de-la-ba [Hyderabad]. In addition, there were several commercial cities, such as Ta-ta [Tatta/Thatta], Ruo-ge-na-qi [Karachi], Lao-she-na [Larkana ?], and Ruo-jie-yi-po [Khairpur]. These all have prospered out of flourishing business activities. The Indus River, while passing through here, divided into multiple tributaries and entered the sea. That facilitated irrigation of the farmland. All the five grains were produced here in abundance and the agriculture was well-developed. The former native king of the local state was very wealthy. The state was conquered by the British in the 23rd year of Daoguang (1843). Of all the states in India, the local people here were exceptionally brave and good at fighting. They were also often hired as sailors to fight against the sea-waves.

The above states are all under the jurisdiction of the Military and Political Governor of Mumbai.

Xi-nan [Ceylon/ Sri Lanka] Island

Xi-nan [Sri Lanka] Island was also known as the 'Lion Country' in ancient times. More than 600 *li* from east to west and more than 1000 *li* from north to south, the inland areas were of unequal heights, ranging from 800 *chi* to 6000 *chi* above sea level. The highest peak was called Ya-tan-zhi Peak [Adam's Peak, Nalathania]. It bred [a natural habitat for] lions. The local Geng-ti [Kandy] people lived in the mountains. In most of surrounding coastal areas migrant Indians lived. The land produced rare products, and it was therefore called the Treasure Island. Chinese merchant ships often came here to trade. During the early Ming Dynasty, it was occupied by the [Arab] Muslims of Mecca. The local leaders joined forces with the Portuguese to drive out the Hui [Muslim] people. Later it became a Portuguese colony. During the Chongzhen period [1627–1644] of the Ming Dynasty, the local leaders invited the Dutch to drive the Portuguese away. All the important commercial cities were then occupied by the Dutch. In the first year of Jiaqing (1796), the British warships arrived and attacked the island. The Dutch were then driven away, and all the island was occupied by the British. The capital was called Ke-lun-po [Colombo]. The British built a fort on the west coast to guard it. The mountain valley road in the north was not good for transportation. Local leaders were cruel and exploitative towards masses. In 1880s, a railway was opened from Kandy to the north-eastern coastal area, and another direct railway line was laid from Kandy to reach Colombo. Every year about 2 million [yuan?] was collected from the road tax.

The Portugese Colonies

E-ya, also known as Ke-wa [Goa] was adjacent to Canara in the southeast and the sea in the west. It was 250 *li* long and 120 *li* wide. It governed three cities. Its capital was called Bang-jin [Panjim]. In its north, new lands with a length of 300 *li* and a width of more than 100 *li* were opened, and ten cities were built over it.

Da-mang [Daman] was at the side of Kai-bai [Cambay] bay. It covered an area of 40 *li*.

Di-yu [Diu] was earlier in Xin-di [Sind]. The place was small but convenient for mooring boats.

The French Colonies

Ben-de-zhi-li [Pondichery] was in the state of Jia-er-na-de [Carnatic/Tamilnadu]. It covered an area of 30 *li*. Ka-li-jia-er [Karikal] was also in the same territory. Ya-na-an [Yaaon] was in Bai-xi-er [Andhra Pradesh, Coromandal coast] region. Shang-de-er-na-ge [Chandernagor] was in the state of Bengal, and Ma-hei [Mahe] was in the state of Ma-le-ba-er [Malabar]. But they were neither a city nor a port, but were only storehouses used for storing and shipping goods.

The Da-ni [Danish] Colonies

Ding-suo-pu-er [Serampore] was in the interior of Bengal, to the left of the Jia-ge-li [Hoogly] river, and Lang-da-gei-ba-er [Tharangambadi] was in the territory of Jia-er-na-de [Carnatic/Tamilnadu].

The Kingdom of Ku-she-mi-er [Kashmir]

The Kingdom of Kashmir was the ancient kingdom of Ji-bin in North India. The *Book of Tang* [*Tangshu*] called it the Kingdom of Jia-shi-mi-luo, and in the *History of the Yuan* [*Yuanshi*] it is referred as Qi-shi-mi-er country. They are all the same. In the past, it belonged to the country of Se-guo [Sikh country] and was ruled by Lun Yasheng [Ranjit Singh]. Later, when the Punjab state was ceded to the British jurisdiction, only Kashmir was not ceded. Its area was still more than 2000 *li*. It bordered with the Ngari Prefecture of Tibet Autonomous Region in the east, Afghanistan in the west, Punjab in the south, and the Pamirs in the north. Its capital was Se-ling-na-jia [Srinagar]. This was built in a valley and was surrounded by mountains from all sides. The terrain was dangerous, with an average altitude of 600 *zhang* and the highest peak of 1700 *zhang*. However, the country was rich, the army was strong, the products were abundant, and the people were rich. It had been a powerful and strong country since ancient times. Surrounded by the Xin-tou River (the upper source of the Sindhu/Indus River), Kashmir confronted the river from three sides. Bordering the Indus River lived an affiliated tribe by the name of La-da-ke [Ladakh]. They belonged to the ancient Yan-da [Tibet?] Country. It was in the territory of Xuandu [Suspended Crossing mountains] which stretched to He-tan [Khotan] in the northeast, and to A-li [the Ngari Prefecture in Tibet] in the southeast, it was more than two-month's journey for both the places. The locals believed in Islam religion. They kept long beards, had tall stature, and dressed up as businessmen while visiting out. They could be seen everywhere in the eight cities in the south and in Tibet. Tibetans called them 'chan tou hui zi [Hui persons with brocaded headband]'.

According to the *Book of Han*, the seat of King of Ji-bin [Kashmir/Kapisha-Peshawar] government was in Xun-xian City. It was 6840 *li* away from the largest seat of local government administered by the Du-hu [frontier Governor/Protector General] in the northeast. It was further 2250 *li* in the east from the Wu-tuo [乌砣/ Wu-cha] State (Wu-cha was also known as Wu-tang [乌塘]; a scholar identified it with Wu-zang-na-dang [乌仗那当] in present De-lie Wei-liao [德列威聊] and other states' region).[78] Except for four or five states, not all the regions, from the south of Pishan county [in Hotan/Khotan Prefecture in Xinjiang] were part of the [Chinese] country during the Han Dynasty. It was recorded that both Da-tou-tong [大头痛 tr. Mountains of the Big Headaches] and Xiao-tou-teng [小头痛 tr. Mountains of the little Headaches][79] consisted of fiery slopes of red earth, and also had three lakes. Both had huge hard rocks and hill-sloping pathways. The cramped space on the pathways was only six to seven *cun* long, and the length of the area was 30 *li*. The road was difficult and dangerous, and most unfathomable. People on foot or on horseback had to hang ropes and pull each other out. After covering more than 2000 *li* like this one could reach Xuandu [tr. Suspended Crossing[80]]. It was said that the monks Faxian of Jin Dynasty [265–420 CE] and Huisheng of the Northern Wei Dynasty [386–557 CE][81] took this route. Monk Xuanzang of Tang Dynasty traveled on this northwest route. While he crossed the Indus River at Bo-luo-er [博罗尔 Balkh?] (also Bian-da-ge-ya 边达哥亚), the Northern Wei master [Hui-sheng] instead crisscrossed the Indus River along lower reaches of the Ba-da-ke Mountains, which was a much longer route.

Gurkha Country [Nepal]

The country of Kuo-er-ka [Gurkha] was also known as the country of Ni-bao-er [Nepal]. The *Book of Tang* mentioned it as Ni-po-luo, and the *History of the Ming* recorded it as Ni-ba-la. The Tibetans called it Bi-bang-zi. In the past it was divided into three parts, namely, Bu-yan, Ye-leng, and Ku-ku-mu. In the tenth year (1732) of Emperor Yong-zheng, they all carried gold leaves to China to pay tribute. During the Qianlong period [1735–1796], the Gurkhas were the most powerful. They merged the other three tribes into one and invaded the Ngari region of Tibet. Duke Fu Wenxiang dispatched troops, defeated them, and demanded payments of indemnities to the Chinese court once every 12 years. Nepal had since then been very respectful and obedient to our country [China] to this day. The country of Gurkha is bordered by Zhe-meng-xiong [Sikkim] and Meng-jia-la [Bengal] in the east, Bai-ha [Bihar] State and Ou-de [Oudh] in the south, De-lie [Delhi] State in the west, and Hou-zang area [lower Tibet/ Ngari region in Tibet Autonomous Region] in the north. It was about 2000 *li* long and 400 or 500 *li* wide country. Its capital was known as Jia-de-man-du [Kathmandu], also called Ba-le-bu, which was derived from its ancient name Bai-bu country. The area under its jurisdiction included Na-li-dan-ba [Mathiyungumbo?/ Nalakomuka?], Ba-ruo-mo [Bairangnia], Gang-pu-er [Janick-poor/ Janakpur], Ha-li-ha-pu-er [Hariharpur] in the south, and Ka-dang in the east. Zha-yan-pu-er [Chyanpur], Yu-dan-zhi [Chitan], and to the west there are Ma-ge-de [Mayakot/ Mulkot?], Gorkha, Ba-er- ba [Palpa], Ka-dang-sa [Khatang] were all cities with flourishing commerce. Along the north side were mountains with high and precipitous peaks that stretched for thousands of miles, collectively known as Xi-mo-li-ya-da-xue Mountains [The Great Himalayan Mountains]. There were four ways to enter Tibet, namely, Ji-long [Kirong], Nie-la-mu [Nyalam/Nola Pass], Rong-xia [Taplang Jong?], and Ka-da [Kagakat]. During the Qianlong period, the checkpost gates were set up, stone posts demarcating border were installed, and troops were stationed to guard it.

In the 23rd year of Zhenguan[82] [649] in the Tang Dynasty, the chief historian Wang Yuance went on an expedition to Tianzhu [India] and issued a war proclamation to beckon troops from neighboring countries. Tubo[83] [the Tibetan King] sent an army of 1,000 troops. The troops were split up at Cha-bo and Luo-cheng (today's Uzbekistan) and broke the defense in three days. In the 17th year of Hongwu (1384) in the Ming Dynasty, Monk Zhi-guang was ordered to be the envoy of the state. He carried the seal book, colored silk, and coins to Ni-ba-la [Nepal] to express goodwill. The Kingdom of Nepal and its neighboring Kingdom of Yongta [Tatar of Xinjiang] both sent messengers to the Ming court to pay tribute. In addition to that, there were rarely any discussion on situation in Nepal in historical records. Their local folk customs and culture were no different from those of the Tang-gu-ta [Tangut].

There were also many lamas. When the British annexed India, leaders of all the surrounding tribes surrendered to the situation. It was only the Gurkha kingdom that was able to maintain its independence by relying on the protection of the Chinese court. Of course, it was also because of its strategic location with difficult access, and brave and valiant people adept in swift movements on such terrain. I [Huang] heard that in the past there was a general named Zang-ke-ba-du [Jang Bahadur],[84] who was good at positional warfare, and his mighty reputation spread far and wide making surrounding countries afraid. The Imperial Court of our country [China] awarded him a title, and the British also honored him by a precious star. At that time, there was a small tribe named La-ke-long, which when suppressed by the British sought help from Gurkha. Zang-ke-ba took the opportunity to annex this place. His younger brother was now in charge of state affairs there.

Zhe-mong-xiong guo [Sikkim] Country

Sikkim was also known as Xi-jin. It was divided between Gurkha and Bu-lu-ke-ba [Lepcha] people. Its territory stretched to about 100 *li*, and the population was between five to six thousand. In the south was Darjeeling, and Tibetans came here for trade. In the north, there were small tribes such as Bai-mu-rong [Zhu-ba-er] and Zha-mu-lang [Chamling] who belonged to lower Tibet's two low land areas, Ding-jie [Dingye county, Shigatse prefecture, Tibet] and Ding-ri [Tingri county, Shigatse].

Bu-lu-ke-ba-pu [Bhutan] Country

The State of Bu-lu-ke-ba-bu-ku [Bhutan] was also known as Bu-Dun. It was adjacent to Zhe-meng-xiong [Sikkim] in the west, Ya-shan [Assam] in the south, the territory of wild Mo-yu [northern people] people in the east, and the Qian-zang [Northern Tibet] and Hou-zang [southern Tibet] in the north. It was more than 1000 *li* long and 500–600 *li* wide. During the Yongzheng period, it sent a tribute to the Chinese court conveying submission to the authority and law of the land. Its capital was named Ta-xi-su-deng (in *Tibet Chronicles* it was called Zha-shi-qu-zong), which was the only two-way road for Tibetan merchants for business and trade exchanges. The southwest was two days away from Du-ji-ling [Darjeeling], and the northeast was three days journey after crossing Du-ji-ling [Darjeeling] to Pa-ke-li [Pari/Phari], and another three days to Jiang-zi [Gyangze valley, Shigatse, Tibet] military camp. The local climate was mild and the products were rich and abundant. It was presented a seal from China engraved in seal script with words, 'the seal of Tang Shi's national treasure'. There were several roads in the north that could lead to places such as Qian-zang [Tibetan upland] and Gongbu [Kongbo'gyamda county, Nyingchi prefecture, Tibet].

(This was inscribed by a field officer from Xinyang, Zhao Yuan yi).

ANNEXURE: SUNDRY THOUGHTS ON INDIA (POEMS) [YIN-DU ZA-XING 印度杂兴]

I.

武帝雄心通大夏，显宗异梦感金精。

轺车持节唐元策，贝叶翻经魏慧生。

重涉昆明三藏路，遍游天竺百王城。

我来不为求经律，万里舆图聚米成。[85]

Wudi[86] carried the lofty ambition of opening a thoroughfare to Daxia,
Xianzong[87] cherished pleasant dreams of the arrival of golden figured Buddha.
Xuanze[88] took the mantle of the Tang's envoy driving a carriage to India,
Huisheng,[89] the Wei monk, explored palm leaves and interpreted the Tripitaka.
Retracing the path of elderly Master San-zang [Xuanzang],
I traveled all over the cities of hundreds of kings in Tian-zhu [India].
I came to India not to obtain Buddhist scriptures,
But to accomplish drawing of maps of thousands of li of this country.

II.

慧光耿耿照震旦，正法千年数未完。

路入罽宾悬渡险，城居舍卫梵宫宽。

恒河东去多歧派，外道西来变异端。

鹿苑鹫峰几尘劫，休将往事问阿难。

The light of wisdom dedicatedly shines over China,
The Dharma[90] uninterruptedly circulates for thousands of years.
The pathway enters Jibin [Kashmir] crossing over the most dangerous
of suspended ropeways,
And reaches Shravasti's[91] spacious hall of the Buddhist Temple.
The Ganges with its many tributaries still flows towards the East,
And carries foreign heretics from the Western region.
The Lu-ye garden[92] and the Ling Vulture Mountain[93] still exist enduring
many disastrous spells,
Yet, now there is no Ananda[94], to talk about Buddhist precepts.

III.

鹰瞵虎视久争雄，割据何年西复东。

大帅全权资坐镇，小邦归命就藩封。

铸金立马功臣像，局鐍调鹦故汗宫。

最是海疆扼形胜，迢迢万里电讯。

In India, Eagles stared, and Lions[95] watched, and each contended for supremacy,
And forcibly fragmented, year after year, the east and the west of the country.
The Grand Master[96] took over all the resources and commanded full authority,
And overturned the destiny of the small states by turning them into vassals.
Commemorated their outstanding heroes by installing their bronze
statues on horseback,
Bolting the ancient palaces of Imperial Mughals for only parrots to move in.
Guarded most of the seacoast from convenient scenic locations,
From a thousand *li* away through communication by telegraph and telephone.[97]

IV.

东竺名都甲谷他，经营百载公班衙。

膏腴沃野三千里，阛阓连云十万家。

五岛迤南侵缅甸，群山直北界支那。

岂惟鸦片居奇久，近日亚山广蓺茶。

In the east was the famous city of Kolkata,
Managed through a Public Office[98] for hundreds of years.
Fertile vast land stretched to more than 3000 *li*,
Households of a large population of 2,000,000 surrounded it.
Five Islands [Wu-dao/India] extended to the south and included Myanmar,
Its northern mountains (Himalayas) bordered with China.
India traditionally produced opium as a special product for trade,
But, how come it had now added tea trees planted in a large area of Assam.[99]

V.

昆仑西去铁门寒，异兽崎嵬见角端。

一战降痕都士坦，千秋仰成吉思汗。

行省征兵追黑石，离宫避暑召黄冠。

藩篱转瞬仍羝触，始信鞭长及腹难。

Genghis Khan terrorized the region from the west[100] of Kunlun to Tiemen,[101]
Where strange beasts[102] lived in remote mountain corners.
A war loomed large on Hindustan,
And Genghis Khan was forever admired for his prowess.
A Yuan province sent conscripts to Heilongjiang,[103]
But he aborted his expedition to acquire black rocks [diamonds],
When he encountered a Yellow hat[104] soothsayer at his summer retreat
[who prophesized],

All the surrounding countries would immediately turn into enemies
like 'horned rams locked in a fence',[105]
And the situation may go "beyond the reach of [his] whip".[106]

VI.

元戎决策复金瓯，万里回疆指顾收。
驿置天山南北路，水分葱岭东西流。
花门突厥归函夏，雄镇伊犁重戍秋。
闻说敦盘联旧好，从容杯酒索荆州。

Yuan Rong[107] decided to restore Jin'ou [Ca Mau, Vietnam],
And recover the vast land of Xinjiang to make the country complete.
Set up Courier Stations on the roads going north and south from the
Tianshan mountain range,[108]
Rivers on the Pamirs flowed from east to west.
The Huamen Turks[109] belonged to China,
And they bravely guarded the Yili region[110] all year round.
It is said that Turpan had old friendly relations with China,
This was like the earlier days when Liu Bei in a feast asked for Jingzhou.[111]

VII.

南洋岛屿似星罗，雄镇新开昔加坡。
粤女打番咸水乐，华人牟利估帆多。
鹊巢鸠占更宾主，蜗角蛮争议战和。
欲借旋螺祈海若，乘槎万里定风波。

Islands of the Nanyang[112] are scattered like stars,
Among them the mightiest is newly opened Singapore.
Women of Guangdong worked in salt water[113] as salt-water girls,[114]
And Chinese men earned much profits by plying sailing boats there.
The British occupied the city like Doves[115] and turned from guests into hosts,[116]
And like arrogant snails[117] struggled with force even for small matters.
I really desired to blow the conch to pray to Hairuo [the sea-god]
To request Him to keep the ship safe and stable in face of the storm in
the middle of the sea.

Notes

1 Huang mistakenly refers to the Governor of the Presidency as Deputy Governor-General.
2 Darjeeling was the erstwhile summer capital during the British rule when Calcutta was the capital of India. After the shift of India's capital to Delhi, Simla became the designated Summer Capital of India and Darjeeling became the summer capital of Bengal Presidency.
3 This appears to be the transliteration of 'judge'.
4 The author's transliteration is probably not correct. He seems to be referring to Calcutta's Pulta-Tallah water works located 23 kilometers away from the city. This was Asia's first surface water-based supply system next to the Hooghly River which became operational in 1868.
5 An ancient unit of length, equal to 8 *chi*.
6 It is a model method found in Chinese calligraphy to decide boundaries of the matter to be copied. It was also called 'Jiu-fang-ge' [Nine Patterns of Square].
7 This refers to the Alipore Zoo which was opened in 1875 and is now one of the largest and oldest zoos in India.
8 Popular animals are often provided pet names in the local language in zoos.
9 The author appears to be confusing bullock cart with imaginative 'deer carts'. In north India it was common to use bulls tamed to pull various types of carts and several agricultural tools and devices leading to the popular observation of India as the land of bullock cart. Some imaginative Buddhist brass sculptures have brass or stone toys depicting deer pulling the cart.
10 Referring to 'Howler Monkey'.
11 Referring to one belonging to Indonesian Orangutans, gorillas, baboons, etc., kinds of mammals which are known to be cannibals.
12 Referring to Pygmy monkeys.
13 His observation is the result of contemporary common racial theories.
14 In *Hou Hanshu*, it is mentioned that the Kingdom of Tiaozhi had lions, rhinoceroses, zebu cattle, peacocks, and giant birds [ostriches].
15 What the author refers to as the Bombay product is actually the Malwa Opium which, unlike the tightly Company controlled Bengal Opium, was in the hands of the princely states of Central India. Indian traders in those states on the basis of current market prices advanced funds to independent cultivators to grow poppy, and purchased all the harvest, processed it, and packed in chests to export through the Mumbai port. Much of this was also smuggled. Princely states earned higher taxes on Opium and the Company benefitted by collecting 'pass/transit tax' on each chest.
16 Vasco da Gama [1460–1524] was a Portuguese nobleman and explorer who opened the direct maritime route between Europe and India when he landed at Calicut [near Kozhikode] in 1498.
17 The author wrongly mentions Fort William as a person by the name of Huo Wei-lian. It was actually linked with the so-called 'Black Hole Massacre' [1756].
18 Robert Clive [1725–1774] was the first governor of the Presidency of Fort William [1757–1760] and was the founder of the British East India Company Rule in Bengal.
19 An-e [translated as Calm-forehead] River, is a Chinese transliterated name of an untraceable local river. But its reference in the context of the Battle of Plassey which was fought in 1757 in a location on the east bank of the Bhagirathi–Hooghly River, a tributary of Ganga, indicates that the An-e is probably this river.
20 Refers to General Hector Munro [1726–1805] who became the ninth Commander-in-chief of Bengal in 1764–1765.

21 This refers to the British expansion during the period of Sir Richard Cooley Wellesley who served as the fifth Governor-General of India between 1798 and 1805.

22 Author's estimate of the year of the establishment of EIC slightly varies because of the conversion of Christian year to dynastic reign year. Throughout his text this variance continues. In this particular case, officially, the year is December 31, 1600. Also the amount of capital invested in the EIC is mentioned differently from those recorded in official documents in pounds. This variation may be due to different conversion method of pound, Spanish dollar, and Chinese yuan. Officially the initial capital was £30,111 which increased to £68373.

23 The officially recorded amount in pound is £3,200,000.

24 This refers to the Charter or Regulating Act of 1833.

25 Huang Maocai reference is to the ancient Chinese description of Wu Yin-du [Five India-s], according to which the ruling territory of Hindustan, during the Islamic/ Mugal period was located in Zhong Yin-du [Central or Middle India] where the capital De-xi was located and the King of the country resided.

26 It is an ancient country in Central Asia; its control area is roughly located in present northeastern Afghanistan and eastern Tajikistan.

27 The Amir or Emir was Sher Ali Khan [1863–1866; 1868–1879], the son of former Amir Dost Muhammad Khan [1826–1839; 1843–1863] during the Second Anglo-Afghan War between 1878 and 1880. This was the period of Great Game marked by the fierce Anglo Russian rivalry for the control of Central Asia for geo-political reason and the establishment of a buffer between the British Raj and the Russian Empire.

28 Huang erred in dates. It was actually September 3, 1879 that the British envoy in Kabul, Sir Louise Cavagnari, and men of his troops were killed by the Afghans in Kabul.

29 Mohammad Yaqub Khan's younger brother was Mohammad Ayub Khan who was Amir during 1879 and 1880.

30 About a thousand miles west of Lhasa, it is known in Tibetan as the Ngari Prefecture of Tibet Autonomous Region and is best known for Mount Kailash, also named Sumeru and Lake Mansarovar, holy places for Hinduism, Buddhism, and Bon.

31 An ancient trading town on the Silk Road, it finds mention in *Hou-han-shu [Book of Later Han]*. The local Islamic regime was established here during the Ming Dynasty when the Shaybanids [a mixed Turkic-Mongolian aristocratic class] established the Yarkent/d Khanate [1514–1713].

32 Lord Dalhousie [1848–1856] was scathingly criticized for the costly war and for raising the demand for compensation 100 times from £1000 to £100,000.

33 Also Translated as *A Brief Survey of the Maritime Circuit,* it was a ten volume [juan] set written by Xu Jiyu which was completed in the 28th year of Daoguang reign [1848]. This along with Wei Yuan's *Hai-guo-tu-zhi [Illustrated Treatise on the Maritime Kingdoms]*, published in 1843, are considered to Trea be the two most influential books of modern China on world history that played a significant role in formation of Chinese ideas on nationalism and modernity.

34 The reference is probably to the founder of Sikhism, Guru Nanak, and a series of other illustrious gurus.

35 Refers to Monotheism of Sikhism.

36 Compiled by Fan Ye, *Book of Later Han [*后汉书 *Hou Hanshu]* records the history of Eastern Han dynasty (25–220 CE).

37 The Yuezhi were the inner Eurasian nomadic confederation probably descending from the Indo-European-speaking (Tocharian) pastoral nomads who exported

jade and horses to Zhou China in the second century BCE and were a prelude to the Da Yuezhi [Great Kushana] after settling in Bactria. [See, Benjamin Craig, 2017, 'The Yuezhi' in *Oxford Asian History Encyclopedia.*, https://doi.org/10 .1093/ acrefore/9780190277727.013.49].

38 The 'Western Sea', referred to as the Da-hai [Great Sea], was the Indian Ocean including the Persian Gulf and the Red Sea [See, John E. Hill, tr., 2003, 'The Western Regions according to *Hou Hanshu*: The Xi-yu-juan' [depts.washington .edu/silkroad/texts/hhshu/ho_han_shu.html}

39 Refers to Vanga in Bengal. The location of Vanga in Bengal or Vanga near the mouth of Indus has been problematized with the use of different Chinese words for it in two separate texts - Pan-qi in *Hou Han-shu* and Pan-yueh in *Weilue*. Chinese texts also use the term Han-yueh country to denote present provincial areas of India's Nagaland, Manipur, and Mizoram.

40 The translation of this and the next passage is based on John E. Hill's online translation of the Kingdom of Tianzhu from the chapter on The Western Regions according to *Hou Hanshu* which has been verbatim referred by Huang Maocai. This is available on depts.washington.edu/silkroad/texts/hhshu/hou _han_shu.html#sec15.

41 This is translated as 'Records of white snake country' and is presumably based on the mysterious surreptitious tales of Fahai – an evil Buddhist monk in the 'Tale of the White Snake', *Baishe Zhuan*.

42 The Three Kingdoms (220–280 CE) is a period of history from the Eastern Han dynasty to the Western Jin dynasty, divided into three regimes: Cao Wei, Shu Han, and Dong Wu.

43 Chinese cartographers identify Funan as a loose network of ancient Indianized states located in mainland Southeast Asia centered on the Mekong Delta that existed from the first to sixth century CE.

44 Su Wu [140–60 BCE] was a Chinese diplomat of the Western Han Dynasty. He remained faithful to his mission and country in the foreign Xiongnu territory despite being detained in a prison under most trying conditions for 19 years.

45 According to Xu Yunqiao's research, the Kouri Kingdom is located on the east coast of the Malay Peninsula. Jiu-li in Malay language is Kuala [= Kuala Lumpur]. See, Xu Yunqiao, 1961, *History of Nanyang*, Singapore World Book Company, p. 222.

46 Kang Tai was a Chinese traveler who journeyed in the middle of the third century from the state of Eastern Wu to Southeast Asia. He together with Zhu Ying documented the existence of Funan in his book *Account of Foreign States in Wu Times* and reported its many similarities with India. [See Tarling, Nicholas 1999. *The Cambridge History of Southeast Asia* Vol 1 Part I (From early times to c. 1500), Cambridge University Press. p. 194].

47 Referring probably to the contemporary Maurya Dynasty, especially Ashok Maurya who played a significant role in the dissemination of Buddhism in nearby countries outside his Indian empire.

48 Large kingdoms or independent states of tribes that came together to form a permanent settlement and state. These arose from the smaller ones from the sixth century BCE onward.

49 Probably refers to a late Gupta King, Buddhagupta [476–495] or Narsimha Gupta [495–?].

50 Zhu Luoda carried and presented his credentials to the Imperial Office of Emperor Liang in Nanjing. This is recorded in *Liang-shu*, Vol. 54. Besides talking about the current good status of both the countries, the Gupta King also mentioned that they are at present time under the protection of Lord Shiva [Shi-po] from the heaven above, people are peaceful and happy; the

family of Gupta belong to the Kshatriya caste, and its kingship has been obtained by inheritance, the ambassador at large is loyal and trustworthy, and he could be trusted. The credential paper also noted that we strongly desire to have friendly relations from generation to generation. At the same time, the ambassador brought in materials like glass utensils, many kinds of perfume, and ancient cowries. See the entry on Qu-duo by Xue Keqiao in *Zhong-yin wen-hua jiao-liu bai-ke quan-shu* [*Encyclopedia of China-India Cultural Contacts*], 2015, Zhong-guo da-bai-ke quan-shu chu-ban-she, vol. 1: 523.

51 At the east coast of the Malay Peninsula.

52 At Surat Thani Province, Thailand.

53 The small and big Gelan was an important transit point between Arab and Chinese merchants. According to the *Ming History,* Its King sent envoys Fuguli and Sumenda to pay tributes in the fifth year [1407] of Ming Emperor Yongle [1402–1424].

54 *Liangshu* [The Book of Liang] mostly records historical events of the Nan-chao kingdom between 502 and 557 CE.

55 Da Qin is the Chinese name in the Han Dynasty for the ancient Roman Empire. The Parthian Empire, also known as the Ā-sa-xi-ci [Assisi dynasty], was a slave empire in the classical period in the Iranian region of western Asia

56 *Zhi-fang Wai-ji*《职方外纪》was a book on geography compiled by the Italian Jesuit missionary Ai-ru-Lue [Guiglio Alleni (1582–1649)] in the third year of Tianqi Qi (1623). It updated an earlier work by Matteo Ricci [1552–1610] entitled *Kun-yu wanguo quantu [Complete map of the Ten Thousand Countries].*

57 Compiled and published by Chinese Scholar official Wei Yuan in 50 scrolls in 1843, this is based on his superior Guangdong Governor Lin Zexu's some preliminary works in the area of world geo-politics, this is considered to be the first modern Chinese work on the West by Xu Jiyu.

58 This was Xu Jiyu's popular book on the world's geography in ten scrolls published in 1848–1849. See endnote 33 above full full reference.

59 Emir Shah Shujah [1785–1842] was a maverick Afghan leader who was the Governor of Herat and Peshawar from 1798 to 1801 and king of Afghanistan for the first time between 1803 and 1809 and the second time between 1839 and 1842. He fiercely competed with Emir Dost Muhammad for the kingship of Afghanistan which brought Persia [Iran], Russia, and the Britain and British India together into some of bloodiest battles and undetermined players linked with the Siege of Herat, Anglo-Persian War, and two Anglo-Afghan Wars in the middle of nineteenth century under the rubric of the Great Game.

60 Da-jian-lu was the major tea-market for the export of Sichuan–Yunnan tea to Tibet and beyond by the land route. The Indian tea because of the less transportation and labor cost competed favorably with Chinese tea. Competition between Chinese and Indian tea led to frequent business confrontations. These occasioned 'Tea Wars' between British India–Tibet and China and 'Treaties' permitting free trade in Tibet. See for details, De Rosthorn, 1895. *On the Tea Cultivation in Western Ssuch'uan and the tea trade with Tibet via Tachienlu.* London: Luzac & Co. Also, interesting is Thomas Thornville Cooper, 1871. *Travels of a Pioneer of Commerce in Pigtail and Petticoats: Or, An Overland Journey from China Towards India.* London, J. Murray.

61 This is how in phonetics Chinese becomes 'Chaaineese'.

62 The full name was Louis Maurice Adolphe Linant de Bellefonds. An explorer of Egypt and the Chief Engineer of the public works between 1831 and 1869, he was popularly known as Linant Pasha.

63 Muhammad Sa'id Pasha, Governor of Egypt owing fealty to the Ottoman Sultan, issued a declaration for the construction of a canal to the French.

64 Sikkim is known as Zhe-ming-xiong in ancient Chinese books.

65 The Tangut people belonged to the Tibeto-Burman family and spoke Tangut language.

66 Appears to be referring to the past Lieutenant Governor of Bengal Mr. Horace Abel Clckerell (1885) who was followed by Sir Steuart Colvin Bayley (1887–1890).

67 It was the capital of the earlier Ahom kingdom.

68 Another much more known river nearby was Phalgu/Falgu formed from the confluence of Lilajan/ Niranjana and Mohan rivers.

69 Under the provision of the Government of India Act of 1833, Agra became the capital of a newly established Agra Presidency administered by a Governor, but by another Act of 1835, it was renamed the Northwestern Provinces with a Lieutenant Governor as head in 1836.

70 One of independent province and a part of the British North-Western Provinces, it consisted of districts of Ajmer and Merwar.

71 Nagari Prefecture in Tibet Autonomous Region was known as A-li region in Chinese. Lake Mansarovar and Mt. Kailash (also known as Mt. Meru or Sumeru) were located here.

72 States forming the Central India Agency.

73 Located in Golkonda region, it was originally named Peddapalli after the Nizam of Hyderabad. The English East India Company established a factory here in 1621. The city was also occupied by the Dutch settlers for trade.

74 The author's reference is to the Anglo-Mysore War in Seringapatam where the King Tipu Sultan [1782–1799] was finally defeated and killed.

75 Mt. Putuo is Chinese rendition for the original Sanskrit name of Mt. Potalaka that was located in the southern coast of India and regarded as the home of Bodhisattva. It is linked with the Buddhist kingdom in south seas widely described in Sanskrit and Chinese mythological Buddhist texts. In Chinese Buddhism, it is one of the four most sacred Buddhist mountains.

76 The small town is known as Kanyakumari, the Virgin goddess. The legend is that Lord Siva was to marry Parvati here, but Lord Shiva failed to come and the marriage did not consummate. Rice and other grains meant for the feast therefore remained uncooked and turned into large stones. The author's use of the name Mi-suo, meaning 'humble grain' in Chinese translation, for the town might be inspired by the legend.

77 This refers to a narrow strip down from the southwest of Bengal along the Coromandel coast, the northern part of which was divided into many circars [subah/prefecture] and the southern part was known as Coramandel. These were occupied by the British and merged with British India's Madras Presidency. There were five important northern circars, namely, Chicacole [Srikakulam], Rajmandri [Rajahmundry], Ellore [Eluru], Mustaphanagar [Kondapalli?], and Murtuzanagar [Guntur]. Huang mentions four contemporary prefectures linked with this region. His rendering of their names in Chinese however does not appear to correspond with Indian names in brackets.

78 In his annotated translation of the History of Former Han Dynasty [Qian Hanshu], Hulsewe discusses various views on its location, that places it in Badakshan, Sarikol, Yarkand region. See, A.F.P. Hulsewe.1979. *China in Central Asia: The Early Stage 125 BC-AD 25*. Leiden: EJ Brill, pp. 98–104. Parallel texts, corrupt copies, and changing names and characters, he mentions, make identification of the location a difficult and complex process. In

such cases, we have noted the names as found in the text copy used in the translation.

79 Huluswe 1979:202 translates that as Hills of Headaches.

80 Huluswe 1979:99 translates as Suspended Crossing.

81 Northern Wei state was established by the leader of the northern Xian-bei tribe, Tuo Bagui.

82 Tang Emperor Tai Zong's reign year [626–649] is known as Zhenguan reign year.

83 Tibetan Tubo Dynasty [seventh to 11th century CE].

84 Jung Bahadur Kunwar Ranaji [1817–1877] belonged to the Kunwar family, and was a Khas Chhetri ruler of Nepal and founder of the Rana Regime in Nepal.

85 Emperor Wudi of the Han Dynasty [141–87 BCE].

86 We are thankful to Prof Xue Keqiao, formerly Professor in South Asian Studies at Peking University, Beijing, for providing explanations for Huang Maocai's sundry poems.

87 Emperor Mingdi of Han Dynasty [57–75 CE].

88 Wang Xuance [seventh century CE] was sent by Tang Taizong as an envoy to India in 648 CE. As referred earlier, the whole episode has been comprehensively dealt by Tansen Sen. 2003. *Buddhism, Diplomacy, and Trade: The Realignment of Sino-Indian Relations, 600-1400.* Honolulu: AAS & University of Hawaii Press.

89 Huisheng was a Buddhist monk who, along with Song Yun, was sent to India by the Empress of Northern Wei Dynasty in 518 CE to collect Buddhist scriptures. They probably went up to Peshawar and Nagarahara [present Jalalabad] and returned in 521 CE. Except for a short narrative by Song Yun, no detailed record of their journey is available.

90 The author's reference is to Satdharma which meant 'the genuine teaching of things as they are' and refers to the exhortation of wisdom that stems from the Buddha Shakyamuni.

91 Shravasti was the capital of the ancient Kingdom of Kosala then ruled by King Prasenjit. It was the place where Buddha lived most after his enlightenment and presented most of his famous sermons.

92 Mrgadvava vana [Deer Park]in Sarnath, Varanasi, India. Buddha delivered here his first sermon on Dharma, i.e., Dhammacakkapavattan Sutta. In Buddhist literature this place is also mentioned as Isipatna/Rishipatttana which Buddha recommended his followers as one of the four sites for pilgrimage.

93 Gridhakuta or Gijjhakuta Mountain also known as Holy Eagle Peal or Vulture Peak in Rajgir [Rajgrha, Bihar, India] is frequently mentioned in Buddhist literature as a place where Buddha delivered important sermons like Prajnaparmithrdaya sutra [Heart Sutra], Saddharma pundrika Sutra [Lotus Sutra], and Surangama Samadhi Sutra [Samadhi or meditation of the Heroic Progression]. Buddha and his disciples often engaged here in Buddhist discourses.

94 Ananda was the first cousin of the Buddha and one of his earliest and beloved disciples and personal attendants. He is referred as the interlocutor as well as the writer of many Buddhist discourses.

95 The Eagle [double-headed or double eagle] probably refers to Russia and used as coat of arms by the Russian military; while the Lion symbolizes Great Britain – the whole scenario is indicative of the 'Great Game' of the contemporary time.

96 Refers to the British Governor-General.

97 The poem highlights the contemporary situation of deep fragmentation of India and the British control of the land through means of modern communication.

98 Refers to the total British administrative structure for hundreds of years.

99 Reference is to Assam tea disrupting the tea trade from Tibet.

100 The poem is based on a legend about Genghis Khan's western expedition that says he encountered an auspicious beast with horns in East India.

101 Tie-men-guan, according to Prof Xue Keqiao, is presumably Termez of Uzbekistan.

102 Referring presumably to auspicious wild beasts.

103 Black rock refers to diamond.

104 Refers to the Daoist priest.

105 The idiom 'The ram touches the fence/domain', as used by Huang Maocai, means that the ram's horns are on the fence and it cannot either advance or retreat.

106 Further, the idiom 'the whip is too long to reach' comes from *Zuo Zhuan's – Xuangong Fifteen Years* that says 'although the whip is long, it is not as belly of a horse' meaning that it is too far away to control. It is said that Genghis Khan wrapped up his western expedition and returned. [This explanation is drawn from Prof Xue Keqiao's communication.]

107 Yuan Rong, the leader, refers to Zuo Zongtang [1812–1885] who regained Xinjiang and Jino'u [Ca Mau] to make country complete. Ca Mau is also metaphor for a complete control.

108 The Tianshan mountain range stretches between Xinjiang and Mongolia and present Kyrgyzstan.

109 The Huihe refers to Huamen Turks [the present Uighur ethnic groups], Hanxia refers to Huaxia and China.

110 The Ili River basin around Turpan in Xinjiang.

111 This refers to an incident that happened at the beginning of the third century BCE when Sun Quan of Soochow joined Liu Bei to repel the attack of Cao Cao in the north. 'At this time, Liu Bei asked Sun Quan to lend Jingzhou [present Hubei] to establish and develop his base. Minister Lu Su advised Sun Quan to agree as this would maintain the alliance with Liu Bei to deal with powerful Cao Cao in the north. Liu Bei thus acquired Jingzhou and also occupied Yizhou [present Sichuan] leading to the beginning of Three Kingdom's Period' [220–265CE] in Chinese history. However, when Lu Su approached Liu Bei for the return of Jingzhou, Liu Bei refused to do so. [We are thankful to Prof Xue Keqiao for the quote and explanation]

112 Nanyang refers to the waters of the South China Sea and Southeast Asia.

113 'Salt water' refers to the place engaged in providing sexual services for the outsiders.

114 'Saltwater girls' refers to the sex workers.

115 'Dove occupies a magpie's nests " is an idiom, which means coming as a guest and then seizing other people's house.

116 The above line is the translation of idiom used in the poem as '"Magpie nested and doves occupied more making guests turned to hosts'.

117 Wo-jiao, an idiom, is used to characterize an arrogant snail. See Zhuangzi's Zeyang, 'whoever has a country on the left corner of the snail are called the Barbarian clan". It means fighting over trivial things.

V

MY HUMBLE OPINION ON TRAVELS [YOU-LI CHU-YAN 游历刍言]

A Panoramic View of Five India-s [Wu Yin-du xing-shi 五印度形势]

The 'Five India-s' denoted the ancient country of Tianzhu [India] which was also known as Shen-du country. It had vast territory. Its terrain was triangular in shape with each side being of 6,000 *li*. Within its territory, there were more than ten large and small countries. They were not united since ancient times. During the early Ming Dynasty [1368–1644 CE] period, the king of Sai-ma-er-han[1] [Samarkand] Di-mu-er [Timur, 1370–1405 CE], who was originally a descendant of Tie-mu-er [Temur Khan, 1295–1307 CE] of the Yuan Dynasty in China, annexed various Islamic tribes in the Western Region. He then invaded India in the south, and attached it to his domain, known as Da-meng-gu-guo [The Great Mongolian/Mughal Country][2]. Its capital was established in the city of De-xi [Delhi] in Zhong-yin-du[3] [Central India]. The Great Mongolian [Mughal] country was spread to more than 20,000 *li* in both length and width, and collected taxes of up to 224 million yuan [?] every year. It was held in deep respect and admiration by every country. During the period of Zheng-de [1505–1521 CE] in the Ming Dynasty, some Portuguese came to the west coast of India for the first time to engage in trade and business. They were later followed one after another by merchants from Holland, Britain, France, Spain, and other countries. However, the power of the Great Mongolian [Mughal] King was formidable, and all feared him. Later, several sons of the Great Mongolian king, however, competed for the throne, and internal chaos and rebellion occurred. Leaders of various local states took the opportunity to become independent. Since then the country gradually disintegrated and its strength declined.

In the 20th year of Qianlong's reign [1756 CE], leaders of the Bengal State conspired with the French to imprison all the British in the territory, and more than half of them were killed.[4] Determined to avenge their humiliation

DOI: 10.4324/9781003505396-6

and loss, the British mobilized their entire country's forces under the leadership of the great general Ji-li-fu [Sir Robert Clive, 1725–1774 CE]. They finally won a great victory at the Battle [Plassey] on the bank of Hooghly River. Observing the formidable power of the British, leaders of all the states of Eastern India came running to surrender. Taking this opportunity, the British conquered many states of Central and South India. In the 30th year of Qianlong [1746CE], the states again rebelled against the British and killed many British. The British dispatched Sa-yi-gu-di [Sir Eyre Cootee, 1726–1783 CE] to recapture the territory. In the tenth year of Jiaqing [1805 CE], the British drove away all the French and Dutch troops stationed in India, and occupied the land captured by France and the Netherlands. Since then, eight to nine tenths of India's territory was seized by the British. After that the Mongolian [Mughal] king also submitted to the authority of the British. His descendants were since then supported by the British, but their reputation was already sullied. The rest of the states either set up prefectures and governed by the dispatched officials, or were downgraded to vassal states that paid taxes.

The British built three ports along the coast. One was in Bengal, which primarily controlled the shipping of eastern India, The other was at Madras which managed the trade of South India, and the third was at Bombay that focused on business in West India. They also introduced important official positions and garrisoned important troops in Ya-jia-la [Agra], Wu-de [Oudh], Ben-ruo [Punjab], Xin-di [Sindh], and Xi-nan-dao [Island of Ceylon/ Sri Lanka]. Trusted officials were appointed as governors and were bestowed with great powers to take various management measures and decisions on their own as the situation warranted. Every year, in winter and spring, the Governor-General stayed in Bengal, and in summer and autumn he went to Ba-le-li [Bareilly?/Shimla?][5] to escape the summer heat. 30,000 soldiers were deputed from Britain and stationed there. There were also about 182,000 native soldiers who either took turns on garrison duty or served as skilled laborers. Half of the soldiers believed in Hinduism and the other half were Muslim. They were kept separated from each other to prevent them from mutually working together to turn into enemies and rising together in rebellion against the British. Yet, mutinies often occurred. Central India and East India were flat, the land was fertile, and the production abundant. Trains and railways stretched to all directions. The capital city of Bengal state was Kolkata [Ka-li-ga-da] which was actually the largest, prosperous and developed city in the southwest Indian Ocean region. There were many high-rise buildings and many means of transportation on the street. More than 800,000 households lived there. They paid land tax, house tax, sign tax, livestock tax, and craftsmanship tax. Tax was levied on even a horse and a cow. Taxes were numerous, yet the majority of people had no complaints about the taxation. What was the reason? It turned out that in the past most of the native kings of local states did not know how to cherish the people, and indulged in endless cruel exploitation. Now with the British management, the people felt like being rescued by them from the middle of deep water and blazing fire, thus enabling them to sleep on a comfortable cool mat. Moreover, revenue from the tax collection was used apart from paying the salaries of officials and soldiers, for all the expenditures on amenities such as roads, bridges, ships, trains, electric wires, coal lamps, schools, hospitals, and other public facilities that brought convenience to the common people. Therefore, nobody complained and everyone was at peace with each other.

South India bordered with the sea and was also full of mountains. The hill people still followed the traditional customs and rituals. The British did not need to use military troops to enforce submission to their authority. Western and northern Indian folk customs on the other hand were fierce and belligerent. The northern India was like Ji-bin[6] that ruled for three generations, and the west India paralleled the Yue-zhi[7] who ruled for three generations. The borders of these two countries were connected. Today, countries of both Sikhs and Afghans could still be called powerful. During the Jiaqing [1796–1820 CE] period, Sikh King Lun-ya-sheng [Ranjit Singh, 1801–1839][8] took initiative on his own to recognize Islam as well as to stop persecution of Hindus and Buddhist gods. He recruited Europeans to train troops for them, and repeatedly crossed the border to the British vassal states. In the nineteenth year of Daoguang [1839 CE] Ranjit Singh died of a sudden illness. His grandson inherited the throne and was also brave and war-lover. In the 22nd year of Daoguang (1842), the Sikh King led the army to attack the south in a big way. Taking advantage of the unpreparedness of the British, they initially won a victory. The British army was then completely defeated. Emboldened by this, other tribes also separately rose to resist the British. This made the British much alarmed and disturbed. There were anxieties whether they could keep control over India. After two years of stalemate, the British commander-in-chief Gao-fu [Sir Hugh Gough 1779–1869 CE] finally defeated the Sikh' army. The Sikhs were then forced to surrender and negotiate, ceding the state of Punjab on the south bank of the La-wei [Ravi] river to the British. The British successively quelled the treasonous states below the Sind state. Every state in India gradually came to respect Britain as the sovereign power. Since the earliest time, the forceful occupation of India was earlier seen as the act of the English East India Company, but now Britain was recognized as the suzerain state and the rule of the British monarch was finally accepted. Afghanistan and Britain had been at war with each other for decades with each sometimes winning or losing. War and peace were intertwined, mainly because of the Russian intervention. Last year, Russia sent envoys to the city of Kabul, but the British envoys were turned away from Afghanistan, so a dispute arose. The British sent troops to

Afghanistan, but because of the cold weather and difficult roads, the British army could not immediately adapt to the situation. But, later it was still able to defeat the Afghan army and capture Kabul. The Afghan king along with his family and property sought asylum in Russia, leaving his son A-gu-bai [Yaqub Khan] to supervise state affairs. Soon after, the Afghan king died of illness, Yaqub Khan succeeded to the throne. He soon had to surrender to the British to negotiate peace, cede land, make reparations, and sign a withdrawal agreement. But the Afghan people were unwilling to accept the defeat, and suddenly launched a mutiny in July, killing a high-ranking British official. Yaqub Khan's younger brother [Ayub Khan] took the opportunity to fight for the throne, putting Yaqub Khan in a dilemma over handling internal and external troubles, and had to give the throne to his younger brother. In fact, it was not impossible for the British military to destroy Afghanistan. The main reason for the British to retain its independence was to use Afghanistan as a buffer, because sections west of Cong-ling [Pamir high plateau], such as those of Hao-han[9], Bu-ha-er[10], Ji-fa[11], etc. were all occupied by Russia. India was only separated by the Xing-du-ge-shi [Hindu Kush] mountain, which was in the territory of Ba-da-ke-shan [Badakshan] country, and was the place where Yuan Taizu's [Ghenghis Khan 1206–1227 CE] Summer Palace was located. The Russians coveted the rich treasures of India and always thought of stratagems to pillage it. They sent people to learn the Indian language, incite and confuse people's heart, and contacted countries such as Persia and Afghanistan to make secret crafty plans. The British strongly resisted that. They sent large troops to guard various important mountain passes and did not slacken off their vigil.[12] I [Huang] just heard that the Russian army was on expedition in the Chu-he area, and the Indian Ambassador ordered leaders in Kashmir to place the troops on garrison duty. The Russians were annoyed that the British were overstepping the time-honored limit. When the two powerful countries confronted each other, the situation became like fighting between a tiger and a dragon with each day after day looking for weapons of war.[13] When Russia attacked Turkey, Britain contained it, and when Britain fought in Afghanistan, the Russians tacitly helped the other. On the surface, the royal intermarriage between the two countries [on 23rd January 1874 between Queen Victoria's son Prince Alfred, and Emperor Alexander II's daughter, Grand Duchess Maria Alexandrovna] appeared very friendly, but behind the scenes they were mutually suspicious and each closely guarded itself against the other.

India began to communicate with China from the Han Dynasty. Han Wudi [148 BCE–86 BCE] once sent envoys from the southwestern minority areas to Shendu [India], but they were blocked at Kunming. Emperor Ming of Han [58 CE–75 CE] dreamt of a golden man with a tall stature and a bright halo on his head, so he sent envoys to Tianzhu [India] to inquire about Buddhist scriptures. Since the Jin [265 CE–420 CE] and Tang [618

CE–907 CE] dynasties, Chinese monks had been going to Tianzhu to seek Buddhist scriptures, mainly through three routes. One was from He-tian [Khotan] to the south to Du-long-chi crossing cliffs through suspended cables and passing through Sha-he and entering Jibin. This was the eastern route which was taken by Monk Fa Xian of the Jin Dynasty and Monk Hui Sheng of the Northern Wei Dynasty [386 CE–535 CE]. The other one went west from Yili[14] [Ili], passed through Huohan [Kokand] to Samarkand, then turned northeast, going beyond Tie-men-du [Termez], crossing Fu-chu-he, and getting over the Hindu Kush Great Snow Mountains entered Kashmir. This was the western route, and it was also the road followed by Monk Yuan-zang [Xuanzang] of the Tang Dynasty, and Monk Qiu Daoren of the Yuan Dynasty traveling from Chang-chun[15]. The third route went up from the southwest of Ye-er-qiang [Yarkand River], moved along many rivers, ascending up the Pamir high plateau to anchor at Sai-le-ku-er [Sialkot], and then crossed the Indus River to the south. This was the middle path and also the route taken by Xuanzang on the way back to China

Studying the history of Chinese military invasion of India or the use of Chinese soldiers against India, it is evident that only Tang Taizong and Yuan Taizu ever sent forces there. In the 23rd Zhenguan reign year [648 CE], Emperor Tang Taizu [Li Shimin] dispatched his right guard under the command of officer and diplomat Wang Yuance to Tianzhu, with Jiang Shiren as his lieutenant. The King of Tianzhu [from Zhong-yin, i.e., Central India] sent troops to resist them. His troops swiftly seized the Tang army's equipments and materials. Wang Yuance retreated to the western region of Tubo [Tibet][16] to stand up against the adversary. He sent an order to call the troops of neighboring countries. Tubo sent thousands of soldiers, and Nepal (that was then known as kuo-er-ka [Gurkha]) sent 7000 mounted soldiers to support. Wang Yuance's army fought with the Tianzhu army for three days respectively at Cha-bo and Luo-cheng[17], defeated them, and captured the Tianzhu king A-luo-na-shun [Arunasva][18]. More than 12,000 men and women were apprehended, and 580 large and small towns were seized. The other example was that of Yuan Taizu (Cheng-ji-si-han [Genghis Khan]) who personally fought in India. He stationed troops on the snowcapped mountains and established Imperial military camps there. He sent his generals to track and subdue Suan-duan [Ali-Sultan/Ali Khalil, d. 1342?] of Ke-fu-cha guo [country of Khwarazmian[19]] to the Shen [Ganges] River area in Central India. *Yuan Shi [The Yuan History]* records meeting of Zhe Bie[20] and Su-bu-tai[21] with Temujin [Genghis Khan] to discuss the movement of Suan Duan [Ali-Sultan], and provides chronological biography of Xian-zong [Emperor Yuan Xianzong], as well as many past expeditions to India which witnessed both swift win and instant loss due to obstructions posed by snowcapped mountains and long distances. The land of Tripitaka [Tibet] and India were intimately close. They were however separated in the middle by numerous high mountains that stretched for thousands of miles. Lofty mountain ranges were perilous. The high and harsh roads were dangerous and difficult. There was no communication channel between first to eight months because of heavy snow enveloping the mountains. This was also the natural barrier that God created to separate China from foreign countries. There was only one most direct road from Darjeeling. That was from Jiang-zi[22] [Gyangze town and county] to the south for three stops to Pa-ke-li [Paheli in Quamdo/Changdu, eastern Tibet]. After crossing the mountain was Bu-lu-ke-ba [Bhutan] Station and then there were three stops to Ta-xi Su-deng [Tashi Samdong?]. From there turning to the southwest and walking again for three stops was Darjeeling. The total distance was more than 500 miles, and one must pass through a narrow passage between India and Tibet.

The leader of Darjeeling had surrendered to the British. The local people had the same language and customs as the Tang-gu-te[23] [Tangut]. The terrain was high and cold. Many rich Indian businessmen had built their summer houses there. The British had set up a consular officer, stationed the deputy commander of the army, and built several bunkers. From Darjeeling to Xi-li-ge-li [Siliguri] took one day by horse-drawn carriage, and then one night by train to Bengal [Kolkata]. The railway mileage was 300 miles, which was about 1000 *li*. The British state was currently stepping up the construction of a direct railway line to Darjeeling which would soon be completed. I [Huang] investigated and found that there was no large place in the city or metropolis to collect and store commodities and goods. The British, however, did not hesitate to superimpose fees and levies to open up the trade route. One must remember that the trade relation between India and Tibet was not a one-off event. The East India Company was passionately engaged in making profit and seizing every opportunity to find ways for that. This certainly was their original primary intention. The British also knew that Tibet was our country's [China's] territory and were not in favor of daring to open up frivolous border conflict. They instead employed hundreds of crafty plots and heavy bribes to make friends with tribes from Bu-lu-ke-ba[24], [Drukpa/Bhutan], and Zhe-meng-xiong [Sikkim] region to trap them to come to their fold. All these tribes were weak and incompetent and could not resist them. The Gurkhas were, however, relatively powerful. Living in dangerous hilly terrain, they were sturdy people with good fighting skills. They relied on the heavenly might of China and received protection. It had been suggested that the Imperial Court should bestow more grace and faith on the Gurkhas to enable them to consolidate this barrier on the border. In the event of a change, the Gurkhas can also be used as the vanguard to resist the British.

In the past, the four passes, namely, Ji-long [Gyirong, Shigaze, Tibet], Nie-la-mu [Nyalam or Yakrushong Tong la], Rong-xi [Rongshar in Tingri, Shigaze, Tibet], and Ka-da [Zanda, Ngari, Tibet], were guarded by ethnic minorities of the Gurkha land [Nepal] and other neighboring countries. As there were no conflicts or incidents, the required management and construction were neglected. Now the time was different, and its momentum too was not the same. In the past, it was not a concern; but in the future, it had to be taken seriously. We must plan ahead and take advance precautions. The frontier defenses should be rectified at Gyantse, Dingri [in Shigatse Prefecture/Central Tibet], and Pakeli to prevent sudden British invasion. As for as the east of Bengal was concerned, the British had opened up a new place called Ya-shan [Assam], also known as A-sai-mi [Assami], which was more than 1000 *li* long and three to four hundred *li* wide. Its north side was close to Bu-lu-ke-ba [Bhutan], and the eastern side was adjacent to the Mo-yu[25] savage/tribal area, the southern side bordered with Myanmar. Its territory was full of mountains. Only the two sides of the Pu-lan-bu-da [Brahmaputra] River were plains with fertile land. In recent years, the land had been reclaimed to grow tea. It was getting more and more prosperous. The British specially hired tea masters from Fujian and Guangdong to train the local people the high skills of cultivating tea. The annual production was now about 100,000 boxes of tea. But the quality was still not as good as that produced in China. According to maps drawn by western countries, the distance of the northeastern border of Ya-shan [Assam] was only two degrees in latitude and 5–600 *li* in diameter from Jiang-ka [Gyantse] and Ba-tang[26]. Recently, the British threatened to open up a road from Assam to Sichuan and Yunnan, the two provinces of my country [China]. But this was based on an erroneous and misleading map of the past, confusing the Ya-lu-zang-bu jiang [Yarlung Zangbo/Tsangpo River] in Tibet with the Pu-lan-bu-da [Brahmaputra] River in Assam. In fact, the Yarlung Zangbo River was the fountainhead of Da-jin-sha-jiang[27] [Great Jin-sha River/Changjiang]. Between estuaries in Myanmar and the big and small tributaries of the Jinsha Rivers, there were several big rivers such as Bing-lang, Long-chuan[28], Lu-yin[29], Lan-cang,[30] and others. Assam in the east, Batang in the west, Jiangka in the south, and Tengyue[31] [Tengchong] in the north constituted the border of the middle section [of Tibet] which was isolated from the world and had been inaccessible since ancient times. Its distance could not be verified. However, when examining the direction of its mountains and rivers, from its longitude and latitude, the length and width should not be less than 2,000 *li*. They were all mountains and cliffs, and there were no ropes to climb along. The water currents in the mountains and valleys were so turbulent that it was completely impossible for boats to pass. More than that, while opening up the mountain to construct a road in ancient Shu country [Sichuan], five of the strongest local persons also could not perform their task in spite of their extraordinary power and strength.

In the southeast of Assam, there were several small tribes called Ge-lu-shi [Garo?], Ge-shi-ya [Kassia/Khasi], Zheng-de-er [Jainitia], and Di-bei-ya [Deori?]. All of them had surrendered to the British. There were new ports in the southern bay called Che-di-gang [Chittagong] and Ai-ke-ya [Akyab] in the state of A-la-gan [Arakan]. The east side of Arakan was called Ba-san [Bassein], Yang-gong [Yangoon], Mo-er-mian [Moulmein], Mo-ni [Mon], and Ti-ni-se-ling [Tenasserim]. All of these were trading ports and were part of the territory of Myanmar. After the reign period of Emperor Dao Guang [1820–1850], they were ceded to the British. Along the coast of 7000 to–8000 *li* from Che-di-gang [Chittagong] to Ti-ni-se-ling [Tenasserim], the British posted officials, stationed heavy troops, and installed communication wire-cables to transmit signals. All of these were under the jurisdiction of the Indian governor. Therefore, the Chinese only knew that the British had occupied India and relied on Indian taxes, but they did not know that they also possessed Burma, all the golden ports along the coast of Siam [Thailand], and the telegraph from India to Xing-jia-po [Singapore]. The uninterrupted flow of information deserved the most attention. The commercial ports of other countries in India include Ke-wa [Goa] and Di-yu [Diu] that were located in the west in Gulf of Kaman [Khambhat], Gujrat, and belonged to Portugal. Leng-pu-er [Rangpur] in Bengal and Da-lang-gei-ba-er [Tharangambadi] in Jia-er-na-de [Carnatic/Tamilnadu] were under the control of Denmark. The two cities of Ben-de-zhi-li [Pondicherry] and Ge-li-ji-er [Karikal] belonged to France. They were located in the state of Carnatic [now Tamilnadu]. The district of Ya-na-an [Yanon] was situated in the state of Ba-jia-xi-er [Coromandel Coast/Andhra Pradesh]. Shang-de-er-na-ge [Chandernagore] in Bengal state and Ba-ha [Mahe] city in Malabar state were respectively only an isolated city and a town. They were used to store and transport goods. Mumbai originally belonged to Portugal and was later ceded to the British. Ma-li-pu-er [Serampore] originally belonged to Denmark and was 40 *li* away from Kolkata. Ba-le-li[32] was close to Houzang area in Tibet and was occupied by Gorkha in the nineteenth year of Jiaqing (1814). The British redeemed it with tens of thousands of taels of gold. The British Governor's Palace there was located at Xin-la [Shimla], and there was a direct railway connection. When major events occurred, all states used telegrams to report the situation to the Governor-General and follow their orders. Although distances were in thousands of *li*, the telegraph signal could be transmitted in an instant, which was no different from reporting the situation face-to-face.

This is the general situation of India. In the past, India was the place where Buddhism blossomed Since the Han and Tang dynasties, Buddhism spread all over the world, and it can be said that it flourished for a while. No one thought that Islam would rise in state of Tianfang [Arab] and gradually spread over the area of Congling [Pamir]. Nowadays, people in India hardly believed in Buddhism and many had converted to Islam. Jiu Lin[33] and Ji Feng[34] were still the same as they were in the past. However, the remains of She-wei [Shravasti] city and Lu-ye-yuan [Mrgdvava/Sarnath] were hard to find. The so-called Light of Wisdom and enlightenment illuminated the universe, but the Pure Land [India] nourished other believers. It was really pathetic!

The Red Sect[35] and the Yellow Sect[36] belonged to the two major sects of Buddhism and were prevalent in the Sanzang [Tibet] area, Inner Mongolia, and Manchuria. In addition, only Myanmar, Siam, and Vietnam adhered to Buddhism. I [Huang] studied Buddhism. With compassion, fasting, and non-violence at its heart it became weaker and weaker. But Islam had been tenacious and persistent, and now there was the Catholicism of Jesus, which strongly competed with Buddhism and Islam. These three religions were as incompatible as were water and fire, and challenged each other. The rise and fall of religions were actually closely related to their status and strength of the world. Some people called India Brahmanical (po-luo-men). In fact, Brahman was the name of the caste rather than the name of the religion. Indians were divided into four classes, the upper caste was Brahmin, and all chief officials belonged to this caste. Soldiers, merchants, and handicraftsmen belong to the next three castes. Castes and occupations were inherited from generation to generation, and the hierarchical order was not allowed to be broken. Once violated, the parents and the people of the country would abandon the individual. Some Indians painted colors on the forehead and at the middle point between the eyebrows. The traditional custom of such tattooing is also a relic of the past.

The name 'Five India-s' was bestowed on India because of its characteristic geographical location. There was, however, no certain boundary between what was east and what was west. The evolution of the term ancient and modern was impermanent, and so were names in Mongolian or Islamic languages. In modern times, it was all changed to English. Looking for and matching place names one by one was impossible. I [Huang] hand-painted the whole map of India, using the current place names for everyone's verification, and I dared not make up and rewrite them in the slightest. However, the place names related to the states of North India and the Sanzang [Tibet] region had been specially annotated in detail. It could be used as a reference for those who would one day in the future examine the history, or for the officials who would manage the border defense.

Notes

1 Samarkand city in Uzbekistan.
2 In contemporary Chinese writings, these Turco-Mongols were referred to as Mongols and the same term was interchangeably used when they invaded and occupied India and established the 'Great' Mughal Dynasty.
3 In the Chinese geographical description of 'Five India-s', Delhi comes under Central India.
4 The reference is to the Black Hole Incident in Kolkata and the subsequent Battle of Plassey in 1757.

5 In the text there is a confusion in the location and transliteration of Shimla/ Simla. The author errs in identifying Simla as Ba-le-li which is the Chinese transliteration of Bareilly. His contextual reference to Ba-le-lei makes it clear that he is describing colonial Simla. In fact, Simla became a British possession after the defeat of Gorkhas in 1815 in the Anglo-Gorkha war. It was also a stop-station on the Hindustan-Tibet Road that was constructed in 1850–1851. In 1864, Simla was officially declared as the Summer Capital of India.

6 Ancient Greeks called Kabul River as 'Kophen', the transliteration of which is Ji-bin. In China from the period of Western Han to Tang Dynasties, Ji-bin pointed out to the river valley between Ka-fei-li-se-tan [Kafiristan/Nuristan] to the source of Kabul River. In some periods, it also included the western part of Kashmir. It was so named because of its kafir [non-Muslim] Nuristani inhabitants who practiced an ancient form of Hinduism [Vedic Religion ?] with local characteristics. They are said to be directly linked with now almost extinct Kalash [Indo-Aryan indigenous people]. After the decline of Buddhism and spread of Islam, they too lost their distinctiveness. Their territory traditionally comprised of portion of Nooristan province in Afghanistan and the lower regions of Chitral in present Pakistan, and spread to the basins of several rivers and mountains.

7 A tribe of Central Asia inhabiting in Xinjiang region. It was linked with the Kushan Dynasty whose rule extended to central India.

8 The author draws attention to the secularism of the Sikh King, Ranjit Singh.

9 Haohan belonged to the ancient Da-wan country [Khanate of Kokand] which was the land of Muslim 'Hui' tribe in the west of Pamir highland.

10 It was also known as the Khanate of Bukhara which was established by the Tajiks, Khwarizm, and Uzbek people around the Central Asian Amu Darya/ River region from 1500 to 1920.

11 Ji-fa's identity is unknown. It is perhaps an abbreviation of Fa-guo [The Dharma Land/Country/India].

12 The author uses the ancient metaphor that literally meant that the official stepped over the sacrificial vessel to serve as a substitute for the cook, meaning to go beyond one's own business scope to deal with other people's affairs.

13 The author's reference is to the continuous war between the states of Qin and Chu during the Warring States Period. Chu remained a major contender for power in China until the final suppression by the Qin.

14 The Ili River basin around Turpan in Xinjiang, is now also known as Ili Kazakh Autonomous Prefecture in Xinjiang.

15 Now, it is the capital city of Jilin province.

16 Tibetan Empire [618–842 CE] was founded by Songtsen Gampo.

17 These are presumably names of two capital cities in the Tirhut/Mithila region of northern Bihar and are linked with the Later Guptas [?] and Lichchavis. The *Jiu Tangshu* refers that after the death of Lichchavi King Narendra Deva, his uncle Vishnugupta usurped the throne and got protection from Songtsen Gampo, the founder of the Tibetan Empire.

18 Wang Xuance was one of the most the famous Tang envoys bestowed with the title 'Grand Master for the Closing Court'. He was deputed to India three times. His second visit to India was in response to the dispatch of a goodwill ambassador to China by the Indian King Harshvardhan [606–647 CE]. But before Wang could reach India, Harsha had died, and his throne was usurped by Arunasva [or Arjun]. The latter was hostile to the Chinese and robbed the gifts and other objects carried by the Ambassador and probably also imprisoned Ambassador Wang Xuance who somehow escaped, and with the help of Tibetans [Songtsen Gampo] and Nepalese attacked Licchavis [Vishnugupta] in Central India, defeated the Indian usurper king, and took him to the Tang Court

as captive. For details see Tansen Sen, 2003, *Buddhism, Diplomacy and Trade*; *The Realignment of Sino-Indian Relations*, 600–1400, Honolulu, University of Hawaii Press. Also see, entry on Wang Xuance in *Encyclopedia of China–India Cultural Contacts*, Vol. II pp. 840–841 in English version. [In Chinese version of the same book Vol II, pp. 682–683.]

19 This is a Turko-Mongolian Sunni Muslim empire in Afghanistan – Persia region of Central Asia.

20 Zhebie/Zhebi [d.1224] is the first fiercest Mongol general who became famous as one of the four tigers or pioneers in the Mongol army.

21 Subutai [1160/1170–1248] is also considered to be one of the ablest Mongol generals and the primary military strategist of Genghis Khan and Ögedei Khan.

22 In Tibetan, its name was: Rgyal rtse in Shigatse Prefecture, Tibet.

23 Dangxiang in Chinese, Tang-gu-de in Chinese transliteration, and Tangut in romanization were the names given to Tibeto-Burman tribes of Yi or Qiang people and their language in the western borderland of China. They had founded the Western Xia or Tangut empire in the tenth century [1038–1227 CE].

24 Bhutan is a Romanized transliteration of Dzongkha/Druk Gyal Khap/Druk Yui used for the local kingdom, lineage, and land. In English translation, it is the Land or Kingdom of Thunder Dragon.

25 Also called Luoyu [珞瑜] or Luoyu [洛渝], in what is now southeastern Tibet.

26 Formerly in Kham province, Tibet and now in Sichuan.

27 Jinsha River is identified as the upper reaches of the Yangtze River or Changjiang in Sichuan and Yunnan.

28 This is also known as Rui-li river in Chinese and Shweli River in Myanmarese.

29 This is also known as Lu-jiang and Nu-jiang in China and the Salween River in Myanmar.

30 Lan-cang River of Qinghai and Yunnan was a part of upper reaches of Mekong River.

31 This is now known as Teng-chong county city of Bao-shan Prefecture in Western Yunnan.

32 See Note #5.

33 This refers to the famous and holy Griddhakuta [Vulture] Mountain Peak of the Buddhist legends in Rajgir [the capital city of Magadh] in Bihar. It was also known as Jie-tou, Jie-feng, Ling-jie-shan, etc. It is said to be the favorite retreat of Sakyamuni where he lived and preached for many years. The place got the name because it resembled a sitting vulture with its wings folded.

34 This refers to the famous Kukkutpada Mountains [now known as Gurpa Hills], close to Gaya, Bihar. It was mentioned by both Faxian [fourth century CE] and Xuanzang [seventh century CE] as Buddha's meditation place, and where according to Buddhist legends, Mahakashyap waited for the Maitreya [Future Buddha] to exchange the 'robe'. China also has Kukkutpada on the Jizu Mountains in Yunnan that was built sometimes in the ninth century CE for devotees unable to go to the original place in India.

35 This is known as the Ningma Sect and is one of the most important and ancient sects of Tibetan Buddhism. Its followers wore red upper garments of ascetics.

36 This refers to the Gelug Sect, which is another important sect of Tibetan Buddhism. In the Tibetan language Gelu means good discipline, and this sect emphasizes strict observance of the precepts. The monks of this sect wear yellow monk hats, so it is also called the Yellow Sect.

INDEX

For Product Safety Concerns and Information please contact our EU
representative GPSR@taylorandfrancis.com
Taylor & Francis Verlag GmbH, Kaufingerstraße 24, 80331 München, Germany

www.ingramcontent.com/pod-product-compliance
Lightning Source LLC
Chambersburg PA
CBHW071121100726
47908CB00008B/2454